Cultural and Political Aspects of Rural Transformation

David R. Smock
Audrey C. Smock

The Praeger Special Studies program—utilizing the most modern and efficient book production techniques and a selective worldwide distribution network—makes available to the academic, government, and business communities significant, timely research in U.S. and international economic, social, and political development.

Cultural and Political Aspects of Rural Transformation

A Case Study of Eastern Nigeria

PRAEGER SPECIAL STUDIES IN INTERNATIONAL ECONOMICS AND DEVELOPMENT

Praeger Publishers   New York   Washington   London

PRAEGER PUBLISHERS
111 Fourth Avenue, New York, N.Y. 10003, U.S.A.
5, Cromwell Place, London S.W.7, England

Published in the United States of America in 1972
by Praeger Publishers, Inc.

74 - 1344

© 1972 by Praeger Publishers, Inc.

Library of Congress Catalog Card Number: 71-165837

Printed in the United States of America

To Our Parents

This study analyzes the cultural and political
aspects of social and economic development in rural
Eastern Nigeria prior to the attempted secession and
the resultant civil war. The economic, agricultural,
and technical components of development efforts in
Africa are popular subjects for discussion and analysis, but the cultural and political sides of rural
development have been relatively neglected. Although
the study focuses upon Eastern Nigeria, our hope is
that the analysis done and the conclusions drawn will
have relevance for other parts of Africa as well.

Most of the data for this study was collected
during the period 1964 to 1966, when the senior author
served as a Ford Foundation adviser to the Community
Development Division of the Ministry of Internal
Affairs and later the Ministry of Rural Development.
However, research conducted by the senior author in
Eastern Nigeria during 1962-63 and by the junior
author during 1966 provided supplementary material.
These rather extended periods of residence, research,
and advisory work in Eastern Nigeria enabled us to
become familiar with a broad cross section of the
area's ethnic groups and rural communities, as well
as to become involved in the planning and implementation of various governmental programs to stimulate
rural development. A visit to the area early in 1971
enabled us to update some of our materials.

In an effort to approach the subject of our study
from a variety of vantage points, several research
techniques were employed. Case studies were done of
such key development programs as community plantations
and resettlement schemes. Detailed studies were also
undertaken of such critical problem areas as land
tenure and cultural traditions that inhibit or encourage the adoption of new farming practices. In addition we evaluated the organization, ethos, and ·

vii

effectiveness of the Eastern Nigerian political system
with regard to its ability to promote rural development. We also made extensive use of survey techniques, with one attitude questionnaire being administered to a carefully selected sample of 480 informants
from a cross section of Eastern Nigerian villages.
An analysis of the survey results indicates differences
in attitudes relating to economic change and development on the part of the various ethnic groups
surveyed, as well as revealing the personal characteristics of individuals who seem to be most favorably
disposed toward social change and economic development. Another attitude survey was administered to
persons in matched pairs of villages, half of which
had been responsive to attempts by the Ministry of
Rural Development to encourage the adoption of development projects, and the other half of which had been
unresponsive. After analyzing the responses of these
two groups, we were able to identify a list of items
from the questionnaire that should have value in
predicting which villages would tend to be responsive
and which ones unresponsive to development efforts.

     Although no two portions of rural Africa are
exactly comparable and development programs have to
be tailor-made for each region, certain features of
Eastern Nigeria enable it to be a particularly
instructive model for other parts of Africa. The
now almost legendary eagerness of the various ethnic
groups of Eastern Nigeria for modernization makes
this area a useful place for experimentation with
programs that may later prove acceptable elsewhere
in Africa. The concluding chapter of the study
assesses the implications of the findings for governmental policy or for other agencies dedicated to
stimulating the reconstruction and development of the
rural areas of Eastern Nigeria and other parts of
Africa.

     In discussing an area where so much has happened
since the time our study ended in 1966, it is difficult to decide upon the appropriate geographical
designations and the appropriate tense in which to
write. In terms of the current political structure
of Nigeria, we should refer to the area discussed as

constituting South-East State, East Central State, and
Rivers State. However, since the study covered a
period before Eastern Nigeria had been divided into
these components, we refer to the area as Eastern
Nigeria. Our use of divisional names also refers to
this pre-1967 period. In selecting tenses, we use
the past tense when discussing institutions and programs that have not reappeared and are unlikely to
do so in the post-war period, while using the present
tense in discussing whatever has been revived and is
likely to persist. For instance, in discussing the
political and administrative structure of that period,
we use the past tense since these forms have not been
resurrected. However, when we discuss governmental
programs for developing the rural areas, we generally
use the present tense, since these are being reinsti-
tuted by one or more of the three state governments.

We are indebted to numerous persons for the
assistance they rendered in the collection and analysis of data contained in this study. Our heaviest
debt is to our Ford Foundation colleagues who also
advised the Eastern Nigeria government on rural
development, Ray Coatswith, Fenton Sands, and the
late Herman Holiday, and to our Nigerian colleagues,
principally N. A. Ndu, Jacob Agwu, and Nelson Nwosu.
In addition, the Rural Development Officers and Peace
Corps Volunteers who were attached to particular
village development projects helped us keep track of
progress on a day-to-day basis. David Heaps and
Frank Moore formulated the project and continued to
give it valuable support. Frank Moore, Francis Sutton,
Archibald Callaway, Elliott Roberts, and Robert Netting
offered valuable comments on earlier drafts of
particular chapters, as did our colleagues in the
field. The students who served as field interviewers
and the villagers who generously gave of their time
to be interviewed are too numerous to name, but their
important contribution to the study needs to be
acknowledged. We are also grateful to R. A. Ogunsua
for the advice he offered on the programming of our
data for computer analysis and to William Foote Whyte
for his help in constructing the questionnaire. The
junior author was also generously assisted by a
grant from the Social Science Research Council to

enable her to analyze some of our material. Finally, we grateful acknowledge the permission granted by the University of Chicago Press and the editors of Economic Development and Cultural Change, The Journal of Developing Areas, and the Bulletin of Rural Economics and Sociology to utilize in this book portions of articles we had written for their journals.

CONTENTS

LIST OF TABLES

LIST OF MAPS AND FIGURES

Cultural and Political Aspects of Rural Transformation

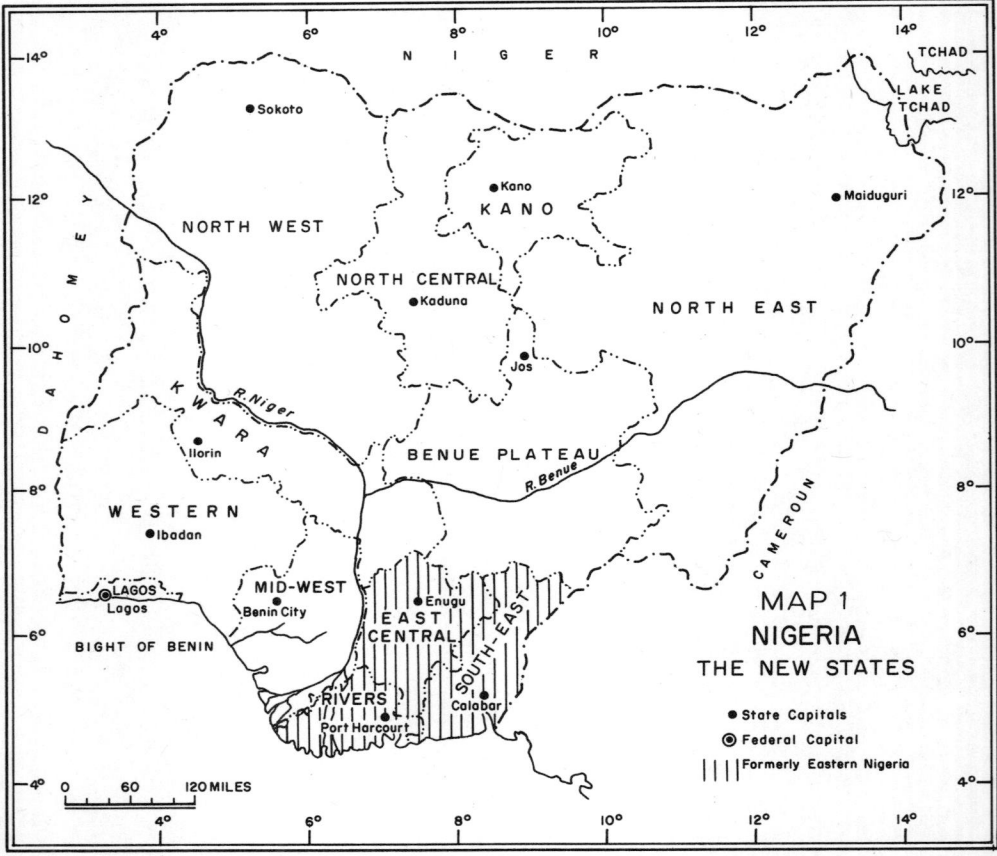

MAP 1

NIGERIA

THE NEW STATES

● State Capitals
◎ Federal Capital
|||| Formerly Eastern Nigeria

N I G E R

TCHAD

LAKE
TCHAD

●Sokoto

NORTH WEST

●Kano

KANO

●Maiduguri

NORTH CENTRAL

●Kaduna

NORTH EAST

●Jos

KWARA

R. Niger

●Ilorin

BENUE PLATEAU

R. Benue

WESTERN

●Ibadan

CAMEROUN

◎LAGOS
Lagos

MID-WEST

Benin City

●Enugu

EAST
CENTRAL

SOUTH-EAST

BIGHT OF BENIN

RIVERS

Port Harcourt

●Calabar

DAHOMEY

0   60   120 MILES

14°
12°
10°
8°
6°
4°

4°   6°   8°   10°   12°   14°

1

INTRODUCTION: TRANSFORMING RURAL AFRICA

With over 80 percent of Africa's inhabitants living in rural areas and depending for their livelihoods on agriculture, the true success of a comprehensive economic and social development program in an African nation is primarily dependent upon the extent to which it contributes to the well-being of those living in the rural areas. Moreover, given the dependence of most African economies upon activity in the rural-agricultural sector, rapid economic growth is principally a function of growth within this sector. Casual observers and itinerant journalists who visit Nairobi and Abidjan can easily be impressed by the magnificence of government buildings and the apparent high standard of urban living. It does not take very careful reflection or calculation, however, to realize what a small portion of the life and activity of African countries can be witnessed in urban areas, and it does not require travel very distant from the capital cities to realize the stark contrasts in levels of development and well-being between the urban and rural areas.

During the initial years of independence, African development programs concentrated on the modern sector of the economy almost to the exclusion of investment in the rural economic base. New government buildings, urban infrastructure, and state-owned industrial enterprises constitute the monuments to development

brought forth during the sixties. To assert that
the lack of attention to the rural sector has been
merely because of the short-sightedness of African
leaders would be to overlook the urban and industrial
bias of the majority of foreign economists and technicians who have advised African governments and
institutions over the past three decades. D. K.
Chisiza neglects the rural roots of most urban
Africans when he states that "the neglect of rural
areas stems mainly from the fact that modern African
political leaders are creatures of the towns."[1]
Regardless of how blame should be apportioned for
the imbalance that exists in development priorities,
there fortunately appears to be growing conviction
within African states that their rural areas must
be given increased attention. Hopefully development
programs in the seventies will restore the balance
by according a new emphasis to rural development.[2]

The case for investing greater resources in the
development of rural areas in Africa is not simply
based on a need to right past wrongs or on the desirability of there being an equitable distribution
of the benefits accruing from economic growth and
modernization. The economic health of the total
economy largely depends upon the vigor of the rural
sector. The dynamic of economic growth in Nigeria
from 1900 to independence in 1960 was based upon the
commodities for export produced by the small farmers
of the country, and the same can be said of many
other African countries as well.[3] Gerald Helleiner
has enumerated the following ways in which peasant
agriculture has contributed and will continue to
contribute to Nigerian economic development: the
provision of foreign exchange and savings for the
development effort; the provision of food, particularly for the growing urban population; the provision
of consumer markets for a growing industrial sector;
the stimulation of linkages with the industrial
sector, both in the provision of raw materials and
through the utilization of manufactured goods required in agriculture; and the stimulation of infrastructure development, such as the building of
roads and bridges.[4]

In recognizing the interdependence between the
urban and rural areas of Africa and the linkages

between agriculture and industry, it is important to remember that the relationships are two-directional. When one advocates increased attention and investment in rural development, a concentration on the rural areas to the point of completely neglecting urban-industrial development is not suggested. This kind of "agricultural fundamentalism"[5] would be to the detriment of both industry and agriculture.

The importance of agricultural development is underscored when one looks at the employment situation Even if significant investments are made in the industrial sector, industrial growth in most African countries is not likely to be able to absorb a very substantial portion of Africa's rapidly expanding population. Harbison has assessed the situation in the following manner:

> Unemployment and underemployment of man-
> power in the modern sector enclaves already
> have reached alarming proportions and no
> alleviation of this situation is in sight.
> Modern factories can absorb only limited
> numbers of workers, and the capacity of
> governments to employ more civil servants
> is limited by growing financial constraints.
> . . . Even under the most optimistic
> estimates of economic growth in the modern
> sectors, therefore, industry, commerce and
> government will be unable to absorb more
> than a fraction of the annual increment in
> the labor force of most African countries.[6]

It has been estimated that Nigeria's industrial sector can provide employment for only 3 percent of the annual increment to the labor force, leaving to agriculture the burden of providing self-employment for most of the remainder.[7] With Nigeria's population expected to grow at the rate of 2.5 to 3.0 percent annually over the next decade, by 1980 the country's population will stand at 86 million, of which approximately 64 percent will live in the rural areas.[8] Added to this rate of population growth, economists anticipate a 1-percent annual rise in per capita food consumption, which will result in a 4-percent annual increase in demand for food.[9] Few nations have been able to sustain this

level of growth in food production, and if Nigeria
is to approach this level, substantial new investments
of both money and ingenuity are required in the rural
areas.

The current slow pace of social and economic
development in the rural portions of Africa does not
simply result from an overemphasis upon industrial
and urban development. The lack of development in
the rural areas largely reflects the formidable
obstacles inherent in the effort. It is tempting
for critics of African development programs to over-
simplify the process of rural and agricultural development, but the continent of Africa is littered with
the carcasses of unsuccessful and abandoned rural
development schemes. The Niger Agricultural Project
in Northern Nigeria, the "villagization" program in
Tanzania, and the attempt to mechanize and commer-
cialize agriculture in the Volta Dam resettlement
scheme typify the well-intentioned but ill-conceived
efforts to transform Africa's rural areas. The few
efforts that can be counted as resounding successes,
like the Gezira scheme in the Sudan, can be pointed
out with relative ease.

The difficulties encountered by governments and
other agencies in Africa in promoting rural development parallel the experiences of other areas of the
world. No state has yet discovered the rosetta stone
to decipher the riddles of rural transformation.
Collectivization of agriculture in the Soviet Union
drastically lowered productivity. The formation of
large-scale communes in China in an effort to bring
the organization and techniques of the factory to
agriculture wreaked havoc on the economy and seriously
disrupted the social structure in the countryside.
India's massive investment in community development
through a tier of elective local councils has failed
to accomplish either of its two goals of stimulating
economic development and reforming the inequities in
the social structure. The recent introduction of
miracle rice and wheat varieties has boosted food
production substantially in many countries, but in
themselves these varieties will not provide sustained
economic growth for the rural areas.

The problems confronting those who would try to achieve a transformation of rural Africa are numerous and varied, and it is always easier to point out the stumbling blocks to success in an ex post facto analysis than in the planning phase or in a feasibility study. Technical limitations involved in increasing agricultural productivity have proved particularly troublesome, and there is a growing realization that much larger investments must be made in Africa-based research in plant breeding, agricultural engineering, agronomy, plant pathology, entomology, and animal husbandry. Production breakthroughs are always accompanied by additional problems of storage, transportation, infrastructure, agricultural credit, markets, and price incentives, as well as problems of organization and administration. Added to problems such as these, one encounters factors that are political, cultural, social, and psychological in origin.

To make an attack on such a wide range of problem areas obviously requires the concerted and co-operative effort of persons from a variety of disciplines. Agriculturalists, engineers, economists, and educators all have important roles to play. Although the roles to be played by the cultural anthropologist, political scientist, and sociologist are not as clearly defined or as universally accepted, these roles are increasingly being clarified and recognized. In speaking of the role of social scientists in stimulating and guiding rural development in Nigeria, H. M. A. Onitiri, Director of the Nigerian Institute of Social and Economic Research, has stated:

> The intellectual community certainly has a
> responsibility for engaging in continuous
> study of various aspects of rural life and
> for taking the leadership in organizing ef-
> fective measures which can help to integrate
> the rural areas into the mainstream of eco-
> nomic development. It is necessary that
> before we start drawing up the next develop-
> ment plan, a good deal of information be
> accumulated on the economic and social con-

ditions of our vast rural areas which are
so far not fully explored. Such basic information is indispensable if programs of
rural development are to feature more prom-
inently in the next major effort for developing the Nigerian economy.[10]

The cultural, social, and political issues in
rural development are the focus of this study.
These factors, although frequently overlooked, very
often bear a close relationship to the technical
problems of rural development, and must often be
analyzed and grappled with by social scientists if
the agriculturalists and technicians are to successfully introduce their innovations. For instance,
traditional beliefs and practices regarding the
ownership, utilization, and inheritance of land are
of critical significance in any effort to change
farming practices in an area like Eastern Nigeria.
The efficient use by farmers of mechanical equipment
requires that plots being farmed be of sufficient
size that the equipment has space within which to
operate without having to be moved frequently from
one small plot to another. Fragmentation of farm
land holdings into small parcels thus inhibits farm
mechanization, and the same is true of attempts to
introduce irrigation. Moreover, if tradition dictates that land not be individually owned and controlled, or that land can only be leased on a short-
term basis, then a farmer hesitates to make permanent or costly improvements to the land. If cultural prohibitions exist against the sale and purchase of land, ambitious farmers have difficulty
acquiring new land, and farmers also face obstacles
in moving from areas of land scarcity to areas where
land is available. The tackling of land tenure
problems initially requires an understanding of
land tenure practices and then imaginative solutions
that must be economically sound while not being
culturally offensive.

Of critical importance in introducing agricultural innovations is an understanding of the social
structure, behavior patterns, and attitudes of peasant
families insofar as these might influence their

receptivity to new ideas, as well as understanding
differences between individuals and groups in terms
of their receptivity. To know which groups might
be more open to experiments with new practices or
new organizational forms can help determine which
groups should receive priority, as well as indicating
the manner in which different ethnic groups should
be approached and educated. The same kinds of questions can be posed in terms of individuals, and
information concerning individual differences in
receptivity can be of substantial assistance to
those organizing agricultural production campaigns
or those recruiting participants for new agricultural
projects. Discovery of what causes differences between villages in responsiveness to change programs
might offer the basis for developing predictive
techniques that could be used in the selection of
potentially receptive villages for participation in
development programs.

     Anthropologists have documented for certain
parts of the developing world the kinds of beliefs
and traditions that constitute barriers to development. Although it is usually the barriers to change
that are emphasized, an understanding of those
cultural elements that might be capitalized upon for
development purposes can also be valuable. Of critical
significance is an assessment of the extent to which
various groups of people are responsive to economic
incentives and are prepared to change their farming
habits or invest in new inputs in hopes of economic
reward.

     In organizing village projects, knowledge of
the political structure and decision-making patterns
within the villages of the area can contribute in
important measure to project success. The continual
search by outsiders, both Africans and Europeans,
for the "chief" in an African village has been the
source of frequent confusion, misunderstanding, and
failure. Village habits and attitudes regarding the
organization of work also need to be considered in
determining how village development projects should
be organized, and whether such projects should be
undertaken on an individual basis, in family units,
or communally. In planning agricultural projects

it is also important to comprehend how rigidly
conceived are divisions of labor by sex, and how
likely it is that men can be enticed into planting
crops traditionally defined as being the responsibility
of women, and vice versa.

In many parts of Africa rural development necessitates some change in settlement patterns. Certain
development projects have encouraged villagers to
move from their scattered homesteads to more centrally
located village sites where social services can be
more efficiently provided and where villages can be
more effectively organized and administered. A
knowledge of the traditional beliefs used to justify
scattered residential units, and the attitudes
regarding alternative settlement patterns facilitates
coping with the initial reluctance to live in nucleated villages. The uneven distribution of population
in many parts of Africa, with overpopulated areas
often being islands in a sea of underutilized land,
offers additional scope for major resettlement efforts.
In contemplating such efforts, a government must deal
with attitudes toward strangers in communities with
surplus land and their traditional mechanisms for
incorporating outsiders, as well as surveying the
receptiveness of individuals and groups from densely
populated areas to resettling elsewhere.

Throughout Africa, governments have assumed
primary responsibility for promoting development.
The nature of the political system, or more specifically its organization, effectiveness, and ethos,
determine both the selection of development programs
and the ability of the government to implement them.
The ethos or attitudes and orientations infusing the
political system significantly influence the priorities and programs enunciated by the government.
However, even a well-conceived program to stimulate
rural development tailored to the cultural predispositions of villagers can easily flounder at the
implementation stage. Since agricultural development
requires that governmental efforts reach the many
small-scale cultivators, the organization and
effectiveness of administrative and political structures constitute a critical variable in the transformation of rural Africa.

It is the concern with these kinds of issues
that has given rise to this study. Although there
is a growing literature on the cultural and social
factors in agricultural development in various parts
of the world, most writers on this subject tend to
delight in recording case studies of projects that
failed when cultural factors were given insufficient
attention. What is required is less ex post facto
analysis and greater attention to the contribution
that social scientists can make to the process of
economic and social development. Several chapters
of this book attempt to illustrate the contribution
that social science can make to the solution of the
sorts of developmental problems enumerated above.[11]

This book focuses upon the cultural, social,
political, attitudinal, and organizational factors
that have influenced and will influence the economic
and social development of the rural portions of
Eastern Nigeria. Mention has been made in the Preface
that certain features of Eastern Nigeria enable it
to be an instructive model for other parts of Africa,
and in turn suggest that this study may have implications beyond Eastern Nigeria. Community development and village self-help programs have a longer
history in Eastern Nigeria than in virtually any
other part of the continent.[12] As evidence of this,
most of the roads and the schools in Eastern Nigeria
were originally built by village labor working voluntarily under village leadership. The first film to
be made on community development in Africa, "Day
Break at Udi," related the story of one portion of
Eastern Nigeria. The distinguished history of self-
help activities in Eastern Nigeria has turned up
substantial evidence of what types of projects succeed and which projects tend to fail in that part
of Africa.

Prior to 1967 the people of Eastern Nigeria
were still feeling their way toward a means of
achieving a full transformation of the rural areas.
Hopefully now that the war has ended, the characteristic dynamism and ingenuity of the people there
will be directed once again toward this end. The
concluding chapter of this study assesses the

implications of the authors' findings for government
policy or for other agencies dedicated to stimulating
the development of the rural areas of Eastern Nigeria
as well as other parts of Africa.

NOTES

1.   D. K. Chisiza, Africa-What Lies Ahead,
quoted in René Dumont, False Start in Africa (New
York: Frederick A. Praeger, 1966), p. 289.

2.   Frederick Harbison makes a similar plea in
his "Priorities in External Aid for African Higher
Education," 1969 (mimeographed), p. 10.

3.   Carl K. Eicher, "The Dynamics of Long-Term
Agricultural Development in Nigeria," Journal of
Farm Economics, 49 (December 1967), 1158-1170.

4.   Gerald K. Helleiner, Peasant Agriculture,
Government and Economic Growth in Nigeria (Homewood,
Illinois: Richard D. Irwin, Inc., 1966), pp. 140-151.

5.   The phrase is from Carl K. Eicher, "Reflections on West Africa's Rural Development Problems
of the 1970's," paper presented at the Symposium on
Africa in the 1980's, Adlai Stevenson Institute of
International Affairs, Chicago, 1969 (mimeographed),
p. 1.

6.   Harbison, op. cit., p. 3.

7.   Frederick H. Harbison, "From Ashby to Reconstruction: Manpower and Education in Nigeria,"
in Carl K. Eicher and Carl Liedholm, eds., Growth
and Development in the Nigerian Economy (East Lansing:
Michigan State University Press, 1970).

8.   Food and Agriculture Organization, Agricultural Development in Nigeria, 1965-80 (Rome:
Food and Agriculture Organization, 1966), pp. 400-401.

9. Carl K. Eicher, "Transforming Traditional Agriculture in Southern Nigeria: The Contemporary Experience," paper presented at the Annual Meeting of the African Studies Association, Bloomington, Indiana, 1966 (mimeographed), p. 2.

10. H. M. A. Onitiri, "Presidential Address--A Proposal for Nigerian Rural Development," The Nigerian Journal of Economic and Social Studies, VIII (March 1966), p. 8.

11. For works that have dealt with the noneconomic aspect of development in rural Africa, see A. I. Richards, Land, Labour, and Diet in Northern Rhodesia, (London: Oxford University Press, 1937); K. D. S. Baldwin, The Niger Agricultural Project (Cambridge, Mass.: Harvard University Press, 1957); John C. de Wilde, et al., Agricultural Development in Tropical Africa Vol. I (Baltimore: The Johns Hopkins Press, 1967), pp. 45-70; Pierre de Schlippe, Shifting Cultivation in Africa (London: Routledge and Kegan Paul, 1956); Thayer Scudder, The Ecology of the Gwembe Tonga (Manchester: Manchester University Press, 1962); William Allan, The African Husbandman (Edinburgh: Oliver and Boyd, 1965); Hans Ruthenberg, ed., Smallholder Farming and Smallholder Development in Tanzania (London: C. Hurst and Co., 1968); Marvin P. Miracle, Agriculture in the Congo Basin: Tradition and Change in African Rural Economies (Madison: University of Wisconsin Press, 1967); Polly Hill, The Migrant Cocoa Farmers of Southern Ghana (Cambridge: Cambridge University Press, 1963); Robert A. LeVine, Dreams and Deeds: Achievement Motivation in Nigeria (Chicago: University of Chicago Press, 1966); Gerald D. Hursh, Allan Hershfield, Graham B. Kerr, and Niels G. Roling, "Communication in Eastern Nigeria: An Experiment in Introducing Change" (East Lansing: Department of Communication, Michigan State University, 1968, mimeographed); Joseph R. Ascroft, Niels G. Roling, Graham B. Kerr, and Gerald D. Hursh, "Patterns of Diffusion in Rural Eastern Nigeria" (East Lansing: Department of Communication, Michigan State University, 1969, mimeographed); Gerald D. Hursh, Niels G. Roling, and Graham B. Kerr, "Innovation in Eastern Nigeria:

Success and Failure of Agricultural Programs in 71
Villages of Eastern Nigeria" (East Lansing: Depart-
ment of Communication, Michigan State University,
1968, mimeographed); and David Brokensha and Marion
Pearsall, The Anthropology of Development in Sub-
Saharan Africa, (Lexington, Kentucky: Society for
Applied Anthropology, 1969).

     12. C. Jackson, Advance in Africa: A Study of
Community Development in Eastern Nigeria (London:
Oxford University Press, 1956).

2

THE
EASTERN REGION
OF
NIGERIA

Throughout this study the frame of reference is Eastern Nigeria. From 1931--when the Southern Provinces of Nigeria were divided into two units with the Niger River as the boundary--until 1967, the Eastern Region constituted a relatively autonomous component within the Nigerian Federation. British colonial policy, with the exception of three brief years--1951 to 1954--promoted the evolution of native authorities and then strong regions rather than a unitary state. The federal system that evolved in Nigeria accorded far more power to the regional components than is usually the case in a federal arrangement. According to the constitutional division of powers in force during the life of the first Nigerian Republic, those governmental functions generally associated with the exercise of sovereignty--armed forces, defense, external affairs, currency, customs and excise duties, external borrowing of money, mines and minerals--and railways, posts, telegraphs, and telephones were vested in the federal level, and all unlisted or residual powers were left for the regions. Under this arrangement the regions assumed responsibility for those subjects relating to development like agriculture, education, public works, and health. Thus to describe and to assess the process of rural transformation in Eastern Nigeria it is necessary to consider regionally conceived and executed programs.

In light of the greater responsibilities of the
regions for resource-consuming activities, the constitution also awarded a preponderance of revenues
to them. Regional governments received exclusive
receipt of the income tax and received back from
federal collectors the export duties collected on
primary produce, import and excise duties on tobacco,
import duties on petroleum and fuel oils in proportion to the amount consumed in the regions, and 50
percent of mineral royalties and mining rents. The
constitution allocated company profits and death
duties to the federal government as its exclusive
field for taxation. In addition it had responsibility
for collecting, and could retain, import and excise
duties other than those levied on tobacco and fuel
oils. Of the money so raised, 30 percent was paid
into the distributable pool along with 30 percent of
the mining rents and mineral royalties. At the end
of each quarter the distributable pool was divided
among the regions with the East receiving approximately one third. After a new revenue allocation
scheme was introduced in the fall of 1965 the federal
government put 35 percent of general customs and
import duties and mineral and mining royalties into
the distributable pool and the East received 30 percent of the total. As a result of this complex formula, each region obtained two thirds of its recurrent
revenues from federally collected moneys.

The configuration of political power reinforced
the tendency for the regions to be strengthened at
the expense of the central government. Nigeria
basically consisted of a series of regional political
systems dominated by single parties. Each of the
major political parties in Nigeria was rooted in one
of the regions and was identified with the dominant
ethnic group there. By wielding the advantages that
office conferred on them, the political parties in
power in each region gradually weakened and all but
eliminated their opponents. The political party in
power in the Eastern Region was the National Convention
of Nigerian Citizens. Since the Northern Region had
a majority of the population of Nigeria, the Northern
People's Congress predominated at the center as well
as in the Northern Region.

The Eastern Region was in some ways a distinct cultural unit also. Although the Region was not ethnically homogeneous--about two thirds of the people were Ibo-speaking and the remaining third consisted of about 40 smaller ethnic groups--the precolonial social and political institutions and cultural orientations of the various ethnic groups in the East had many traits in common, as Chapter 3 will demonstrate. These similarities are further heightened by comparing the small autonomous, segmentary socio-political systems of the East with the centralized and Islamized states predominant in the North and the urban, pyramidal kingdoms characteristic of the West. Owing to the nature of the precolonial political systems in the East, the British encountered far greater difficulties there in attempting to regularize administration. Moreover, the relatively similar nature of the traditional cultural orientations of the Eastern peoples engendered relatively similar responses to the new order that evolved under colonial rule.

COLONIAL RULE

European traders began dealing with groups presently incorporated in the Eastern Region in the seventeenth century, first for slaves and then primarily for palm oil. From the seventeenth to the middle of the nineteenth centuries, the ships of European slave traders carried away several million unfortunate prisoners from the area. Contact with the Europeans was usually confined to a few trading communities in the Niger Delta area, where slaves were procured from middlemen in the interior.

The first British colony in what is now Nigeria was established in 1861 when Lagos was annexed, ostensibly to end the slave trade along the southwestern coast. After a conference in Berlin in 1885 sparked a scramble for colonies in Africa by stipulating that no annexations would be recognized as valid unless they were accompanied by effective occupation, the British hastened to exclude other powers from the Niger Delta by establishing a protectorate over the coast between Lagos and the Camerouns in 1885 and

then extending it inland in 1893. Participants at
the Berlin conference had acknowledged British claims
to the Niger Basin area, and in 1900 the newly named
Protectorate of Southern Nigeria was placed under the
supervision of the Colonial Office, which was given
the task of establishing an administration. Six
years later the Colonial Office joined the Protectorate
of Southern Nigeria with the colony of Lagos to form
the Colony and Protectorate of Southern Nigeria. In
1914 the British then amalgamated this unit with the
Protectorate of Northern Nigeria, thus bringing the
territory of Nigeria into being.

     Although the British had expanded to the present
boundaries of Nigeria by 1914 and placed the territory
under a single administrator, the Northern and Southern
Provinces remained separate units until 1946. The
higher officials of the two separate bureaucracies
in the North and the South met only once a year at
the annual session of the legislative council in
Lagos. Northern bureaucrats favored a separate pattern
of development for the emirates in the North, which
would preserve their indigenous Islamic political
systems. The two groups of administrators even spoke
different official languages--Hausa in the North and
English in the South.

     As High Commissioner for the Northern Protectorate
from 1900 to 1906, Lord Lugard adopted the system of
indirect rule since he lacked sufficient personnel to
govern directly. Under the system of indirect rule,
as practiced in the North, the emirs continued as the
executive instruments of government. The British
administrators assigned to the emirates were expected
to guide and supervise the native authorities, but
not to assume direct power. The British imposed
only such limitations on the emir that they considered
necessary to preserve British overlordship: prohibitions on the emir raising an army, arming the
police under his control with modern weapons, and
appropriating land for public purposes. In addition
the British administration retained the right to
review and approve legislation.

     The hinterland of the Eastern Region was one of
the last areas of Nigeria to be pacified. Between

1902, when the British dispatched troops to destroy
the important religious oracle at Aro Chuku, and 1914,
when the amalgamation of the Northern and Southern
Protectorates under a single governor took place, they
sent 20 military expeditions into the area. Only after
World War I did the British complete the division of
the East into provinces under the jurisdiction of a
provincial commissioner, divisions administered by a
divisional officer, and native court areas presided
over by the divisional or district officer with a bench
of warrant chiefs to advise him. The nature of the
precolonial societies in the East, particularly the
autonomy of each village and the general lack of centralized authority both in the village and over the
area, made it difficult for the British to apply the
principles of indirect rule and govern through existing
units of government. When British administrators could
not find traditional chiefs with whom they could deal,
they appointed cooperative individuals and vested them
with authority.

The first system of administration in the Eastern
Region ended in 1928 with a series of disorders, which
are often referred to as the Aba riots. These disorders were provoked by a variety of factors including
a dislike for the concentration of authority in warrant
chiefs (who were not accountable to the community) and
the economic hardships caused by the decline in palm
oil prices and the introduction of direct taxation.
The establishment of a system of administration based
on smaller, supposedly more traditional units followed.
However, these native authority councils often did not
reflect the boundaries of traditional communities both
because the prior official anthropological surveys were
perfunctory and because the precolonial units were too
small. British administrators then assumed that the
continued ineffectiveness of the system of indirect
rule through native authority councils in the East
could be countered by merging the small units into
larger ones. In the late 1930's British administrators
therefore began to "encourage" native authority areas
to federate into larger and hopefully more viable units.
units. Since these larger native authority councils
were also ineffective, the government replaced them in
in the early 1950's with a system of local government
patterned after British models of local government.

Intensive missionary activity began later in most of the East than in the West among the Yoruba. Although missionaries opened stations in two Eastern communities, in the Efik community of Calabar and the Ibo community of Onitsha in 1845 and in 1857 respectively, missionaries did not reach the Ibo and Ibibio communities in the interior until well into the twentieth century. Once Christian missionaries penetrated the Eastern hinterland, though, they attracted a proportionately greater number of converts in a shorter period of time than elsewhere in Nigeria. In the 1953 census, half of the population in the Region registered as Christian as compared with 37 percent in the West.[1]

Since missionaries were the primary bearers of western culture and education, the major ethnic groups in the East lagged behind the Western Yorubas in producing an educated elite. When the British administration moved into the Eastern hinterland, it often employed educated Efiks or Onitshans as inter-mediary agents. Also in the coastal centers of administration and commerce, Efiks and Onitshans monopolized the best positions open to Africans, along with the far more numerous educated Yorubas. The vast majority of Easterners found themselves treated with contempt in their initial contacts both with the African elite and with the Europeans in the towns, because of their lack of education and the relative simplicity of their traditional culture.

It is likely that this perception of low status and relative backwardness precipitated the intensive campaign for self-improvement of many Ibo and Ibibio communities in the 1930's. Unlike in the Western Region or in the other parts of Africa where the opportunities for education usually came with little local initiative, the rapid expansion of educational facilities in the East resulted from communal efforts to open schools and endow scholarships for outstanding young men. Communities built schools that were then staffed by the missionary societies. The wide educational gap separating Easterners from the more advanced groups quickly closed. During the 1930's educational facilities expanded at a faster rate in

the Eastern Region than anywhere else in Nigeria.
The return of Eastern barristers and doctors from
abroad after World War II ended the predominance of
the Yoruba in the educated professions. The 1953
census showed that by that time the rate of literacy
in the East, 16 percent, almost equalled that of the
West, 18 percent. Once the East became self-governing
under the colonial administration in 1957, the Eastern
Government regularly spent approximately 42 percent
of its annual budget on education in order to eradicate
any remaining difference.[2]

ECONOMIC DEVELOPMENT

     Until recently the East appeared to be relatively
poorly endowed in economic terms. The population
density of the East was one of the highest for an
agricultural area in the world. According to the
1963 census, the regional population density attained
more than four times the Nigerian average and along
the Onitsha-Mbaise axis reached over 1,200 people
per square mile. The poor quality of the soil made
many parts of the East unsuitable for some of the
lucrative cash crops, like cocoa, that were introduced
elsewhere along the West African coast.

     Along with palm oil products, Eastern Nigeria's
greatest potential asset was its people. After the
pacification of Nigeria made long-distance travel
possible, Easterners began flocking to the towns in
search of new economic opportunities as traders and
laborers, and after they received some education, as
clerks and administrators. Since the major early
commercial and administrative centers, with the
exception of Calabar, were located outside of the
East, members of Eastern communities often migrated
to the West and the North. By 1966 some 2 million
Easterners out of a total population of approximately
12 million resided outside the Region.[3] Several new
urban centers also grew up in the East: Enugu, the
regional capital and center of the coal mining industry; Port Harcourt, the East's major port and industrial center; Onitsha, a trading center with the
largest market in Africa; and Aba. However, the
ambitiousness of the people combined with the lack

of existing opportunities for advancement in the
rural areas of the East encouraged large numbers
of Easterners to emigrate, thus depriving the East
of some of its most talented citizens.

Statistics compiled during the 1950's showed the
East to be less developed economically than the West
but in many ways to be more advanced than the North,
where the exclusion of the Christian missionaries
and the conservatism of the emirs had retarded the
rate of development. When revenues were regionalized
according to the principle of derivation under the
1954 constitutional reforms, the reapportionment of
revenues reduced the proportionate share of the East.[4]
Furthermore, since the East earned its export revenues
primarily from the products of oil palms growing wild,
its financial base seemed somewhat less elastic than
the West's with its cocoa and the North with its tin,
cotton, and groundnuts. The other major agricultural
products of the East, yams and cassava, were consumed
internally. The report of the International Bank
for Reconstruction and Development published in 1955
listed a per capita income of £N21* for the East as
compared with £N34 in the West and £N17 in the North.[5]

The discovery of oil in commercial quantities
in the East transformed its economic outlook. In
fact the oil boom caused many people to forget that
until recently the East had a relatively poor resource
base. Oil companies began prospecting in the East
in 1938 and finally discovered commercially profitable
oil fields in 1956. By 1958 Nigeria entered the ranks
of oil exporters. Six years later oil became the
most valuable Nigerian export, surpassing the cocoa
grown in the West. In 1965 oil exports were valued
£N68 million, approximately two thirds of which
derived from oil fields in the East and the remainder
from the Mid-West. Prior to 1967, when the outbreak
of the war temporarily halted oil production, Shell-
British Petroleum, the largest oil producer in Nigeria,
had invested some £N150 million, mostly in the East,

---

*£N = Nigerian pound. One £N = $2.82.

and achieved an annual output of 15 million tons.[6]
Since the East received almost two thirds of the
revenues from its oil production, the regional government had considerably more money available to it after
1958. For example, in 1964-65 the respective revenues
raised by the regions were approximately £N26 million
in the North, £N23.4 million in the East, £N18.8
million in the West, and £N5.8 million in the Mid-
West, giving the East the highest per capita resource
base.[7]

     While the production of oil gave the Eastern
government more revenue to invest in development
schemes, it did not alter the basic economic patterns
in the rural areas. Little of the money and few of
the benefits from the oil industry flowed back to
the village dweller. Despite its investment and
production, Shell-British Petroleum employed a total
of only 4,000 people in both the East and the Mid-West.
Hence statistics for the East during this period are
somewhat misleading since they inflate the real per
capita income. According to figures released in 1967
the gross national product of the Eastern Region was
£N552 million and its per capita income was £N38.4,
calculated on the basis of a population of 14 million
(which was probably somewhat inflated).

     In addition to oil production, the East had
coal mining and several other light industries. Coal
mining in the East began in 1917. The collieries
at Enugu, which were managed by the Nigerian Coal
Corporation, sold the coal principally to the Nigerian
and Ghanaian railways. Even before the civil war
halted production, the coal mining operations there
had several major problems deriving from dieselization
of the railways, low quality of the coal, and high
cost of production. Light industries in the East included brewing, lumbering and saw milling, manufacturing of cement and asbestos cement products, tire
manufacturing, and a small steel rolling mill.
Several processing industries were financed and
managed by the Eastern Nigerian Development Corporation
(ENDC). However, many of these ENDC enterprises were
not operated profitably, and by 1963 the ENDC had
sustained losses of £N1.3 million.[8]

The cities and villages in the East were linked
by one of the best road systems in Africa. As a
result of the large investment in roads in the 1958
to 1962 regional development program, in which transport was allocated 28 percent of the capital outlay,
the road mileage figures for the East increased to
17,722 miles, 1,443 of which had a bituminous surface.
By 1966 the East had one mile of road for every 1.8
square miles of territory making most villages accessible during the dry season, except for those in the
riverine areas of the Niger Delta and the areas east
of the Cross River. According to one geographer,
Eastern Nigeria had "the best-developed road system
in Nigeria and probably the densest network of comparable size on the African continent."[9]

By the early sixties the East was a good example
of the uneven type of development that typifies so
many new states. The oil installations and the
small-scale industries in the urban centers contrasted
sharply with the virtually unchanged technological
and economic conditions in the countryside, where
approximately 80 percent of its people lived. Although the East had one of the highest levels of
educational development in Africa or Asia--with a
primary school enrolment of 1.25 million and over
3,000 secondary schools by 1967--and one of the
largest crops of highly trained manpower--with some
700 lawyers, 600 engineers, and 500 doctors by 1967--
the heavy investment in education (more than 40 percent of the government's recurrent expenditure) did
not directly lead to a transformation of the economy.
Most of the 50,000 students who left primary school
each year, as well as the secondary school and university graduates, flocked to the cities rather than
becoming farmers. By 1965 there were approximately
350,000 unemployed school-leavers, and many analysts
projected a crisis by 1970 brought on by the high
numbers of jobless, partially educated Easterners.[10]

Development planning for Eastern Nigeria, as
with the performance of most government functions,
was primarily undertaken by the regional rather than
the federal government. Development planning in
Nigeria by the colonial administration began in 1944

in response to the request by the Secretary of State
for Colonies that all British dependencies prepare
development proposals during the next ten years for
their respective territories. This initial aggregate
of proposals, which was to cover the 1946 to 1956
period, soon became outmoded by political events.
The establishment of a federation in 1954 caused
planning to be regionalized. Detailed projective
planning, to the extent that it was ever engaged in
during the life of the first Nigerian Republic,
therefore reflected a regionally oriented perspective.
Even the 1962 to 1968 development program, which
was described as a National Plan, "was no more than
four separate plans formulated, decided, and presented
by each of the four governments with, no doubt, some
recognition of common objectives and economic targets."[11]

As in most new states, the economic development
programs prepared by the regional governments in
Nigeria more closely resembled a catalogue of priorities and projects than a blueprint providing a
detailed, comprehensive strategy for development.
The shortcomings of these programs resulted from
several factors: the difficulties involved in
obtaining information relevant to the planning process,
the inadequacy of planning institutions and personnel,
and the unsuitability of the political process for
comprehensive planning.[12] The absence of facts
essential for planning led Wolfgang Stolper, head
of the federal economic planning unit from 1960 to
1962, to entitle his book deriving from that experience
Planning without Facts, and by this Stolper meant
more than a dearth of relevant statistics.[13] His
title also referred to the difficulties the planners
had in posing the critical questions, so that the
required information would be forthcoming. Moreover,
the regional government had to rely on an administration whose organization and personnel were more
suited to maintaining law and order than planning or
promoting development. The Eastern government did
not fundamentally reform the administrative set-up
inherited from the colonial regime despite static
orientation. In addition, none of the regions established a scheme of government service specifically
for economists who might supplement the generalist

orientation of most civil servants. Perhaps most
significantly, as one Nigerian economist has stated:

> Even at the regional level, the leadership,
> though in full control of their regions,
> did not appear to understand its pro-
> cesses. Development to many of these
> political leaders meant the provision of
> social services and a pork-barrel distri-
> bution of industrial projects. It mat-
> tered very little whether the satisfac-
> tion of purely political considerations
> was at the expense of rapid growth in
> the GDP.[14]

Following regionalization in 1954, each regional
government prepared a development program for the 1955
to 1960 period. Owing to the shortage of funds for
capital investment, the Eastern government merely formulated the barest outline of a development plan in contrast to the more detailed plan for expenditures published by the Western Region. When the export of oil
transformed the economic outlook of the East with
regard to revenues, the government revised the original program to cover the 1958 to 1962 period, quadru-
puling projected capital investment from £N5.2 million
to £N20.7 million. The largest component of the
1958 to 1962 plan was for transport, which constituted
28 percent of the capital expenditure, followed by
water, which was 17 percent, and trade and industry
at 9 percent.[15] A variety of difficulties encountered
by the Eastern government prevented it from fully
implementing the plan. A shortage of engineers,
architects, and supervisory personnel delayed the
execution of transport projects. A time lag of six
months to a year between the placing of orders for
materials and equipment and their arrival further
postponed progress on all kinds of projects. Nearly
£N2.6 million of the funds budgeted for the 1958 to
1962 program were carried over for the 1962 to 1968
plan period.[16]

The objectives set in the 1962-68 Eastern Nigeria
Development Plan gave priority to productivity rather
than infrastructure. The Eastern government, as did

the other regions, assigned first priority to agriculture with a proposed investment of £N36.8 million
(34 percent of the total) in agriculture, animal
husbandry, fisheries, and forests during the life of
the plan. Manufacturing and processing industries
were second, representing £N13.5 million or 12 percent
of the total development budget. The plan accorded
third priority to technical training and education
in order to train the technical manpower needed to
attain the other targets. The government expected
to contribute £N51.5 million of the projected costs
of the plan and make up the £N45.9-million deficit
through external aid.[17]

    The planned investment by the government did
not precipitate rapid development for several reasons.
The total investment was not sufficiently large
and was often expended on projects that benefited
few people. Furthermore, many of the enterprises in
which the government invested operated at a deficit,
and some of the sectors, like education, which consumed a large portion of government expenditure, did
not have immediate productive economic derivations.
Finally, expectations of external aid proved to be
overly optimistic.

                THE INSTITUTIONAL FRAMEWORK

    Until the military take-over in 1966, the insti-
tutional framework of the Eastern Region resembled
the central Nigerian structures since both were based
on the Westminister parliamentary model bequeathed
by the British. Eastern Nigeria, like the other
regions, had a popularly elected House of Assembly
and a House of Chiefs. The members of the House of
Assembly were elected from multimember constituencies
until the 1961 regional election when the East was
reapportioned into 146 single member districts. As
Chapter 3 will indicate in more detail, the precolonial political systems in the East did not have
chiefs who wielded permanent executive authority.
Hence, initially, the Eastern Region did not have a
bicameral legislature. However, the Eastern government succumbed to public demand and established a

House of Chiefs in 1959 so that the Eastern Region
would not lack anything the other two regions had.
In the East the House of Chiefs served as a ceremonial
institution. The Constitution vested the executive
authority of the region in a governor, who was appointed by the president of Nigeria on the advice of
the Eastern premier. In practice the premier and
his council of ministers exercised executive authority.
The governor could only act on the advice of the
premier.

After the 1954 regionalization of the government
structure, separate civil service, marketing board
apparatus, and development corporations were established in the East. The Eastern Civil Service Commission set the conditions for recruitment, transfer,
dismissal, and discipline for the public services in
the East. Following this regionalization of the
civil service, members appointed to posts in the East
tended to be of Eastern origin, as was the case in
the other regions. The Eastern Nigeria Marketing
Board controlled the export of the palm oil, palm
kernels, cocoa, beniseed, soybeans, groundnuts, and
copra grown in the region in order to stablize producer prices during a single crop season and to
minimize fluctuations between seasons. By maintaining
a monopoly on the export of agricultural produce,
and particularly on the marketing of the palm products,
which in 1962 constituted about 90 percent by value
of the region's exports, the Marketing Board could
also attempt to control and improve standards of
quality. In addition, the Marketing Board accumulated
financial reserves from the difference between the
world price of the commodities and the amount paid
to producers which could then be employed to foster
economic development.

For purposes of administration, the Eastern
Region was originally divided into 5 provinces, and
then in 1958 the 5 provinces were redivided into 12
provinces, each of which was headed by a provincial
commissioner. The provinces were subdivided into
29 divisions, 107 county council areas, and some
7,000 villages. The county councils had the responsibility for providing local services and undertaking

certain local public works projects. The 900 subordinate local councils generally failed to perform
any significant functions.

POLITICS IN EASTERN NIGERIA

     Politics in Eastern Nigeria was inexorably linked
to the fortunes of the National Convention of Nigerian
Citizens (NCNC), the dominant political party in the
region. The NCNC originated in 1944 as a coalition
of existing organizations that had joined together
to work for self-government for Nigeria. As the
first mass political party in Nigeria, the NCNC
always claimed to be a national rather than a regional
political party. While the NCNC continued to maintain
the national orientation and aspirations of its
founders, its solid base support after 1951 was
confined to the Eastern Region, and after its establishment in 1964, the Mid-West Region. When the
party formed in 1944, it had a Yoruba president, and
up to the time of its dissolution in 1966 by the
military government, the NCNC always had national
officers from several regions and ethnic groups.
However, the party tended to be identified with Nnamdi
Azikiwe, an Ibo who was its first general secretary
and its president after 1946. Although Azikiwe considered himself a Nigerian, rather than an Ibo,
political leader, in the Western and Northern Regions
and among some of the minority (or non-Ibo) communities
in the East the NCNC came to be viewed as a predominantly Ibo political party.

     Initially the NCNC received the warm support of
all politically conscious groups and individuals in
the East. When the party organized for the 1951 election, Nnamdi Azikiwe chose to stand from a constituency
in Lagos, the federal capital, and Eyo Ita, an Efik,
was considered to be the leader of the NCNC in the
East. Contrary to its expectations that the NCNC would
win a majority of seats in both the East and the West,
the results of the election left Azikiwe as leader
of the opposition in the Western House and Ita as the
head of the government in the East. The ensuing dispute between Azikiwe and certain ministers in the

Eastern government, led by Ita, over continued participation in the political system established under the
Richards Constitution ended with the bitter expulsion
of the Ita group. Expelled Ibo supporters of Ita
eventually rejoined the NCNC, but many of the politicians from other ethnic groups formed another political party, the United National Independence Party.
Although the NCNC eventually regained strong electoral
support in the minority areas, it never achieved the
earlier allegiance and spontaneous popularity from
most of the people there. Its large electoral major-
ities reflected the expedient assessment of the
inhabitants of these areas that it was advantageous
to cooperate with the dominant regional party.

     In theory the NCNC was a mass party of individual
members, who were organized in local branches and
directed by the decisions of the national party con-
ventions as conveyed by the officers and secretariat
organization. However, even in the Eastern Region
the local organization of the party was always tenuous,
and coordination between the regional bodies and
branches was virtually nonexistent. At no time did
the NCNC invest the requisite time or resources for
establishing a strong branch organization. To a
great extent, the early success of the NCNC in the
East and the absence of an effective opposition there
eliminated the need for party leaders to actively
concern themselves with its organizational weakness.
The only strong opposition to the NCNC came from
independents who bolted the party, usually over the
issue of nominations. Most of the independents
sought to rejoin the NCNC after the election.

     One frequently heard comment about Nigerian
politics is that parties relied on mass participation
of a communal nature in their core regions. In order
for party on a gemeinschaft or communal basis to
evolve, members and supporters had to "conceive of
their party as an extension of the social order into
which they have been born and to which they attribute
spiritual or mystical significance."[18] Once membership in such a party became integrated into a total
world view, supporters would view opposition to that
party by other members of the community as a form of

antisocial conduct. Ethnic solidarity did sometimes constitute one source of support for the NCNC,
but as Richard Sklar and C. S. Whitaker, Jr. observed,
ethnic affinity by itself did not give rise to communal participation.[19]

   The NCNC rarely received such a gemeinschaft
allegiance from its supporters, even from rural Ibo
communities. Ethnic solidarity existed primarily
at the level of the local community and only tenuously
for the more-encompassing ethnic groups. The Ibo,
Ibibio, and Ijaw identities developed relatively
late and consequently were not traditional forms of
allegience. Political competition in the East rarely
invoked these residual pan-ethnic identities. Instead,
regional politics revolved around efforts by representatives of local communities to gain amenities
for their constituents. These local representatives
sometimes formed alliances within the NCNC, but these
political blocs usually reflected provincial or
divisional rather than ethnic boundaries. While the
NCNC did receive support from an overwhelming majority
of Ibo (and non-Ibo Eastern) people, many of them
did so because of the advantages they believed they
could reap. When communities invoked the need for
political solidarity they based their actions on
rational calculations of political benefits and not
on the mystical quality of membership in the NCNC.

   The local orientation of political participants
made the NCNC prone to dissension. In conflict situations provoked by local communal tensions, loyalty
to the primary community generally outweighed allegience to the political party. Hence the NCNC
suffered in every election from the defection of
supporters who voted for independents from their
community. Branches frequently became engrossed in
purely local matters, like the competition between
two subgroups for dominance in the community, ignoring
or resisting the directives of higher NCNC bodies.
The absence of a strong, mystical, irrational
gemeinschaft attachment to political parties also
left them vulnerable to religious and class conflicts,
as well as to communal tensions. Disputes arose in
Eastern Nigeria and within the NCNC over the issues

of whether public support for parochial schools
should entitle the government to prescribe standards
and curriculum and whether the government should
restrict the expansion of parochial schools, despite
the support of both Catholics and Protestants for
the NCNC. Electoral contests for the party's nomi-
nation and the competition for appointed positions
also engendered conflicts between Catholics and
Protestants.

     The political parties in power in all regions
of Nigeria consolidated their positions primarily
through manipulating the advantages that accrued
from control over the government. The regionalization
of marketing boards and public corporations afforded
the NCNC access to patronage over and above its ability
to direct the regional distribution of resources and
amenities to local communities. The Eastern Nigeria
Marketing Board appointed firms and individuals as
licensed agents to buy agricultural produce, which
the Board then exported for resale abroad. Although
licenses were supposed to be issued on the basis of
commercial criteria, political good will often had
to be present to expedite the transaction. For
example, in 1958 the Marketing Board did not reappoint
as soybean buying agent a previously licensed firm,
whose head had become a leading financial backer of
the new, opposition Democratic Party of Nigeria and
the Cameroons (formed by some dissident Ibo politicians who quickly returned to the NCNC fold).[20]
By channeling Marketing Board funds into the African
Continental Bank, the Eastern government enabled the
bank to extend credit to some Eastern businessmen.
Again political factors often influenced the decisions
as to which businessmen would receive loans from the
African Continental Bank or the public corporations.

     The NCNC combined the promise of the carrot with
the fear of the stick. In the Eastern Region candidates based their campaigns on the promise to build
more schools, roads, and hospitals and to bring
electricity to their constituents. Campaigning in
the Eastern Region, Premier Okpara was reported as
saying, "I will give you all the amenities you require
but you must first vote for me. Booty of war is

always shared after the war."[21] People commonly
believed, and often with justification, that the
regional government would refuse to allocate development funds to areas that voted for opposition parties.
Constituents also expected rewards in the form of
more amenities for their faithfulness in continuing
to return party candidates to the regional and federal
legislatures.

CREATION OF NEW STATES

On January 15, 1966, a group of dissident junior-
and middle-grade officers assassinated the Northern
and Western Regional premiers, kidnapped and killed
Prime Minister Sir Abubakar Tafawa Balewa, and seized
key facilities in Kaduna, Enugu, and Ibadan. By the
next day, General J. T. U. Ironsi gained control of·
the situation, since most of the army remained loyal
to him. A rump of the federal Council of Ministers
then convened and decided to invite the army to take
over the government, which they did. General Ironsi
suspended the apparatus of government established
under the constitution and installed a military regime
with a Supreme Military Council at the center and
military governors in the four regions.

The events following that original coup and
the installation of the Ironsi regime are both too
familiar and too complex to warrant repeating here.
In May 1967, following a countercoup, three waves
of disorders in the North resulting in the deaths
of several thousand Eastern Nigerians, and abortive
constitutional conferences, Lieutenant-Colonel (now
General) Gowon, the head of the Supreme Military
Government, announced the division of Nigeria into
12 states. The Eastern Region of Nigeria became
three states: an Ibo East Central State, a predominantly Ijaw Rivers State, and a largely Ibibio
South-East State. Colonel Ojukwu, who claimed to
receive a mandate from the Eastern Consultative
Assembly to declare Eastern Nigeria a sovereign and
independent state, used the decree by Gowon as a
pretext for secession. On May 30, 1967, Ojukwu proclaimed Eastern Nigeria the "Republic of Biafra."

The cessation of hostilities with the surrender
of the secessionists in January 1970, has enabled
the Federal Military Government to implement fully
the decree dividing Eastern Nigeria into three states.
It will take several years to assess fully the consequences of the traumatic experiences brought by war
and their implications for political, economic, and
social development. However, events following the
war strengthen the prospect that the future will
bring reconciliation, reconstruction, and the opportunity for development.

Although Eastern Nigeria as such no longer exists,
its successor states have inherited its experience
with rural development. The cultural context, the
potential for development, and the options remain
largely the same within the new state boundaries.
The dynamics of rural development as described in
this study, however, pertain primarily to East Central
and South-East States, since the different ecological
conditions of the Rivers State require alternative
approaches.

NOTES

1. Census of the Eastern Region of Nigeria, 1953
(Lagos: Government Statistician, 1954); Population
Census of the Western Region of Nigeria, 1952 (Lagos:
Government Statistician, 1953). The detailed figures
from the 1963 census have never been published.

2. For a more detailed analysis of the role of
missionaries in the development of education in
Nigeria, see James S. Coleman, Nigeria: Background
to Nationalism (Berkeley and Los Angeles: University
of California Press, 1958), pp. 91-166.

3. Approximately this number of people came
fleeing back to the Eastern Region after the distur-
bances directed against Easterners in the North and
the West in 1966. While no detailed breakdowns are
available, it seems that Ibibio and Ijaws, along with
Ibos, emigrated to other parts of Nigeria in numbers

proportionate to their relative share of the Eastern
population. The 1963 census figure for the East was
12.4 million people. Some sources assume therefore
that after the 1966 repatriation the population of
the East was about 14 million. However, it is likely
that some of the 2 million emigrants returned to the
East in 1963 to be counted. Moreover, all of the
1963 census figures in Nigeria were probably inflated.

4. Richard L. Sklar, Nigerian Political Parties
(Princeton, N.J.: Princeton University Press, 1963),
p. 134.

5. The Economic Development of Nigeria (Baltimore: The Johns Hopkins Press, 1955), p. 616.

6. Barry Floyd, Eastern Nigeria: A Geographic
Review (New York: Frederick A. Praeger, Inc., 1969),
pp. 263-269.

7. Estimates of the Government of the Federation
of Nigeria, 1964-65 (Lagos: Government Printer,
1965).

8. On the modern industrial development of
Eastern Nigeria, see Floyd, op.cit., pp. 254-277,
312-313.

9. Ibid., p. 292. For more on the pattern of
communications in Eastern Nigeria see pp. 289-306.

10. On this point, see Ukpabi Asika, "Rehabilitation and Resettlement," paper presented at the
Conference on National Reconstruction and Development
in Nigeria, Ibadan, 1969, p. 8; and Floyd, p. 259.

11. Adebayo Adedeji, "Federalism and Development
Planning in Nigeria," paper presented at the Confer-
ence on National Reconstruction and Development in
Nigeria, Ibadan, 1969, p. 13.

12. See Chapter 5 for a more detailed discussion
pertaining to how the administrative structure and
political process affected rural development.

13.   Wolfgang F. Stolper, Planning without Facts:
Lessons in Resources Allocation from Nigeria's De-
velopment (Cambridge, Mass.:   Harvard University
Press, 1966), pp. 6-16.

14.   Adedeji, op. cit., pp. 21-22.

15.   Eastern Region of Nigeria, Revised Development
Programme 1958-62, Official Document No. 13 of 1960
(Enugu: Government Printer, 1960).

16.   Eastern Nigeria Development Plan, 1962-68,
Official Document No. 8 of 1962 (Enugu: Government
Printer, 1962), pp. 6-7.

17.   Ibid., pp. 8-17.

18.   Richard L. Sklar and C. S. Whitaker, "Nigeria," in James S. Coleman and Carl G. Rosberg, Jr.,
eds., Political Parties and National Integration in
Tropical Africa (Berkeley and Los Angeles: University
of California Press, 1964), p. 620.

19.   Ibid., p. 620.

20.   Ibid., p. 634.

21.   The statement is quoted in John P. Mackintosh,
Nigerian Government and Politics (London: George
Allen and Unwin, Ltd., 1966). p. 525.

3

**PRECOLONIAL
SOCIETIES
AND
THEIR
TRANSFORMATION**

Sources commonly described the population of
the Eastern Region of Nigeria as constituted by three
large ethnic groups--the Ibo, the Ibibio (including
the Efik), and the Ijaw--and up to 40 much smaller
ethnic communities, many of which were located in
Ogoja Province. According to the 1952 census, Ibos
comprised approximately 61 percent of the population
of the region, Ibibios 15 percent, and Ijaws 3 percent.[1] These ethnic labels currently employed to
designate the major groups in the Eastern Region
did not evoke recognition from most of their members
until late in the colonial period. Prior to the
imposition of colonial rule, the territorial area
that was to be incorporated into Eastern Nigeria was
inhabited by a multitude of small, autonomous communities ranging in size from about 200 to 8,000.
In the dense forests that cover much of the region,
in the swamps, and on the small islands in the Niger
Delta, the allegiance and identification of the people
reflected the primacy of the self-contained small
village.

Some communities did acknowledge cultural bonds
with contiguous villages deriving from a common
ancestry. Ibo villages so related often formed a
village-group with a central meeting place containing
a shrine to Ale, the earth goddess, and a market.[2]
Ibibio villages subscribing to a common myth of
origin usually had a shared tutelary deity and totem.[3]

37

In most cases, however, these kinship bonds did not
give rise to the emergence of effective political
units. Components of Ibo village groups sent representatives to intermittent meetings regarding the
common shrine and market place but usually did not
have other permanent political institutions regular-
izing relations or sponsoring joint activities.
Although Ibibio communities often shared a common
name and considered themselves a cultural unit, the
clans did not generally constitute effective political
entities capable of unified action. Each village
in the region jealously guarded its independence and
regarded most of its neighbors as potentially hostile.
Somewhat like the relations inherent in the European
state system in the seventeenth and eighteenth centuries, each village stood in a state of opposition
to or armed neutrality with most adjoining communities.

Hence prior to the colonial period, the Eastern
Region did not exist as a unified political, economic,
or cultural entity. This does not, of course, imply
that the self-contained communities lacked similar
social and political institutions or that they were
totally isolated from one another. As the following
discussion will show, the available ethnographic
data reveals many institutional resemblances among
the different linguistic groups. According to G. I.
Jones, communities often did recognize a kind of
system of law governing relationships between them.
When violations occured, the wronged community would
more frequently respond with economic sanctions than
by the use of force, because war was so costly and
usually indecisive between these evenly matched
groups.[4] Moreover, religious diviners, craftsmen,
and traders did travel through large parts of the
area. Research has also shown that a system of
distributive trade in slaves, foodstuffs, salt, and
crafts developed over the centuries connecting the
hinterland with the delta.[5]

Eventually one marginal Ibo group, the Aro, came
to dominate the hinterland trade, primarily through
their manipulation of the oracle located at Aro
Chuku. The emergence of this oracle as the most
universally respected and feared throughout the Ibo

territory occurred simultaneously with the rise of
the Aro as the middlemen in the slave trade. When
some individuals and communities could not resolve
a dispute or when a person or groups wished to appeal
a decision, they sometimes journeyed to Aro Chuku
to consult the deity. The penalty imposed by the
Aro through the deity for a negative decision was a
fine to be paid in slaves, supposedly eaten by the
Chuku, but in actuality sold to the coastal dealers.
Hired mercenaries also gathered slaves for the Aro.

The economic influence of the Aro over other
forms of trade derived from the series of settlements
they established along the main training routes. The
presence of the Aro in an area usually insured a
peace in which trade could flourish. There were
three kinds of Aro settlements, each entailing a
different relationship with the indigenous community.
Those founded along the main trade routes or on the
fringes of communities did not directly interfere in
the affairs of the neighboring villages. Larger
settlements located adjacent to central market places
dominated the management of the market, but did not
infringe upon the autonomy of the community in other
respects. Some large-scale Aro settlements displaced
the governing institutions of the surrounding villages,
transforming their inhabitants into vassals.[6]

The activities of the Aro did not initiate a
sense of common identity or unity among the communities
they harassed. Nor can their trading empire be considered a political system in any normally accepted
definition of that term.[7] Furthermore, since Aro
control encompassed only a small portion of the
communities now designated as Ibo, even if one con-
siders their trading hegemony to be a proto-political
system, the Aro failed to unify the territory later
included in the East. While the extreme political
fragmentation did mask certain institutional and
cultural similarities, these shared traits and the
bonds that linked the disparate communities should
not be overemphasized. The eventual acceptance of
a common ethnic identity by linguistically related
groups owed more to the social forces unleashed
during the colonial period than to the underlying
traditional configurations.

PRECOLONIAL SOCIAL AND POLITICAL
INSTITUTIONS

The fragmented nature of the precolonial pattern
of authority presents fundamental difficulties in for-
mulating models of the traditional societies. Since
there were over 600 separate communities among the
people now called Ibo and probably about that many
constituted by other ethnic groups, considerable variation must have existed. Classifications of the Ibo
and Ibibio peoples divide them into numerous subgroups
on the basis of dialect, customs, and institutions.
In their seminal work on the Ibo and Ibibio speaking
peoples, Daryll Forde and G. I. Jones, for example,
enumerate five major Ibo divisions and six main Ibibio
groups. It is difficult to generalize about the Ibo
or Ibibio ethnic blocs as a unit, let alone include
them in a general discussion with the other smaller
ethnic groups in the region.

Furthermore the knowledge about the precolonial
societies is superficial at best and virtually nonexistent for many of the communities. Since no docu-
ments or reports describing the traditional societies
prior to the coming of European traders exist, anthropologists have attempted to reconstruct the precolonial
baseline by examining villages that seemed not to have
undergone much social change and by collecting oral
histories and legends. Most of the anthropological
research completed has been single village studies
from which social scientists have tried to generalize
about entire ethnic groups. Moreover, little field
work of any type has been conducted on many of the
smaller ethnic groups in the region. With these qualifications in mind, a discussion of the precolonial
social and political institutions of the Ibo, Ibibio,
and Ijaw follows.

As previously indicated, the village was the
operative level of most social and political institutions for the ethnic groups residing in what was to
become the Eastern Region. If present village size
approximations reflect precolonial dimensions, Ibo
villages averaged about 5,000 people, Ibibio 500, and
Ijaw 250 or less.[8] Members of Ibo and Ibibio villages

recognized a common mythological ancestor, the founder
of the village, thus making the village a kinship
unit. Some Ijaw villages, like the Kalabari, did
not acknowledge a common ancestry for the community's
various lineages. Instead, village unity derived
from a sense of territorial isolation, political
autonomy, and cultural distinctiveness.9

Even when all members of a village traced their
ancestry to a common founder, the kinship organization
emphasized divisions within the community. Throughout
the area, most communities had a segmentary social
structure consisting of several coequal groups having
a weak superior or none at all. The basic social
unit was usually a patrilineage, a kinship group
comprised of all the descendants in the male line of
a particular individual. Some communities had a
system of double descent whereby kinship obligations
and inheritance were traced through both the father's
and the mother's lineages. In a few Ijaw communities,
whether a child belonged to his father's or mother's
line depended on the size of the dowry the father
had paid since only "big dowry" marriages conferred
rights over the children to the man's side. There
were also a few isolated instances in the area where
communities were organized according to matrilineages,
i.e., kinship units incorporating all the descendants
in the female line of a particular woman.

Irrespective of the descent system on which they
were constituted, the lineal segments of a village
were the basis of the social organization. Each
lineage undertook the tasks of social control and
arbitration of disputes among its own members, as well
as arranging for their participation in cooperative
endeavors. In addition to performing ceremonial
functions as the intermediary between the living
members of the lineage and their ancestors, the lineage
head sometimes represented individual members and
the kinship unit in its relations with outsiders.
Hence, for the most part, members of a lineage conducted their affairs internally without reference
to any other institution or individual within the
village. In some Ibibio and Ijaw villages the lineal
segments, (which anthropologists refer to as wards)

operated as autonomous political, as well as social,
units. Lineage heads tended to be vested with moral
authority and ritual obligations rather than with
political power. In some communities the oldest
member of the lineage automatically assumed its head-
ship when the office was vacant, unless he was found
objectionable. In other communities the lineage
head was selected by the members for his leadership
abilities.

     Among the few Ijaw and Ibibio communities that
turned from their traditional pursuit of fishing or
farming to trading with European merchants, the
lineage organization developed into an economic and
fighting unit. In the Ijaw communities of Bonny,
Kalabari (New Calabar), Opobo, and Nembe (Brass),
an individual wealthy enough to man and maintain
a costly war canoe could found a new canoe house.
If the canoe house was successful and expanded economically, successful members often started a new
house, which was subordinate to the older trading
corporation from which it derived. The heads or
chiefs of the main and the subordinate houses were
elected by the other members and could be deposed
if they did not exhibit commercial and administrative
ability. Nevertheless, the heads of the houses
exercised a great deal more power than the lineage
heads in the villages.

     The Efik-Ibibio settlement of Calabar similarly
had houses (ufok) based, at least originally, on the
patrilineage. Since the Efik farmed as well as traded,
their houses were also landholding and residential
units. Houses went raiding up the Cross River for
slaves and then either sold them to Europeans or
used them as laborers on their land or plantations.
When the position became vacant, elders chose the
new head of the house from the suitable male members.
As among the Ijaw trading communities, the commercial
activities of the house tended to concentrate more
power in the head than he had previously held.

     To compensate somewhat for the vertical division
of the village into segments based on descent, three
other types of organizations developed in most of

the communities: age groupings, title and/or secret
societies, and village assemblies. Age organizations
differed in their complexity, workings, and importance
from area to area. In most communities all children
born within a certain period of time, frequently
three years, became members of a male or female age
set. When the members of the age set reached some
age, often about 15, they formally initiated the
unit by taking a name and beginning to meet regularly.
Since female age sets did not have any significant
functions in many communities, they usually ceased
operating following the initiation. In contrast,
the male age organizations, which included both the
sets constituted every three years and the groups
formed by cooperation among several age sets, performed much of the communal work in the village and
in so doing helped to integrate the society.

In addition to the boys under 15, there were
three other categories of males in the villages:
the juniors, or the age group on the threshold of
recognition, the middle age group of young men, and
the elders. The junior age group usually prepared
a feast for the village to mark the arrival of their
maturity and assumption of communal duties. Most
tasks requiring communal labor, like clearing paths
and defending the village, were assigned to the
middle age group. In most communities the senior
age group or elders formally administered the village.

Title and secret societies also cut across
kinship segments because they generally accepted any
member of the village who could pay a prescribed
entrance fee. Somewhat less commonly, war societies
brought together the ablest fighting men, again
regardless of their lineage affiliation. Most villages
had at least one title and one secret society, and
many had several. A title was a manifestation of
wealth, since entrance to a society usually depended
on either the provision of a large feast for the
members or elaborate "second burial" (funeral) rituals.
In contrast to the title societies, secret societies
were primarily secret cults of supernatural beings.
They would attempt to propitiate the spirits by
holding ceremonial masquerades and pageants. Although

entrance to the secret societies also depended on
the payment of a fee, in many cases the fees were
sufficiently low that most of the men in the village
could join. Some of the title and secret societies
accorded ranks to members in terms of gradations
based on age or wealth.

In many communities, title and secret society
members assumed political roles. Since the acquisition
of wealth conferred social status in many of the
communities, other members of the village considered
title holders to be leading citizens. Thus title
holders often exercised a great deal of influence
in the formulation of political decisions. If all
the men in a village were members of its secret society, the village elders, who were also the leaders
of the society, disciplined other members in the
name of the supernatural being to whom the society
ministered. The Ekpe society of the Efiks, a secret
society with grades depending on fee payments, became
a paramount political force in Calabar. Decisions
of the chief (Obong) regarding trade with Europeans
often required the acquiesence of the Ekpe Society
and could only be appealed to them. Members of the
Ekpe society also enforced the decisions, sometimes
with violent sanctions.

Despite local variations, matters concerning
the entire village were decided by a village meeting
or council which intermittently exercised political
authority for the village. As G. I. Jones indicated
in the report on chiefs and natural rulers that he
wrote for the Eastern government, "one of the most
striking features of this survey has been the uniformity of the traditional form of local government
throughout the region."[10] Among many Ibo communities,
when the assembly met, every adult male could attend
and voice his opinions. After the preliminary
discussion, the elders of the village retired to make
a decision. This decision, however, had to be approved
by the assembly before it became operative. Moreover,
political leadership was only theoretically the
conciliatory prerogative of the elders. When the elders
withdrew to formulate their decision, they allowed
certain "natural leaders" to influence the outcome.

These "natural leaders" have sometimes been compared
with American political bosses because they depended
on their skills as arbitrators and their capacity to
perform services for their supporters to retain their
influence. In a segmentary society with its inherent
proclivity for disputes between lineages and individuals, political leaders could rarely stabilize their
position. As soon as he lost his ability to represent
successfully the interest of his supporters in
negotiations with similar leaders within his village
or from adjoining communities, he lost his influence
base.

In most Ibibio and Ijaw communities, on the
other hand, the village assembly or council was
attended only by the members of the most senior age
sets. Less information detailing the dynamics of
these council meetings exists than on the Ibo.
According to Robin Horton's account of Ijaw government, "Acquisition of influence in the assembly is
one of the chief preoccupations of the male villager's
life; and he seeks this influence by trying to com-
bine the support of his lineage members with that
of his age-mates, nonlineage kin and friends."[11]
Since all members of specific age groupings in the
village participated in these assemblies or councils
as equals, it seems very likely that "natural leaders"
emerged to mold the decision-making process in most
communities.

Consequently, chieftancy as it is normally con-
ceived--i.e., a person occupying an inherited position
of permanent executive authority--did not exist in
most precolonial Eastern communities. With certain
exceptions, such as the Onitsha kingship and the Ijaw
and Efik trading communities, the precolonial political
systems lacked a differentiated administrative structure and permanent elective or hereditary political
offices. Many of the communities, however, did
recognize an individual as the traditional head of
the village or village-group, who embodied the unity
of the group. Aside from assuming this symbolic
function, the head of the village, who was designated
by a variety of titles, did not perform even the roles
inhering in the limited chieftancy of the traditional

pyramidal political systems, like the Yoruba in
Western Nigeria. The village headman, for example,
rarely had any elaborate religious functions, even
though every group tended to have a tutelary spirit
of its own. Unlike the pattern prevailing in the
pyramidal political systems, the village headman
did not pronounce the decisions of the village
councils or assemblies in order for them to become
sanctioned as the law of the community. Moreover,
as the description of the village assemblies and
councils indicated, the deliberative and executive
functions of a community were exercised collectively
by all male members of the community or specific age
sets or covertly by natural leaders.

     In most communities, succession to the headship
depended on a combination of factors relating to
age and descent. Often the head of the village or
village-group came from one lineage or a few lineages
among whom the succession rotated. Sometimes the
eldest male member of the senior lineage automatically
assumed the office when it became vacant by death
or, in the case of a few Ijaw and Ibibio villages,
deposition. (In almost all communities title holders
and the village headman would lose their positions
if they committed certain offenses.) In many communities the rules governing succession were altered
by considerations pertaining to the suitability of
the candidate: his social standing, wealth, character
and popularity. In many Ijaw villages the personal
qualities of the candidate displaced all other criteria
in determining the selection.[12]

     Onitsha, a traditional Ibo community on the
Eastern bank of the Niger River, had a political
system resembling the kingdom of Benin, from which
the Onitshans claimed descent. While the Onitshan
king was vested with many more ceremonial functions
than a village head and while his position was imbued
with religious significance, his actual political
powers were limited. Richard Henderson has described
the traditional political system of Onitsha as "a
system of compact village-groups which combines an
ideology of 'divine kingship,' theoretically possessin
centralized controls, with retention of a genealogical

segmentary political system."[13] As in the case of
segmentary political systems found throughout the
area, lineages retained control over their land,
houses, shrines, and internal dealings. Within the
separate village units, individuals and groups com-
peted for the office of chieftancy, which was based
on achievement. Age sets and age groups crosscut
and integrated the villages, and during crises these
age organizations could sometimes mobilize the Onitsha
population.

Not only was the actual power of the king limited
by the segmentary nature of the society and the independent authority of the sub-chiefs and the age
organizations, two thirds of the men of the Onitsha
community were eligible for elevation to the kingship,
thus often engendering intense competition and
bargaining over the succession. Moreover, recent
research into oral history and early historical records
has indicated that in the centuries prior to coloni-
zation the Onitshan political system underwent an
evolution that increased the scope of achievement
criteria and eroded the prerogatives of ascribed
status. This evolution benefited the sub-chiefs and
accentuated the trend towards decentralization at the
expense of the king.[14]

The centralization of power among the Efik in
Calabar and the Ijaw living in trading ports was an
adaptive response to the needs of the elaborate
trading system that developed. In Calabar European
traders demanded some mechanism for assuring that
trade contracts would be honored so that the procedures
and conditions of the slave trade could be regularized.
The Efik responded by establishing a chief as their
only recognized representative in dealings with the
European traders. Gradually the elected chief and
the subordinate heads of the various trading houses
gained considerable political power, partly through
the respect they were accorded by the European
traders.[15] Besides playing a role in regulating
trade, the kings of Bonny, Opobo, Kalabari, and Nembe
acted to prevent any of the trading houses in their
communities from attaining a dominant position by
counterbalancing the power of the expanding trading
house through aligning with several of its rivals.

TRADITIONAL VALUES AND ATTITUDES

The dearth of research and accurate information
on other aspects of the traditional cultures makes
the ethnographic data available on social and political
organization seem like a cornucopia. Some anthropologists have researched aspects of culture taken
in a narrow sense, that is, ceremonies, marriage practices, and religious observances. Broader and more
significant dimensions of culture, however, such as
the norms, orientations, values, and attitudes underlying and infusing the institutions and processes of
the societies, have generally been neglected. In
part this reflects the training and orientation of
the anthropologists who have done field work in Africa.
Also a researcher concerned with traditional values
and attitudes would confront almost insurmountable
obstacles. Few areas in the region have been left
untouched by aspects of modern life. The rapid
Christianization and expansion of educational facilities in the East in the past century have rendered
most potential informants inaccurate interpreters
of their traditional culture. Moreover, the research
techniques necessary to elicit attitudes and values
tend to be more time consuming, expensive, and
methodologically controversial than the participant
observation and use of informants relied on to gather
information regarding social and political organization.

Interpreters of Ibo culture have emphasized
its receptivity to change and achievement orientation.[16] According to these interpretations, Ibo
society conferred an equality of opportunity on its
members. Children did not inherit their parents'
role or social status in the community, but instead
embarked on their own career path in search of wealth
and the prestige associated with it. Hence competition ensued in all spheres of life between individuals
and between segments of the community. The predisposition toward individualism and excessive competition was, however, somewhat offset by strong corporate
loyalty and acceptance of obligations to the community.
With its emphasis on achievement, individual choice,

and alternate paths, the underlying world view of
the Ibo incorporated the very essence of the open
system--change. The Ibo perceived a dynamic world
in which all things underwent change and were subject
to manipulation, even man's relationship with the
spiritual order. Consequently, according to these
interpretations, the precolonial Ibo culture embodied
many of the characteristics considered to inhere in
modernity. Underneath the facade of simple or "primitive" institutional development dwelled a very
"modern" value orientation. The transformation of
Ibo society during the colonial period therefore was
a function of the interaction between traditional
patterns of response and the changed environment with
its new opportunities.

Although more work has been done on Ibo culture
than on the other ethnic groups in the East, the
highly generalized accounts of the Ibo pose many questions that cannot be answered. The fragmented nature
of the traditional Ibo sociopolitical systems and
the absence of even a sense of common identity among
the communities now classified as Ibo-speaking promoted
considerable diversity. Classifications of the Ibo
commonly divide them into several categories, which
sometimes are individually referred to as tribes.
Yet virtually no attempt has been made to distinguish
the culture of one Ibo subgroup from another beyond
detailing certain ceremonial differences. The elevation of these descriptions of the highly ambitious,
energetic, innovative, and individualistic Ibo into
a stereotype has doubtlessly influenced subsequent
researchers, who have interpreted their findings to
fit the mold and thus emphasized the uniformities
rather than variations.

Available data suggest that the Ibibio and Ijaw
peoples shared many of the cultural traits now
associated with the Ibo. Again the reader should
be forewarned that this conclusion is based on limited
sources and fragmentary information. The results
of the attitude survey the authors undertook of
villagers in Eastern Nigeria, which will be discussed
in subsequent chapters, also support the hypothesis
that many similarities currently exist, and probably

have existed for many years, between the value orientations of these three groups.

Portrayals of the Ibo, especially those that deal with political dynamics, have emphasized the significance of achievement criteria in contrast to the ascriptive or inherited status inhering in most traditional societies. As the preceding description of the precolonial social and political institutions prevailing throughout the East indicated, Ibibio and Ijaw communities also had ample opportunities for individual advancement to positions of overt and covert leadership. All communities shared a concern about the suitability of candidates for certain offices. Moreover, none of these segmentary societies seem to have been divided into hereditary classes that would have permanently limited the opportunity for advancement of some of their members. Entrance to secret societies often depended on nominal fees that virtually all members of the community could afford. Membership in title societies reflected the wealth accrued by individuals through their own initiative. Historical accounts of the outstanding Ibibio and Ijaw trading communities in the area reveal the same rewards for individual initiative and enterprise that are attributed to the Ibo. Opportunities for individual advancement were, however, denied to slaves in most of the communities. Those describing Ibo equality often neglect to mention that in precolonial times many of these communities had domestic slaves, which were a sign of wealth, and cult slaves. While domestic slaves were often absorbed into lineages and could amass wealth, they were denied political and personal rights and could always be sold or offered as a sacrifice. Cult slaves also suffered the penalty of social ostracism from which they could not be redeemed. Most of the slaves the Efik acquired were Ibos, whom they employed in large groups to work their plantations. Efik slaves and the slaves owned by the Ijaw trading communities could sometimes buy their freedom and occasionally rose to prominent positions.

While communities varied considerably in their religious practices and in their perception of the

nature of the spiritual world, none of the groups
seemed to have been preoccupied with religious concerns. The absence of an other-worldly orientation
is shown in the fact that wealth was highly valued
and vigorously sought after in all of the communities.
Moreover, their world views did not present individuals or groups as the victims of an unalterable
fate. Although other groups might not have embraced
the highly manipulative and contractual relationship
to the gods attributed to Ibo communities, few, if
any, perceived man as powerless with regard to altering
the effects of the spirits. Even the Kalabari Ijaw
with their complex nations of spiritual forces and
layers of reality believed that "It is men who make
the gods important," since the strength of an individual god could be built up or reduced to insignifi-
cance through intensive worship.[17]

     W. T. Morrill has attempted to explain the rise
of the Ibo immigrants to a position of economic
predominance in modern Calabar as owing to differences
between Ibo and Efik society, particularly in regard
to the respective attitudes toward work, the emphasis
on achievement, and the willingness to participate
in new institutions. According to Morrill, "No work
is 'beneath' an Ibo's dignity. Only sloth is."[18]
In contrast to the Ibo attitude toward work, the Efik
residents of Calabar considered manual labor (except
farming) to be degrading and preferred to be unemployed rather than accept work thought to be
undignified. Morrill's description of traditional
social patterns stresses the Ibo reliance on achievement and the Efik acceptance of ascription. His
depiction of the contemporary social patterns in
Calabar contrasts the tendency for Ibos to form and
participate in the activities of ethnic-improvement
unions with the inability of the Efik community to
found and sustain a single organization to represent
their interests.

     In his analysis of the traditional Efik social
system, however, Morrill attributes less scope to
achievement criteria than other research imputes.[19]
Moreover, Richard Henderson's penetrating critique
of Morrill's work demonstrates that in his analysis

Morrill confuses attitudinal and value factors with
the nature of the social and political structures
and particularly the greater specialization in traditional Efik social and political structures with
a cultural narrowness or rigidity. Henderson's data
also indicates that there are some marked similarities
between the Onitsha Ibo and the Efik in terms of
occupational structure, predilection for certain kinds
of work, and participation in such new social organizations as ethnic-improvement unions. Hence Henderson
concludes that certain Efik and Onitshan characteristics may reflect the early exposure of the two
communities to Christianity and modern education during the nineteenth century and their subsequent
privileged positions under colonial rule.[20]

TRANSFORMATION OF THE TRADITIONAL SOCIETIES

Chapter 2 outlined some of the political and
economic changes the Eastern Region underwent during
the colonial period and the life of the first Nigerian
republic. This section will attempt to suggest the
impact of a unified regional administration, the high
rate of Christian conversion, and the spread of
modern education on the traditional societies. It
will concentrate on three aspects of this transformation: how these factors have affected the autonomy
and integrity of the village, how they have impinged
on the existing social and political institutions,
and how they have modified certain dimensions of the
belief systems and value orientations. As with the
portrayal of the traditional institutional framework,
the analysis here can only generalize about regional
trends.

With the imposition of colonial administration
as described in Chapter 2, the once autonomous village
communities of Eastern Nigeria were incorporated into
larger administrative units. Following the abolition
of the warrant chief system after the Aba riots, an
attempt was made to create larger administrative units
at the local level which reflected traditional social
groupings. In fact, these reforms had the effect of

grouping together villages with no geneological links
and no prior experience of cooperative effort under
the label of "clan." The motive behind the creation
of clans was that the traditional village communities
were thought to be too small in size to constitute
effective administrative units. Villages also lost
some of their autonomy as a result of the reforms
that introduced competitive elections. Since a single
community was too small to provide an effective
political base within a constituency, villages tended
to break out of their shells and cooperate with
neighboring villages in an effort to promote the
election of those candidates who could be counted
upon to represent the interests of their local community or group of communities. At the same time,
new economic opportunities lured large numbers of
villagers to urban centers throughout Nigeria. Even
though those living in urban centers, who came to
be known as "sons abroad," did not break their ties
to their home communities, this process of emigration
further undermined the insularity of the rural village.

     As a result of these various political, social,
and economic forces, village communities began to
expand their horizons and broaden their social
identity. While primary loyalty remained with the
village community, individuals and even whole communities also began to perceive themselves to be
members of other, more inclusive units. After a
system of county councils had been created as the basic
unit for local representative government, particular clans composed of several village communities
within a county council area would struggle as a
unit within the context of competition for amenities.
For purposes of political competition in urban
elections, broader ethnic groupings consisting of
residents from particular administrative divisions
or provinces became operative. Despite the tendency
of analysts to refer to so-called tribal units, such
as the Ibo, Ibibio, and Ijaw peoples, these labels
were relatively meaningless for many years and only
rarely have been operative sources of identity within
Eastern Nigeria. The remolding of traditional
social identities into categories more appropriate
to the wider political, economic, and social system

that was developing resembled the process of identitive
generalization observed in many other parts of Asia
and Africa. [21]

Communities in Eastern Nigeria responded to the
threatening erosion of communal solidarity by establishing new organizations that linked the emigrants,
or sons abroad, with the home village. The emigrants
to an urban center from a particular home community
frequently founded a mutual aid association to help
them cope with the strange and sometimes hostile
urban environment and to provide them with financial
aid and support in times of emergency. In many cases
these urban-based associations then became imbued
with the desire to improve economic conditions and
to promote educational development in their home communities. To effect the necessary coordination and
communication with the home village, many of these
associations organized a branch organization in the
home village and then formed a federation of the
various urban branches. The activities of the member
branches were coordinated through a yearly conference
held in the home village to which all units sent
representatives. Despite the similarity in basic
structure, however, considerable variation existed in
the organizational sophistication and the activities
of the many ethnic-improvement unions that sprang up
in both rural and urban portions of Eastern Nigeria.

Somewhat similar mutual aid associations with
an urban base have been formed in many parts of Africa
and Asia, but the pattern of ethnic-improvement unions
that evolved in Eastern Nigeria is unique in several
ways. Unlike what prevailed elsewhere, the ethnic-
improvement unions in this case have developed strong
links with their rural homes and have often become
instruments of rural transformation. Moreover, the
complexity of the organizational structure and the
variety of levels within the political system upon
which a particular association might be based are
other unusual features of the Eastern Nigerian
situation. In contrast to the rather infrequent
occurrence of such associations elsewhere, a majority
of communities in Eastern Nigeria have organized
ethnic-improvement unions. [22]

Several analysts of economic and political
development in Eastern Nigeria have referred to the
propensity of Ibo communities to organize ethnic-
improvement unions, but they usually fail to mention
similar associations among other ethnic groups. To
some extent this bias reflects a tendency to concentrate on the Ibo and neglect other ethnic groups as
a result of the fact that the Ibo constitute approximately two thirds of the population of Eastern Nigeria
and are one of the three major ethnic groups found
in Nigeria. Furthermore, little data of a comprehensive nature have been collected on ethnic associations.
However, one survey of 71 villages (52 Ibo and 19
Ibibio) in 30 county council areas revealed that
Ibibio villages are more likely to have ethnic-improvement unions than Ibo villages, since 79 percent of
the Ibibio villages had such unions as against 69
percent of the Ibo villages. Far from cooperation
on village development projects being exclusively an
Ibo cultural trait, this same survey indicated a
somewhat greater propensity among Ibibio villages
to organize cooperative village projects. For example, Ibibio villages surveyed completed an average
of 4.21 projects and Ibo villages 3.46.[23] One of
the questions in the attitude survey the authors
conducted among Eastern Nigerian villagers (the results
of which are discussed in detail in subsequent
chapters) asked whether "In the past few years, have
the people of this village all worked together on
some project, such as road building, building a
maternity, etc." While 85.3 percent of the Ibo
respondents answered yes, 98.1 percent of the non-Ibo
respondents, including Ibibio, Ijaw, and Boki,
answered affirmatively. Hence the formation of
ethnic-improvement unions and organization of village
development projects is broadly characteristic of the
communities in Eastern Nigeria and not a pattern
confined to Ibo communities.

The introduction of Christianity has threatened
the unity of some communities. Many of the traditional
religious rituals reinforced the solidarity of the
village by affirming the common kinship bonds and by
providing ways for villagers to jointly mark significant communal and individual occasions, but the

conversion of villagers brought new kinds of divisions
to the community. Because missionaries usually for-
bade converts from participating in traditional
rituals and such institutions as the secret societies
that were associated with these ceremonies, the pagan-
Christian split widened. Later, when the various
missionary societies began to compete for converts
in the same area, new kinds of sectarian differences
further divided communities.

Villages have reacted to the intrusion of these
new divisions in a variety of ways. In communities
where most people converted to Christianity, the
churches have provided alternative forms of integration
through religious and ceremonial activities. In some
places the activities of ethnic unions have served
as a cohesive force. Sometimes traditional religious
ceremonies have been successfully transformed into
new civic rituals. In other cases the mutual tolerance
of the Christians and pagans, or perhaps the absence
of preoccupation with religious matters has minimized
the divisive impact of religious differences.

The very rapid spread of primary education during
the 1930's and 1940's also made a dramatic impact
on the villages of Eastern Nigeria. However, it is
not easy to distinguish the impact of education from
that of Christianity and migration to urban centers,
since attendance at mission schools has been the
principal basis for conversion to Christianity, and
much of the migration from villages to cities has
been by those who attend primary school. Nevertheless,
it has provided greater exposure to Western culture
and value, it has broadened the horizons of both
children attending school and their families, and
it has instilled in many villagers the spark of dis-
content, which has led them to want a more economically rewarding and more Western way of life both
for themselves and for their families and villages.
Education has also provided the basis for social
and occupational mobility, as well as exposure to
improved agricultural practices. Although divisions
have occurred within some villages between those who
were literate and those who were not, these differences have not caused the friction engendered in

several other developing countries, largely because those who have not attended school respect those who have, even when substantial difference in age are involved.

In the new social, political, and economic order some traditional institutions have lost their vitality. In highly Christianized communities villagers no longer join secret societies and sometimes do not participate in the age organizations, because they view their ceremonial accompaniments as pagan. Many younger men prefer to spend the large initiation fees required for membership in the title societies on education for members of their families or for the construction of modern homes, thus depleting the ranks of potential members.

Again in this sphere the villages of Eastern Nigeria exhibit both individual variability and adaptability. Some communities have resuscitated moribund masquerade societies and age organizations to perform nontraditional functions. Among some more traditional Ibo villages, title societies and age groups coexist alongside more modern ethnic-improvement unions, and rarely have the voluntary organizations or government-sponsored local and county councils supplanted the village assembly as the supreme decision-making body for the community.[24] In contrast to this organizational pluralism and fragmentation of authority, in some relatively acculturated Ibo areas ethnic-improvement unions have become the paramount arbiters of communal af-fairs.[25]

Despite the impact of Christianity and modern education, the predominant trend is one of cultural continuity rather than disruption or marked conflict. To a considerable extent this continuity reflects the remarkably "modern" character of precolonial orientations and values in Eastern Nigeria. In fact, one can argue that the receptivity in Eastern Nigeria to Christianity and Western education has itself derived from certain of these traditional cultural dispositions. Hence Simon Ottenberg's statement about the Ibo: "Paradoxically, of all Nigerian

peoples, the Ibo have probably changed the least
while changing the most."[26] This statement characterizes other ethnic groups in Eastern Nigeria
as well. Modernization has often resulted from
utilization and adaptation of basic cultural patterns
to new conditions and opportunities rather than the
erosion of traditional responses and values and their
substitution by new ones.

In conclusion it should be stressed that the
precolonial institutional and cultural patterns
endowed Eastern Nigeria with many assets for future
economic and political development. The absence
of any large-scale traditional political units eventually facilitated the administrative unification
of the region under the British and then contributed
to the meaningfulness of the political process by
allowing groups to compete on an equal basis. The
inadequacy of the small insular community and its
institutions in the larger regional context promoted
the acceptance of new forms of identity and the
adoption of more suitable institutional forms. Subsequent chapters will more fully evaluate the contribution of traditional precolonial cultural patterns
to economic development, but it should be clear at
this point that the enthusiasm for innovation has
fitted Eastern Nigerians for citizenship in the
modern world even before colonialism and political
independence brought the modern world in their wake.

NOTES

1. In arriving at these ethnic proportions, the
classification of Daryll Forde and G. I. Jones in
their The Ibo and Ibibio-Speaking Peoples of South-
Eastern Nigeria (London: Oxford University Press,
1950) was employed which designated the Anang and the
Efik as Ibibio subgroups. The Eastern government
never authorized the publication or use of the 1963
census figures because it rejected them as inaccurate.
For the earlier census breakdowns see Population
Census in the Eastern Region of Nigeria, 1953.

2. The portrayal of the Ibo people in this chapter comes from field work and from the following sources: K. Onwuka Dike, Trade and Politics in the Niger Delta: 1830-85 (London: Oxford University Press, 1956); Forde and Jones, op. cit., M. M. Green, Ibo Village Affairs (2nd ed.; New York: Frederick A. Praeger, 1964); G. I. Jones, "Ecology and Social Structure Among the North-Eastern Ibo," Africa, XXXI (April 1961), 117-134; G. I. Jones, "From Direct to Indirect Rule in Eastern Nigeria," paper presented at a seminar at the Institute of African Studies, University of Ife, Nigeria, 1964; G. I. Jones, "Ibo Age Organizations with Special Reference to the Cross River and North-Eastern Ibo," Journal of the Royal Anthropological Institute, XCII (July-December 1962), 191-211; G. I. Jones, Report on the Position, Status and Influence of Chiefs and Natural Rulers in the Eastern Region of Nigeria (Enugu: Government Printer, 1956); C. K. Meek, Law and Authority in a Nigerian Tribe (London: Oxford University Press, 1937); Simon Ottenberg, "Ibo Oracles and Intergroup Relations," Southwestern Journal of Anthropology, XIV (Fall 1958), 294-317; Simon Ottenberg, "Ibo Receptivity to Change," in William R. Bascom and Melville J. Herskovits, eds., Continuity and Change in African Cultures (Chicago: University of Chicago Press, 1962), pp. 130-143; Victor C. Uchendu, The Igbo of Southeast Nigeria (New York: Holt, Rinehart and Winston, 1965).

3. The portrayal of the Ibibio-speaking groups in this chapter comes from observation and from the following sources. Daryll Forde, ed., Efik Traders of Old Calabar (London: Oxford University Press, 1965); Forde and Jones, op. cit.; Jones, Report on the Position. . ., op. cit.; John C. Messenger, Jr., "Religious Acculturation Among the Anang Ibibio," Comparative Studies in Society and History, V (July 1963), 424-448; Donald C. Simons, "Sexual Life, Childhood and Marriage among the Efik," Africa, XXX (April 1960), 153-165.

4. G. I. Jones, "From Direct to Indirect Rule in Eastern Nigeria," p. 9.

5. G. I. Jones, The Trading States of the Oil Rivers: A Study of Political Development in Eastern Nigeria (London: Oxford University Press, 1963), pp. 13-16.

6. See Ottenberg, "Ibo Oracles and Intergroup Relations," particularly p. 301.

7. For a contrary and highly disputed point of view see Robert F. Stephenson, Population and Politica Systems (New York: Columbia University Press, 1968).

8. Jones, The Trading States of the Oil Rivers, p. 16.

9. Sources on the Ijaw-speaking people used for this chapter include the following: Robin Horton, Kalabari Sculpture, (Apapa, Nigeria: Department of Antiquities of the Federal Republic of Nigeria, 1965); Robin Horton, "The Kalabari World View: An Outline and Interpretation," Africa, XXXII (July 1962), 197-220; Jones, Report on the Position...; Jones, The Trading States of the Oil Rivers; Kay Williamson, "Changes in the Marriage System of the Okrika Ijo," Africa, XXXII (January 1962); 53-60.

10. Jones, Report on the Position. . ., p. 6.

11. Horton, Kalabari Sculpture, p. 2.

12. Jones, Report on the Position. . ., pp. 7-15.

13. Richard N. Henderson, "Onitsha Kingship Succession: Traditional and Contemporary Patterns in Ibo Politics," paper presented at the annual meeting of the African Studies Association, Philadelphia, 1965.

14. Richard N. Henderson, "Generalized Cultures and Evolutionary Adaptability: A Comparison of Urban Efik and Ibo in Nigeria," Ethnology, V (October 1966), 365-391.

15. For a more detailed discussion of old Calabar see particularly Forde (ed.), Efik Traders of Old Calabar.

16. For interesting discussions of this aspect of Ibo culture see Robert A. LeVine, Dreams and Deeds: Achievement Motivation in Nigeria (Chicago: University of Chicago Press, 1966); Ottenberg, "Ibo Receptivity to Change"; and Uchendu, The Igbo of Southeast Nigeria.

17. For discussions of Kalabari religion see Horton, "The Kalabari WorldView."

18. W. T. Morrill, "Immigrants and Associations: The Ibo in Twentieth Century Calabar," Comparative Studies in Society and History, V (July 1963), 437.

19. See Forde; Jones, Report on the Position..., pp. 33-35.

20 Henderson, "Generalized Cultures and Evolutionary Adaptability."

21. See for example Clifford Geertz, "The Integrative Revolution: Primordial Sentiments and Civil Politics in the New States" in Clifford Geertz, ed., Old Societies and New States: the Quest for Modernity in Asia and Africa (New York: Free Press of Glencoe, 1963), pp. 105-157.

22. See Audrey C. Smock, Ibo Politics: The Role of Ethnic Unions in Eastern Nigeria (Cambridge, Mass.: Harvard University Press, 1971).

23. Gerald D. Hursh, Niels C. Roling, and Graham B. Kerr, "Innovation in Eastern Nigeria: Success and Failure of Agricultural Programs in 71 Villages of Eastern Nigeria" (East Lansing: Department of Communication, Michigan State University, 1968, mimeographed), pp. 228-229.

24. David R. Smock, "Changing Political Processes among the Abaja Ibo," Africa, XXXVIII (July 1968), pp. 281-292.

25. For a study of two such communities see Audrey Smock.

26. Ottenberg, "Ibo Receptivity to Change," p. 142.

4

**AGRICULTURE
IN
EASTERN
NIGERIA**

Despite developments in the industrial sector
and attempts by the government to encourage industrial
development, agriculture in the three successor states
to Eastern Nigeria still employs over 75 percent of
the working population, and approximately the same
percentage of the region's land area is devoted to
agriculture.[1] Before the oil industry developed into
the region's principal source of export revenue, over
90 percent of the region's exports consisted of agricultural produce. More than 50 percent of the region's
domestic output still originates in the agricultural
sector.[2]

The setting for Eastern Nigeria's agriculture
consists of an area with rainfall ranging from 140
inches per year in the south to 60 inches in the
north (see Figure 1). Natural vegetation varies from
mangrove swamps in the Niger Delta and the coastal
belt to derived savannah in the northern portion,
with gradations, including lowland rainforest and
heavily wooded savannah, bridging these two extremes
(see Figure 2). Differing levels of rainfall and

Portions of this chapter originally appeared,
in slightly different form, in Economic Development
and Cultural Change, Vol. 18, No. 1 (October 1969)
© 1969, The University of Chicago. All rights
reserved.

FIGURE 1

Mean Annual Rainfall in Eastern Nigeria

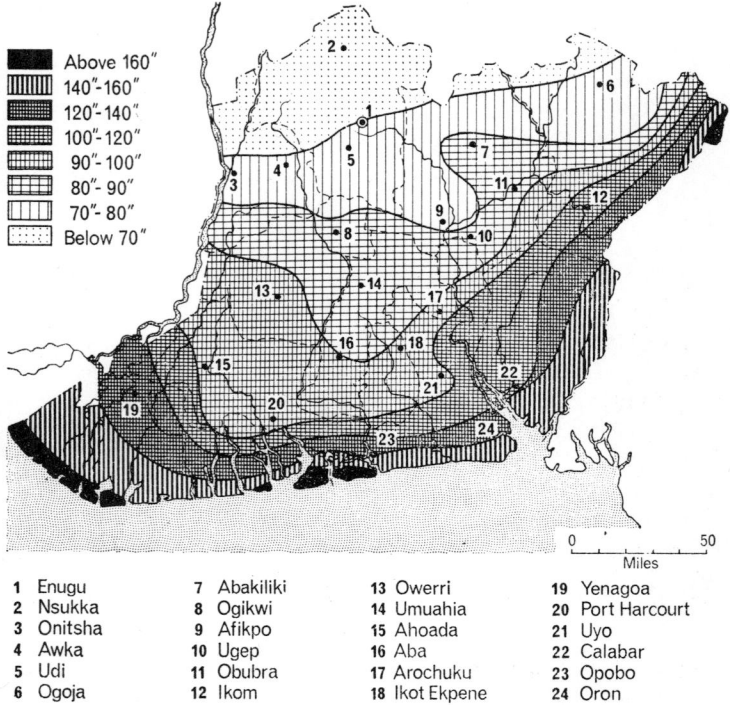

1 Enugu	7 Abakiliki	13 Owerri	19 Yenagoa
2 Nsukka	8 Ogikwi	14 Umuahia	20 Port Harcourt
3 Onitsha	9 Afikpo	15 Ahoada	21 Uyo
4 Awka	10 Ugep	16 Aba	22 Calabar
5 Udi	11 Obubra	17 Arochuku	23 Opobo
6 Ogoja	12 Ikom	18 Ikot Ekpene	24 Oron

Source: Barry Floyd, Eastern Nigeria: A Geographic Review (New York: Frederick A. Praeger, Inc., 1969), p. 145.

FIGURE 2

Vegetation in Eastern Nigeria

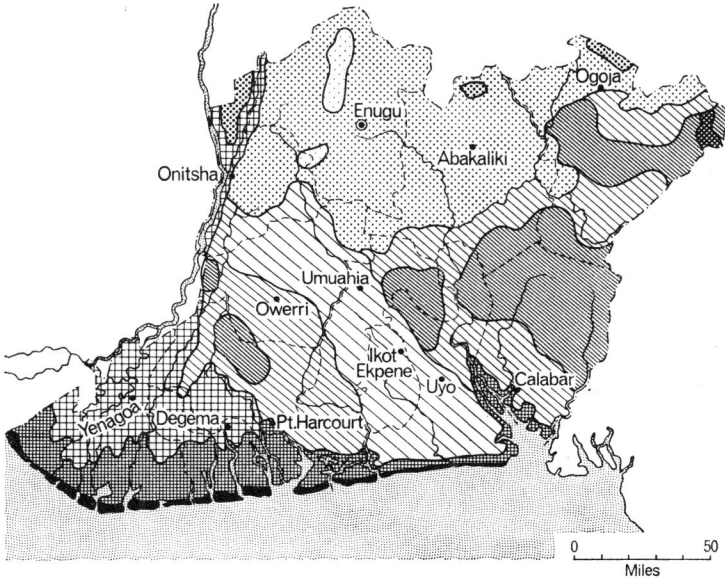

I MANGROVE FOREST AND COASTAL
  VEGETATION
  ■ Beach Ridges with Fresh Water Vegetation
  Salt Water Swamp with Mangrove Forest
II Fresh Water Swamp and Rain Forest
III LOWLAND TROPICAL RAIN FOREST
  Largely unmodified
  Partially modified
  Greatly modified (oil palm 'Bush')

IV DERIVED SAVANNA
  (WOODLAND-SAVANNA MOSAIC)
  Sizeable 'relict' outliers of Rain
  Forest
  Wooded Grassland
  Open Grassland
V Montane Rain Forest and
  Grassland

Source: Barry Floyd, Eastern Nigeria: A Geographic Review (New York: Frederick A. Praeger,
Inc., 1969), p. 154.

65

soil types found in various parts of the region give
rise to important variations in cropping patterns
and farming methods. The principal food crops, which
include yams, cassava (manioc), maize (corn), cocoyams
(taro), and other vegetables, are cultivated throughout the region, but some predominate in some areas
and others elsewhere. Yam and cassava constitute
the staple foods in most of the region, with such
minor sectional variations as plantain being the staple
in some areas east of the Cross River. Oil palms,
although most heavily concentrated in the high-rainfall
areas of the south, grow throughout the region and
are exploited for palm oil, palm kernels, and palm
wine (a widely consumed, mildly alcoholic beverage).
Palm oil and palm kernels provide Eastern Nigeria
with its principal agricultural exports, while cocoa
and rubber comprise the other principal agricultural
export commodities.

Some of the region's agricultural exports derive
from government and privately owned plantations, but
well over 90 percent of Eastern Nigeria's agricultural
output is produced by individual farm families on
small landholdings utilizing traditional farming
practices. Aside from the cultivation of tree crops,
farming is undertaken within a system of shifting
cultivation in which a particular plot is farmed for
one or more years and left fallow for a period sufficient for natural regeneration. When the field is
again ready for cultivation, the growth of natural
vegetation is cut and burned, so that a new planting
cycle can commence. Despite the fact that the farmer
moves from one plot to another, his life is in no
sense nomadic and does not involve his moving his
place of residence, which shifting cultivation (also
called slash and burn agriculture) does entail in
some parts of Africa.

Population density is extremely high in most of
the farming sections of the region, with densities
reaching over 1,200 persons per square mile in some
areas of intensive cultivation (see Figure 3).[3]
However, the 12 million persons living in Eastern
Nigeria are not evenly distributed over its surface
area of 30,000 square miles, and in some farming

FIGURE 3

Population Density of Eastern Nigeria, 1963
(estimated number of persons per square mile)

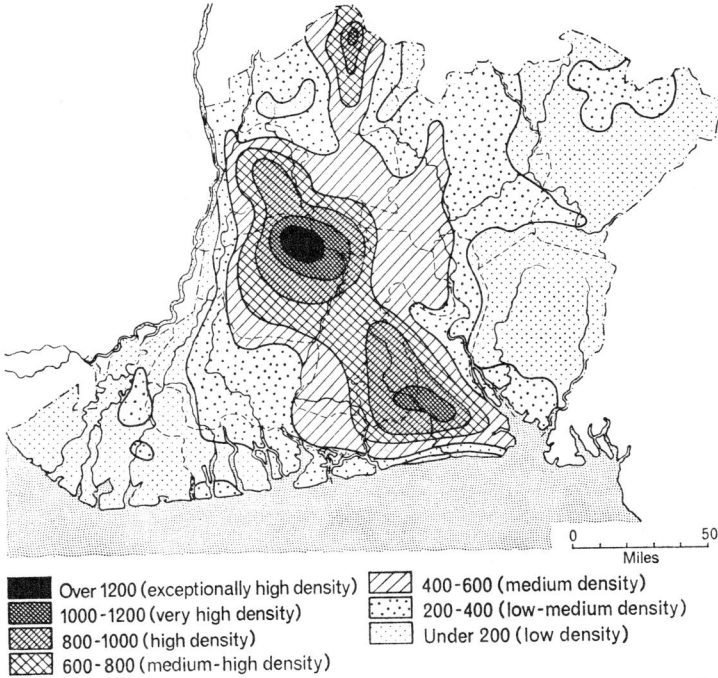

Over 1200 (exceptionally high density)   400-600 (medium density)
1000-1200 (very high density)   200-400 (low-medium density)
800-1000 (high density)   Under 200 (low density)
600-800 (medium-high density)

Source: Barry Floyd, Eastern Nigeria: A Geographic Review (New York: Frederick A. Praeger, Inc., 1969), p. 40.

sections the density drops below 10 persons per square
mile. Some of this unevenness in population distribution reflects differences in suitability of land
for cultivation, but it is also a function of differing
rates of population growth and variations in the land
area controlled by particular ethnic groups. Because
of the scarcity of land and the technologically simple
manner in which farming is conducted, per capita incomes average only about $100. Differences in wealth
exist, but poverty is the prevailing state. However,
the poor are not at the mercy of rich landlords, since
most farmers control their own land and few wealthy
landlords are found.

TRADITIONAL AGRICULTURE

As already mentioned, aside from a few commercial
plantations managed by the Eastern Nigeria Development
Corporation and by some foreign companies, along with
some government-operated farm settlements, agriculture
in Eastern Nigeria is predominantly smallholder,
peasant agriculture.[4] The basic features of this
agriculture do not differ significantly from what
prevails in other parts of the humid tropics in Africa,
in that a system of shifting cultivation and bush
fallow is followed, and a farmer cultivates his land
without the assistance of animal power or machinery,
having as basic tools a machete, one or more hoes,
and a digging stick.

Of the principal food crops mentioned above,
yams have traditionally been the most important and
the most culturally valued, but within the last 30
years cassava production has overtaken yam production
in many areas. This shift has resulted from the
economic advantages of cassava over yams, which include
its ability to grow on less-fertile soil, the ease
of cultivation, the convenience of storage (it can
be left in the ground until needed), and the growing
demand of urban dwellers for cassava products. The
unfortunate aspect of this shift results from the
very low protein content of cassava, which is vitually
pure carbohydrate as compared with the slightly greater
nutritional value of yam. As evidence of the decline

in yam production, in two of eight farming areas that
were surveyed almost no yams are now grown, although
they are still highly valued as food.[5] Differences
in soil, climate, and food preferences in the various
parts of the region give rise to important variations
in the types of yams grown, and this variation is
found with other crops as well.

In addition to yams, cassava, cocoyams, and maize,
other food crops include rice, okra, fluted pumpkins,
various types of melons, various types of beans, red
pepper, eggplant, bitter leaf, and tomatoes. Rice
has been introduced only within the past 20 years,
but its popularity is growing rapidly.[6] Among fruits
found are bananas, oranges, pawpaw (papaya), mangos,
pineapples, plantains, coconuts, grapefruit, and
avocados. As with oil palms, most of the fruit trees
in Eastern Nigeria are self-seeded.

Because of the prevalence of tsetse flies, the
vectors of trypanosomiasis, only resistant species
of livestock can be kept. The most important of these
are chickens, sheep, and goats, and most farmers have
a few chickens and either some sheep or goats. In
addition, some villagers raise ducks, pigs, and dwarf
cows, although primarily for family consumption rather
than for sale.

As in all agricultural areas, Eastern Nigerian
villages have clearly defined agricultural calendars.
Clearing and burning of the bush (undergrowth) in
preparation for planting is done between January and
March, which is the second half of the dry season.
By this time it has not rained for a sufficiently
long period that the grass and shrubs are dry and
can be cut and burned easily. Moreover, there is
little chance of new undergrowth emerging between
the time of burning and the time of planting. In
places where the bush is not thick and consists
mostly of grass, burning takes place within a week
or two after cutting. The exception to this occurs
where the land to be cleared is so heavily wooded
and the rains so frequent that a longer period must
elapse between clearing and burning before the bush
can dry sufficiently to burn.

Preparation of the soil and planting begin with the first rains in March and April, and cover a four- to eight-week period. Although yams are usually the first crop to be planted, variations exist since each community has its own ideas about the order in which crops should be sowed. No two of the eight areas surveyed followed exactly the same pattern, and the greatest variations occurred in the time chosen for planting cassava. The most widespread practice is for cassava to be planted sometime between September and January on a piece of land from which yams have recently been harvested; but in some places cassava is planted in separate fields at about the same time yams are planted, while elsewhere it is intercropped with yams in June or July. Although some of these variations in planting patterns result from ecological differences, others seem merely to reflect distinct cultural traditions.

Clearing and planting require the most sustained and difficult activity of the agricultural year. Once the yams have been planted, they need to be trained up stakes and weeded before the preliminary harvest, which in most localities commences in August and September. In this harvest the heaps of certain varieties of yams are opened so that the main portion of the tuber can be cut. The remainder of the tuber is covered again so that auxiliary tubers can develop more fully and be harvested between September and November for use as seed yams.

Maize is usually harvested in July and August, and cocoyams in December and January, but no specific period is prescribed for harvesting cassava. In addition to communities differing as to when they plant cassava, communities and individual farmers have divergent notions on how long cassava should be left before harvesting. Although it may be left for as little as 9 months or for as long as 24, most farmers harvest after approximately 12 months of growth. The exact period depends upon the variety of cassava grown, the tradition in a particular locality, the urgency of a family's need for food, and fluctuations in the market demand for cassava.

As with agricultural calendars in most parts
of the world, in Eastern Nigeria some periods of
the year are considered periods of intensive activity,
others are thought of as periods of light activity,
and the remainder is viewed as a period for inactivity
and rest. Although in most communities only the broad
guidelines of the agricultural calendar are imposed
by tradition, in some villages specific leaders set
the exact dates for the performance of certain tasks.
For instance, in one community surveyed the yam priest
determines the times for clearing, planting, and
harvesting of yams. Following instructions received
from the family heads in the village, the yam priest
performs certain ceremonies that signal the time to
commence has arrived, and no one is allowed to begin
before these ceremonies have been performed. In
another village surveyed the village elders meet to
determine exactly when the farmers of the village
should plant and then harvest their yam crop.

Farming is an enterprise carried on by the nuclear
or the polygynous family, with a careful delineation
made by each community as to which tasks fall to a
man and which are assigned to his wife or wives. A
bachelor usually farms with his father or a brother,
but once he marries he and his wife start farming
as an independent family unit. Although occasionally
a man and his wife might share tasks, each job is
generally assigned to one or the other, and it would
be unsettling for a man to do a woman's work very
frequently, or vice versa. In most places, a man's
responsibilities are confined to clearing and burning
the bush and cultivating yams, which entails making
mounds, planting, staking, and harvesting. His wife
is expected to undertake certain tasks connected
with clearing and burning, plus planting all crops
other than yams, and carrying all crops from the
farm to the house. In those communities where few
yams are grown both men and women plant cassava,
although they maintain separate fields rather than
sharing the labor. It is clear from this analysis that
women have substantial responsibilities in the family's
farming enterprise. In fact in many communities
they spend more time on farming activities than the
men do.

Men offered two explanations when asked why they consider the cultivation of yams to be their exclusive prerogative. The first explanation usually given is that yams are the most highly valued crop, and thus their production is reserved to the males of the community. They also claim that planting, staking, and harvesting yams require more physical exertion than comparable jobs for other crops; since yams involve the hardest work, the stronger sex is obligate to assume this responsibility.

Along with farming responsibilities being care-fully divided between man and wife, farm income is divided as well. When a man sells his yams, the proceeds are for him; and when his wife sells her crops (cassava, okra, maize, pepper, cocoyams, etc.) the money is hers. In turn, both man and wife have financial responsibilities, with each having types of goods and services they are expected to purchase or provide the family. Most men and women do not reveal to their spouses the size of their incomes, nor how they spend the money in excess of what is required for family use.

Although farming is basically an enterprise for the nuclear family, farmers often receive assistance from relatives and age-mates on a reciprocal basis. In some places groups of relatives or age-mates organize themselves into work teams and move from one man's field to another's, planting or staking yams. In other places a few friends will help a man in time of need, and then he will repay them by workir an equivalent period on each of their farms.

Hired workers also constitute an important labor input. The laborers usually have their own farms but complete their work early in the season so that they can hire themselves out for a few days or weeks. As a result, farmers almost never engage labor on a year-round basis, but do so to perform such specific tasks as clearing bush, mound-making, and planting. Farmers from some sections, like Abakaliki, spread throughout the region during the farming season to work as laborers, earning wages ranging from three to five shillings a day plus meals. Wages are calculated in some places on the basis of piecework, with so much being paid per 100 yam mounds produced or per acre of bush cleared. In some villages more farm work is done by hired laborers than by the farmers themselves. Despite the fact that such a heavy burden of farm work falls to women, laborers are rarely hired to assist with women's work.

Except where farm plots lie close enough to a farmer's hut to be easily mulched, plots are rarely cultivated on a continuous basis, with the bush-fallow system being almost universally practiced. The most widespread pattern is for a newly cleared piece of land to be planted with yams and intercropped with maize or cocoyams and minor crops. Although in some localities yams are planted two years in succession and in other places cocoyams are seeded following the yam harvest, in most places cassava is planted on the plot after the yams have been harvested. Following harvest of the cassava most land is allowed to be fallow for a period that is specifically defined for each locality, but which ranges in different areas from two to ten years. The length of the fallow cycle depends upon the fertility of the soil and the availability of land. Where land is scarce the fallow cycle is short, and as population density increases fallow cycles throughout the region become increasingly shorter.

Since a minimum of five years of fallow are generally required for full restoration of soil fertility, the abbreviated fallow cycles found in most parts of the region result in the steady depletion of soil fertility and a continuous decline in crop yields.[7] Although it is easy to condemn the bush-fallow system for its inefficient utilization of land and tempting to advocate its replacement by a system of permanent cropping, considerable research remains to be done on such problems as crop rotation and the maintenance of soil structure and soil fertility before the bush-fallow system can be legitimately criticized and abandoned.

Farmers generally have plots in scattered places and during a particular year the pattern of planted

and fallow plots looks like patchwork. However, a
few villages subscribe to a more rigid system of land
use, in that all the land in the village is divided
into several large sections, with each farmer having
one or more plots in each section. In these instances
the whole village follows the same fallow and rotation
cycle, so that everyone is planting yams in a particular section one season and in another section the
following season. Passing down the paths that divide
these sections, one sees land lying fallow on one
side of the path and hundreds of yam plots on the
other side of the road, while another planted section
contains only cassava.

Most farmers plant several plots in a single
year, and many farmers were found planting in eight
or ten different places. These plots are generally
small, with the average size in the more densely
populated areas being between 1/25 and 1/5 of an
acre. The total amount of land a man and his wife
plant in a given year usually does not exceed 2.5
acres, although occasionally a farm of four or five
acres was found.[8] The amount of land planted depends
both on the availability of land and on the labor
resources the farmer has at his command. The man
who is able to plant more that three acres usually
has several wives or employs several laborers. Table
1 indicates the average landholdings within one
community in Okigwi Division.

A farmer's various plots are usually located
some distance from one another and some farmers have
to walk six or eight miles to reach their scattered
parcels of land. A village's farming area might
also be located some distance from the settlement
area, either because the land immediately adjacent
to the settlement has been farmed too intensively
and has lost its fertility, or because the settlement
is so large that some of the villagers must go a
great distance if they are to secure sufficient land.
In most cases where the farm land is distant from
the settlement, farmers build small huts near their
farm land so that they can spend several days at a
time there during periods of intensive activity.

TABLE 1

Average Farm Size in Uboma,
Okigwi Division

	Acres	No. of Plots
Under crops	2.91	14.70
In fallow	4.76	14.82
Tree crops	0.16	0.85
Average total holding	7.83	30.37

Source: H. A. Oluwasanmi, I. S. Dema, et al.,
Uboma: A Socio-Economic and Nutritional Survey of a
Rural Community in Eastern Nigeria (Bude, Cornwall:
Geographical Publications Ltd., 1966), p.84.

Although most farmers own the major portion of
the land they cultivate, some acquire farm land
through short-term leasing arrangements. Rent payments
vary widely in different localities, and some land
was discovered being leased for as little as two
shillings per acre and other land for as much as £N5
per acre. Patterns of land ownership and alternative
means of acquiring new land are discussed in Chapter 6.

The standard farming implements are the machete,
hoe, and iron or iron-tipped digging stick, and in
some places various types of knives and axes are also
used for agricultural purposes. The men and women
in most localities use differently shaped hoes, with
the man's hoe being larger than the woman's. Although
one finds considerable variation in the types of hoes
used in different parts of the region, all the hoes
are of the short-handled variety, with the blade
usually meeting the shaft at less than a 90-degree
angle. Because of their design, they are more easily
used for scooping and scraping than for hacking.

Since machetes are factory made, they exhibit little
variation in size and shape, and the same holds for
the locally made digging stick. From this inventory
of tools, it is apparent what a limited array of
equipment a farmer has at his disposal. Mention has
already been made of the fact that a farmer cultivates
his land without the assistance of animal power or
power-driven machinery.

Each of the communities we surveyed has clearly
defined traditions that prescribe which crops are
to be interplanted with which, whether planting should
be done in rows or at random, how large yam and cocoyam mounds are to be, and how often weeding should
be done. These patterns differ significantly from
one community to the next. Although minor variations
are found among farming methods employed by the farmers within a given community, these differences are·
small when compared to the discrepancies found in
intervillage comparisons. One region-wide generalization that can be made is that practically no one
manures or irrigates his crops, and very little
mulching is done either.

The following brief descriptions of farming
practices investigated in three villages illustrate
the variations in practices in different localities.
In Oban (Calabar Province) virgin land is readily
available and is often cleared for a new farm.
Once the forest and shrubs have been cleared and
burned, yams, plantains, and minor crops are planted.
For planting, a small hole is opened in the surface
of the earth and then the seed is covered with
dirt. This simple process leaves most of the surface untouched and unbroken, with only enough soil
scraped together to make yam mounds 6-8 inches high.
Planting is done in rows, and no order is apparent
in the way the various crops are mixed and interplanted in a field. In plots that have been planted
with yams one year, cocoyams, cassava, and minor
vegetable crops are planted the next. The manner of
cultivation in the second year of planting is comparable to cultivation in the first year. Plants
are spaced a considerable distance from each other
and one has the impression of farming being carried

on in a rather casual manner. Since land is plentiful most families have only two large farm plots,
and no one has a garden close to his dwelling or
"compound."

In Akoliufu (Bende Division) farmers have yam
plots, cassava plots, cocoyam plots, and compound
plots that usually contain yams and vegetables of
minor importance. The yam plots are generally interplanted with vegetables, but there is no mixture of
crops in the cocoyam plots and the cassava plots.
Yam mounds are 18-24 inches high and are spaced at
distances of 6-24 inches from each other, although
they are not arranged in orderly patterns. Vegetables
interplanted with yams include beans, maize, okra,
and pepper, all of which are planted in such a way
that their vines climb the same stake as the yam vines.
In preparing the yam mounds, farmers cultivate the
whole surface of the plot. After the yams and the
interplanted vegetables have been harvested, either
cassava or cocoyams are planted in their place, with
the cassava cuttings and the cocoyam seeds being put
into the old yam mounds.

In Affa (Udi Division) there are yam plots with
an admixture of vegetables, plots exclusively for
beans, plots exclusively for cassava, plots for minor
vegetables, and compound gardens that are used
exclusively for cocoyams. Every family plants at
least one of each of these types of plots each year.
In the yam plots, maize is planted in the mound with
the yam, while the other interplanted vegetables are
planted around the base of the yam mound. The mounds
themselves are 14-15 inches high and are arranged in
rows. Water yams, a type of yam not found in Oban
and Akoliufu, are planted as a border crop around
the edges of the yam plot. Following the yam harvest,
cassava is planted in the yam plot, and when cassava
is planted it is planted alone, without intercropping.

Someone familiar with modern agricultural practices
in the temperate zone is likely to be disturbed by
the rather chaotic appearance of farming plots in
Eastern Nigeria, with various crops planted in the
same field and with little apparent order in the

location of mounds and plants. These practices do,
however, have certain advantages. De Wilde has
described some of them:

> By planting a succession of crops with
> varying planting times, rooting habits and
> maturities, the cultivator may make better
> use of his or her time, permit plants to
> tap the nutrients in various soil layers
> more effectively, distribute the risks due
> to vagaries of climate or incidence of
> pests and diseases, assure a more regular
> food supply and gradually, as the season
> progresses, cover the soil so well with
> vegetation that there is more effective
> protection against the effect of sun and
> rain and comparatively little need for the
> time-consuming job of weeding. Moreover,
> as long as only 'unimproved' varieties of
> crops are available or are used, the total
> yield from a given area may well be higher
> than when a single crop is planted in pure
> stand.[9]

As previously mentioned, palm oil and palm
kernels constitute Eastern Nigeria's principal
agricultural exports, and oil palm trees grow in mos
parts of the region. Palm oil, which is used domes-
tically for cooking, also makes up an important and
nutritious ingredient in the diet, as does palm wine
Since most oil palms are self-seeded and not cultivated, little attention is paid the palms until
harvest time. Although palm fruits are harvested
throughout the year, the greatest production takes
place during the months of March and April. Oil
palms are concentrated in the southern portions of
the region where the rainfall is greatest, and in
some areas their density reaches 100 trees per acre.
In parts of the northern savannah the density drops
below 10 trees per acre, and in these drier areas
they tend to thrive along river valleys and on compound land close to dwellings.[10]

Although obviously no variations in patterns
of cultivation are found with self-seeded palms,

arrangements concerning ownership do diverge. In
some communities all palm trees are considered village
property and can only be harvested on certain
designated days. In some of this localities the
harvest benefits village development projects, while
in other villages the fruits a man collects on harvest
day belong to him. Elsewhere the individuals or
families on whose land the palms grow own them, and
their produce belongs exclusively to the landowners.
Although villagers in some areas refuse to climb
palms and thus either hire laborers to harvest them
or cut the trees down to get the fruit or wine, in
most parts of the region farmers climb their trees.
According to the culturally prescribed division of
labor, climbing is exclusively the work of men. In
some communities the pounding and processing of fruits
to obtain oil is the joint work of a man and his wife,
but in other areas this is a woman's work and she is
consequently the one who benefits from the sale of
the palm products, even if her husband has climbed
the tree to cut the fruit. In the more economically
developed portions of the region, owners of screw
presses, hydraulic presses, or steam-powered oil mills
buy the fruits from farmers and process them.

Fluctuations in rainfall constitute the hazard
most frequently cited by farmers interviewed as the
major cause of poor production. Farmers say that
some years it rains too much and other years it rains
too little, although the likelihood of excessive
rainfall is greatest in the southern part of the
region, while the northern portion is more likely to
suffer from insufficient rainfall. Insects, such
as yam beetles, also pose problems, along with such
animals as antelopes and such rodents as the cutting
grass. In some rainforest areas elephants can devour
a farmer's total planting within a few minutes.

Since most crops are consumed shortly after
harvest and since cassava can remain in the ground
until needed, yam is the only major crop that requires storage for an extended period. Almost all
farmers in Eastern Nigeria have yam barns in which
the yams are tied to a lattice-work bamboo structure.
Some villages have a single, communal yam barn for

all the farmers of the village. The crop requiring
the greatest amount of processing is cassava, which
can be processed and prepared in a variety of ways.
All cassava processing, however, involves extraction
of the poison that the different varieties of cassava
possess in varying degrees.

Rarely is an individual farm or a village completely self-sufficient in agricultural produce, and
to permit the buying and selling of farm goods
villages generally hold a market every four to seven
days. Wholesalers who wish to buy yams, cassava, or
palm produce attend these markets to purchase a
farmer's excess crops. The food and agricultural
goods most frequently bought by villagers for their
own use on market days include fish (fresh, dried,
or tinned), meat, salt, rice, onions, and leaf tobacc
for snuff.

To insure that no evil spirits and no animals
harm their crops while they are growing, non-Christians often perform ceremonies and sacrifices at the
beginning of the farming year. Farmers also commonly
hire rain-makers and rain-chasers, and some non-
Christians consult diviners to determine which plots
they should plant. Overall, however, religion does
not play a large role in farming or in decisions
relating to farming operations.

                    AGRICULTURAL DEVELOPMENT

Given the low level of technology and the lack
of scientific information possessed by the peasant
farmers of Eastern Nigeria, the low level of productivity and the resulting rural poverty are not
surprising. It is difficult to predict the agricultural potential of Eastern Nigeria, because it is
hard to know at this point which of the technologica
economic, and cultural problems confronting agricultural development efforts in the region can be
surmounted and which can not. However, it is likely
that agricultural productivity can be increased
several fold, once existing scientific information
is disseminated and utilized and once additional

technical and cultural barriers are overcome. Since
this study focuses upon the cultural and political
factors of achieving rural transformation, an attempt
is made to give some balance to the discussion by
summarizing in this section the research priorities
in the technological and economic spheres.

Since significant technological breakthroughs
have been achieved with the oil palm, it is only a
matter of time before the production of palm oil
increases substantially. The improved oil palm
varieties that have been developed at the Nigerian
Institute for Oil Palm Research can out-produce wild
varieties by 500 percent. Once the new international
Institute of Tropical Agriculture in Ibadan has had
a chance to tackle critical problems relating to food
crop production, breakthroughs comparable to those
achieved with wheat in Mexico and with rice at the
International Rice Research Institute in the Philip-
pines should be attainable. Despite the generally
poor quality of the soil in Eastern Nigeria, the
heavy rainfall in the southern portion makes that
area suitable for such tree crops as oil palms, rubber,
and cocoa, while the drier northern portions have
considerable potential for food production, particularly rice, cassava, and yams. The high population
density in Eastern Nigeria will continue to inhibit
rapid increases in per capita income, but if a means
can be found for redistributing some of the region's
population as well as slowing the population growth
rate, and making more productive use of those fertile
areas in the Cross River basin that are now only
scarcely populated, some of the constraints posed by
land scarcity could be broken.

Technological, economic, and sociological research constitute the principal prerequisite to
significant improvements in agricultural productivity
and increases in rural income. The colonial government in Nigeria concentrated its agricultural research
activities on the tree crops that contributed to
export earnings. Very little imaginative or productive
research has been conducted on annuals or food crops,
and this field needs to be given increasing attention.
Plant breeding work is required to produce not only

higher-yielding varieties, but also varieties with
higher protein content. Such crops as cassava are
very popular as food and have high yield potentials,
but very low nutritional value. Protein deficiency
occurs commonly in the humid tropics, and the most
satisfactory solution in tsetse fly areas seems to
be plant crops with higher protein content.

Probably the maintenance of soil fertility and
structure comprise the most perplexing technical
problems facing agricultural scientists in the humid
tropics. Some means needs to be found of maintaining
soil fertility and structure as an alternative to
shifting cultivation and bush fallow, which permit
the utilization of only a fraction of one's landholdings in a given year. Simple crop rotation and
use of fertilizer, which serve this purpose in the
temperate zone, have not thus far provided the answer
in the tropics. Only a limited amount is known about
the responsiveness, or the reasons for the unresponsiveness, of various crops to fertilizer application
in Nigeria.

According to the Consortium for the Study of
Nigerian Rural Development: "Currently, there is no
acceptable alternative to the age-old practice of
shifting cultivation (bush fallow) on which the agriculture of the tropics is now based. Suitable
alternatives must be found. Lands in the tropics are
beginning to be recognized as the world's most attrac
tive undeveloped agricultural resource, but one
currently being used far below its potential."[11]
With increasing population density and resulting land
scarcity, fallow cycles are shortened to the point
that the soil cannot be completely regenerated by
natural means. This is another reason why an alternative must be found to shifting cultivation and
enlightenment sought regarding the problems surrounding soil fertility.

Some increases in agricultural production could
be achieved simply through the application of practic
already well established elsewhere in the world.
Examples include more frequent weeding and mulching,
wider and more regular spacing of plants, and better

soil conservation practices. However, casual observers
from temperate areas often exaggerate the significance
of these changes and tend to underestimate the magnitude and scope of the research still required.

Virtually no significant research has been
undertaken on the agricultural engineering problems
faced by farmers in Eastern Nigeria. If hoes and
machetes are inefficient, tractors are usually difficult to use and maintain and are excessively costly.
Farm machinery more sophisticated than hoes and
machetes but less complicated and expensive that
tractor-drawn equipment needs to be developed. In
Northern Nigeria oxen are providing a successful
alternative to manpower and machine power, but in
Eastern Nigeria they are subject to attack by tsetse
flies and thus cannot survive for long periods.

Moreover, no easy substitute for the slow manual
methods of clearing hardwood forests have yet been
developed that are economically feasible and even
owners of commercial plantations usually resort to
the use of axes and allow stumps and roots of trees
to rot naturally rather than removing them mechani-
cally. The importance of farm machinery is not simply
to relieve the almost inhuman burdens imposed on
both men and women in the rural areas of Eastern
Nigeria. In places where sufficient land is available
for expansion of farm operations, the limiting factor
in farm size is the amount of work that the farmer
and his family can perform during periods of peak
activity. Simple machinery that could improve a
farmer's work output might permit significant increases in the amount of land put under cultivation.
Improved and expanded systems of irrigation and
water control could also lay the basis for important
production increases both for crops--such as rice--
that require water control and for dry-season farming.
Very little irrigation is presently found.

Problems of food processing and storage also
cut into agricultural production and farm income.
Post-harvest waste results both from spoilage and
insect infestation. Post-harvest losses in perishables
frequently range between 10 and 50 percent.[12] Without

irrigation and without adequate methods or facilities
for storage, many foods are available only for limited
periods during the year, although the temperatures
of the area permit year-round plant growth.

    In addition to the research problems of a techni-
cal and engineering variety, economic issues also
need analysis.[13] A more thorough understanding of
the factors influencing the prices of agricultural
commodities in the region would provide a basis for
organizing profitable production campaigns in particular commodities. Certain past food crop production
campaigns have resulted in nearly disastrous drops
in prices because insufficient information was available concerning market potentials. Careful assessment
of the economic implications employing newly developed
plant materials, fertilizers, insecticides, and other
farm inputs is also required before production campaigns can be successfully mounted by the Ministry
of Agriculture. Without such analysis, farmers might
be encouraged to use materials that could turn out
not to be of economic benefit. Another price issue,
which has been the subject of debate for many years,
concerns what percentage of the export price of palm
oil and palm kernels sold on the world market by the
Eastern Nigeria Marketing Board should go to the
peasant producer. The difference between the Marketing
Board sales price and the amount that goes to the
farmer has served as an important source of governmental revenue, but some analysts argue that if a
higher percentage of the world market price went to
the farmer it would provide an incentive to increase
production.

    Microeconomic studies of peasant farming opera-
tions might point the way to more efficient management
and more effective utilization of a farmer's labor.
Moreover, answers could be found to the problem that
has perplexed many planners of agricultural projects,
i.e., the size of farm a man and his wife can efficiently and economically operate, given existing or
improved crops and tools. Careful assessment of the
agricultural potential of each section of the region,
plus a fuller understanding of the agricultural
economy of the region as a whole could facilitate the

development of a plan to stimulate greater crop
specialization by area and by individual. This would
lay the basis for the commercialization of agriculture
as well as increases in productivity.

To assure that the results of the research efforts
prescribed above are effectively translated into increased agricultural output and higher farm incomes,
linkages are required between the research institutions
and the farmers. This can be accomplished through
improvement of the extension service as well as by
other types of educational programs. Training in
agriculture must be developed further at the University
of Nigeria and at Nigeria's other universities, along
with the training of extension workers and the introduction of agricultural content into the primary
school curriculum, since the primary school is the
principal contact the peasant family has with the
school system. Finally, the establishment of liaison
or coordinating councils would facilitate the necessary
interchange between the educational, research, and
extension institutions concerned with agriculture.

AGRICULTURAL DEVELOPMENT PROGRAM

When discussing agricultural development it is
important to remember that agriculture has probably
never remained completely static in Eastern Nigeria,
and that even in the precolonial era agriculture was
almost continually undergoing changes and improvements.
The most dramatic change has been in the introduction
of cassava. Most communities in Eastern Nigeria were
not acquainted with cassava 50 years ago, but now it
is the most important crop in the region.[14] Tomatoes
and new varieties of yams and beans have also spread
throughout the region without assistance from any
government program. Mention is made earlier in this
chapter of the rapid spread of rice, which also
gathered its initial momentum without governmental
encouragement.

The pace of change has increased considerably,
however, as a result of research and extension programs
as well as production programs organized by the

Ministry of Agriculture, particularly since independence in 1960. This study makes no pretense of
offering an exhaustive analysis of the economic,
biological, or technical prospects or progress of
agricultural development in Eastern Nigeria, and thus
no systematic treatment is given to the various
development programs that have been introduced by the
Ministry of Agriculture. Yet, as a means of indicatin
the types of options open to the farmers of the region
and the types of new technology and organizational
forms that have been introduced, this section briefly
surveys programs of the Eastern Nigeria government
in the agricultural sphere. A more detailed analysis
of some of the programs appears in Chapters 7, 8,
and 9.

The 1962-68 Eastern Nigeria Development Plan
stated the government's principal concerns within
the field of agriculture and indicated the relatively
high priority given agricultural development:

> With over 50 percent of the Region's output
> in the agricultural sector alone, it follows
> that no serious improvement in the pace of
> over-all progress can be made unless very
> strenuous efforts are made to raise pro-
> ductivity in agriculture. Such increases
> must manifest themselves not only in the
> exports but also in food crops: the growth
> of industry could be retarded if food
> production (in Nigeria as a whole) is not
> expanded significantly. The aim is not
> to make the Region self-sufficient in food
> but to increase the protein content of the
> diet and to raise and diversify the pro-
> duction of those crops for which the
> Region has natural advantages. One of the
> main objectives of the 1962-68 Plan is
> therefore the modernization of agricultural
> methods through the adoption of improved
> techniques, intensified agricultural
> education and changes in land tenure.[15]

Over the plan period, government expenditures
were concentrated on three types of programs in the

agricultural sector. The first was farm settlements,
by means of which 4,200 farmers were eventually to
be settled in 6 settlements at a total cost of
approximately £N7 million. Each settlement was designed to have 720 farmers living in 6 villages.
The settlements averaged 12,000 acres in size and
individual holdings ranged between 15 and 20 acres,
depending upon whether the commercial crop grown was
rice, oil palm, cocoa, citrus, or rubber, or a combination of these. The hope was that net farm incomes
would rise to between £N300 and £N500 when the
settlements were in full production.[16] By the time
the civil war started the farm settlements had only
been operational for four years, and thus it is
impossible to give a full assessment of their economic
viability at this point. However, it is quite clear
that the per capita capital investment required by
the farm settlement is enormous when compared to the
total population and the total needs of the region.
A program that only assists 4,200 farmers and yet
consumes approximately 20 percent of the capital
spent on agricultural projects during the development
plan period cannot be considered a sound investment.[17]
Moreover, some question remains whether settlements
will turn out to be viable economic units or profitable
for the individual settlers.

The second major governmental investment in the
agricultural sector has been plantations of the
Eastern Nigeria Development Corporation (ENDC), whose
operations include industrial subsidiaries as well.
ENDC was assigned responsibility by the government
for planting 104,200 acres in plantation crops over
the 1962-68 period, and by late 1966 nearly 62,000
acres had been planted on 23 plantations.[18] Tree
crops planted in these plantations include oil palm,
rubber, cocoa, and cashew. Unlike many government
plantations in other parts of West Africa, ENDC
plantations tend to be well managed and have the
prospect of profitability.[19] The exact returns will
not be known until the trees have a chance to mature
fully, and profits will depend upon world prices,
which tend to fluctuate rather widely for all of
these commodities. A study done in 1965 projected
that the return to the government from ENDC oil palm

plantations would average 7 percent over a 36-year
period.[20] The extent to which this projection would
be affected by the lower prices for palm oil and
kernels prevailing more recently has not been estimated.

Despite the fact that the cost of establishing
an acre of ENDC plantation was considerably less than
the cost per acre of a farm settlement, the financing
is still very burdensome, and the economic benefits
fall primarily to those receiving wages from ENDC.
Most economists who have studied agricultural development in Eastern Nigeria now conclude that the most
productive use of government funds in the agricultural
sector lies in those programs that offer assistance
to large numbers of peasant farmers.[21] The program
holding the greatest prospect for dramatic results
is the Oil Palm Rehabilitation Scheme. Following
the development by the Nigerian Institute for Oil
Palm Research of the improved varieties of oil palm
previously mentioned, which promise, with proper
cultivation, increases in oil palm production of up
to 500 percent per acre, the Eastern Nigeria government devised a scheme aimed at stimulating planting
of this new variety. One of the principal problems
that had to be overcome in launching this scheme
was that the vast majority of oil palms in Eastern
Nigeria are self-seeded and wild, and thus the farmers
of the region have not had experience with planting
and caring for oil palms. Their experience has
generally been limited to harvesting and processing.

Under the rehabilitation scheme, farmers are
given the seedlings of the improved variety plus the
required fertilizers free of charge. Since the scheme
was originally conceived as a means of rehabilitating
existing wild palm groves, a subsidy is also paid
the farmer as an incentive to cut down old wild palms
and plant new ones, as well as to assist the farmer
until his new palms start bearing after five to seven
years of growth. As it has turned out, most of the
land planted under this scheme has not previously
had oil palms growing on it, but the subsidy is still
paid. Over a five-year period the subsidy totals

£N10 per acre. The subsidy payment has the added
value of assuring that proper agricultural practices
are followed, since the subsidy payment can be with-
held if the palms are not planted and cared for
according to the manner prescribed by the Ministry.
Aside from the costs of government administration
and supervision by extension agents, the estimated
cost to government of this scheme is £N18 per acre,
much less than the investment in ENDC plantations or
farm settlements costed on a per-acre basis. Since
the government, through statuatory Marketing Boards
and direct taxation, receives approximately 40 percent
of the world market price of exported palm oil, the
government will eventually receive back from the
increased production of palm oil more than it has
invested in the rehabilitation scheme. In addition
to being the least costly means of increasing oil
palm production, the scheme has also resulted in the
largest acreage planted of any government program as
indicated in Table 2. Comparable schemes exist for

TABLE 2

Target Acreage and Actual Planting
Under the Three Oil Palm Development
Schemes in Eastern Nigeria

Scheme	Target Acreage 1962-68	Planted Acreage (as of March 1967)
Oil Palm Rehabili- tation Scheme	60,000	49,951
ENDC Estates	40,000	29,100
Farm Settlements	16,320	5,353

Source: Malcolm J. Purvis, "Report on a Survey
of the Oil Palm Rehabilitation Scheme in Eastern
Nigeria-1967" (East Lansing: Consortium for the Study
of Nigerian Rural Development, Michigan State
University, 1968, mimeographed), p.4.

peasant plantings of cocoa and rubber, but their
popularity among farmers has not matched that of the
oil palm scheme.

Despite the success of the Oil Palm Rehabilitation
Scheme, its impact has not been nearly as great as
it could be if certain problems, particularly those
relating to various aspects of the land tenure system,
could be overcome. Chapter 7 discusses the community
plantation program launched in 1964 to enable large
groups of peasant farmers to participate and thereby
increase the acreage planted and the number of farmers
benefiting from the scheme.

In addition to the programs for increasing
production of palm oil and kernels, cocoa, and rubber,
all of which involve tree crops and an export market,
the Ministry of Agriculture is also engaged in various
production campaigns relating to locally consumed
food crops.[22] To increase the production of rice,
improved rice varieties are distributed to existing
peasants producers, and efforts are being made to
improve water control through government subsidized
small-scale irrigation schemes. Improved varieties
of cassava are also being introduced by the Ministry
of Agriculture and distributed throughout the region.
The Ministry of Agriculture distributes higher-yielding
maize varieties to the farmer and then the government
purchases the maize crop produced by these seeds at
a fixed price for use in poultry and livestock feed.
Some of this maize is eaten locally, but most is
sold to the government since it is yellow rather than
the white maize to which the farmers are accustomed
and it also has a different texture than the traditional varieties.

Jute and tobacco are being experimented with
on a pilot basis to test their biological and economical potential in the region. The Market Garden
Division of the Ministry of Agriculture tests,
multiplies, and sells vegetable seeds, and vegetable
production is increasing, although at a slow rate.
Various methods of plant protection are being tested
and introduced to farmers on a trial basis. The only
insecticide used in significant measure is Aldrin

dust, which is primarily effective with yam beetles. The Ministry of Agriculture also sells fertilizers for use on cassava, maize, yams, and oil palms at a subsidized price to encourage use. Although sales totaled only 500 tons in 1967, they are increasing. Attempts have been made to introduce poultry on a commercial basis, and by 1966 egg production had increased to the point that no eggs were imported from outside. However, costs of production are so high and the market for eggs so limited that the chances for expansion are limited. Initial hopes that poultry would provide the answer to the protein-deficient diet of the Eastern Nigerian villager have proved to be unfounded. Limited effort is also being made to encourage the production of pigs and other livestock.

Table 3 indicates the breakdown of expenditures by the Eastern Nigeria Ministry of Agriculture from 1962-67 and thus serves as an index to the priorities given various projects and programs.

SOCIAL AND CULTURAL FACTORS AFFECTING AGRICULTURAL DEVELOPMENT

In introducing the discussion of social and cultural factors, the authors want to state their conviction that peasant farmers in Africa are not so tradition-bound that they are unresponsive to economic incentives, and that in most instances where economic betterment conflicts with social and cultural influences, the economic factors prevail.[23] There does appear to be evidence of a "target income" mentality in some parts of Africa, in that when some minimum level of income has been attained substantially higher prices are required before the farmer is prepared to exert the effort required to achieve additional output.[24] William Jones, however, has persuasively demonstrated the general responsiveness of African peasant farmers to economic incentives.[25] Of Nigerian farmers Helleiner has stated:

Nigeria is an area in which [economic man] has demonstrated his presence in many areas.

TABLE 3

Proportional Distribution of Estimated
Expenditures, 1962-67
(Eastern Nigeria Ministry of Agriculture)

1. Directed investment	
a. Settlement projects	21%
b. Government plantations	47
c. Cattle ranches	1
4. Processing and marketing	4
5. Extension	
a. Smallholder tree crop development	11
b. Rural development schemes (community plantations)	4
c. Cattle: veterinary services, disease control	1
d. Poultry development	1
6. Research and investigation	2
7. Education and training	2
8. Credit	4
9. Miscellaneous and unclassified	1
Total	99%

Source: Jerome C. Wells, "Government Agricultura[l] Investment in Nigeria: 1962-67" (Ann Arbor: Center for Research on Economic Development, University of Michigan, 1968, mimeographed), pp. 23, 28, and 31.

The whole history of the introduction and
vast extension of cash cropping in Nigeria
is one of peasant response to improved
incentive--in particular, changed terms of
trade between leisure and goods. But the
Nigerian peasants have also demonstrated
rapid and sophisticated response to much
shorter-run price incentives.[26]

Noneconomic factors loom largest when the economic return is not sufficiently dramatic,[27] and
instances of supposed resistance to innovation often
turn out upon closer analysis to be explainable in
economic rather than cultural or attitudinal terms.[28]

While keeping the above qualification in mind,
an analysis of agricultural development in Africa
that disregards the social and cultural factors is
seriously deficient. The authors' experience in
Eastern Nigeria has confirmed this, and the purpose
of this section is to illustrate the significance
of these factors. But it is also emphasized that
these social and cultural factors can be contributors
to agricultural change and development as well as
being inhibitors.[29] Thus if one is to offer a balanced
analysis of these factors, one must consider both
negative and positive factors.

Cultural Factors Encouraging
Development

One cultural factor that facilitates the acceptance of innovations and in turn encourages agricultural change is the passion for the accumulation
of wealth that prevails in the region. In some
African societies farmers are reluctant to acquire
or display wealth for fear that they will be accused
of having become rich by nefarious means or for fear
that others may become envious and bewitch them.[30]
Okoko claims that he found this fear among some of
the Efiks and Ibibios he studied, but it is absent
among the Ibo and it is not generally a significant
factor in Eastern Nigeria.[31]

The rather flat or nonhierarchical character
of the social structure is another positive influence
Most farmers in Eastern Nigeria control their own
land and work for themselves, and thus are not stifle
by the kind of feudal social structure prevalent in
many parts of Latin America and Asia.[32] Since they
do not have to share their farm incomes with a landlord, a hacendada, or a chief, the farmers of Eastern
Nigeria benefit directly from any increase in production or profit.

Although Everett Hagen is incorrect in assuming
that all traditional societies are hierarchical and
ascriptive, his assertion is valid that a hierarchica
social organization and positioning by ascription
constitute impediments to change and development.[33]
When an increase in production and in turn an increas
in a farmer's income does not enhance his social
status, he has little incentive to accept innovations
and assume new risks. But as described in Chapter
3, most societies in Eastern Nigeria are in the
advantageous situation of having little social strati
fication and of using achievement rather than
ascription as the primary basis for positioning.
Thus if a man becomes a prosperous farmer he will be
accorded prestige and influence, which in turn offer
powerful incentives to diligence and experimentation
with new agricultural practices to achieve a higher
income.

Respect among the young farmers for the older
men of the community is not so intense that it has
an inhibitory influence on agricultural advance as
it does in some parts of the world. Although age
does provide one of the bases for status determination, a young man is usually prepared to adopt new
practices on his farm if they are perceived as being
in his self-interest, regardless of the attitudes
of the community elders. A study in Asia that inquired whether farmers would use commercial fertilize
if their fathers disapproved of the practice revealed
that most young farmers would bow to their fathers'
wishes.[34] The authors' investigations indicated that
this phenomenon did not prevail in Eastern Nigeria.

What might be termed a "sense of family continuity through time" also contributes to agricultural development in Eastern Nigeria. A farmer generally wants to glorify his family, to have his name revered by his descendants, and to give his children a boost. As a consequence elderly men are willing to plant oil palm and rubber plantations that will not begin to yield revenue for several years and will financially benefit only their children, not themselves.

The relative lack of intrusion of religion and superstition into agriculture also facilitates agricultural change. Although certain ceremonies are performed by practitioners of traditional religions in connection with their farming activities, and although later in this chapter mention is made of superstitions that tend to inhibit change, on the whole religion and superstition do not constitute formidable obstacles. In some societies the changing of agricultural practices necessitates restructuring the farmer's whole metaphysical system,[35] but the Eastern Nigerian farmer can retain most elements of his traditional religion and still adopt modern farming techniques. Moreover, Christianity is spreading so quickly that within a generation the traditional religion will most likely be a negligible force as far as agriculture is concerned. The extent to which economic factors override religious traditions and sentiments can be seen in the gradual displacement of yams by cassava as the principal crop. In many parts of the region the traditionally unchallanged significance of yams in the diet and economy meant that yams were elevated to sacred status, and they continue to play a central role in religious ceremonies. Despite the mystical aura surrounding the yam, cassava is in the process of superseding the yam as the principal crop. The fact that cassava gives higher per-acre yields, requires less work, and presents fewer storage problems is considered more significant than the religious status of the yam, and as a result cassava production increases every year.

The value placed on hard work constitutes another

positive factor. Work is valued not only as a means
to increased production, but as a value in itself.
Comments regarding the desire of farmers in various
parts of Africa to avoid exerting any extra effort
occur frequently in the literature, but they are
generally inapplicable in this part of Africa.[36]
This is not to imply that Eastern Nigerian farmers
perform difficult or strenuous tasks merely to enhanc
their prestige in the community. Farmers continually
assess the importance of work to be done in terms
of its contribution to production and profits. What
we are asserting is that when increased production
requires hard work and the performance of difficult
tasks, most farmers do not retreat. Moreover, one
does not find the excessive division of labor that
results from the reluctance of certain castes or
classes to perform unpleasant tasks in some parts of
the world.

Cultural Factors Inhibiting
Development

In the preceding section it was asserted that
there is a widespread willingness to experiment and
to accept new practices, but at the same time certair
traditions persist. Moreover, while most elements
of the population are progressive, some are conservative. For some farmers the recommendation that
they change their farming habits is tantamount to
suggesting that they disown their forebears and be
unfaithful to their history. The farmers of Abia
in Bende Division have small hoes, and the yam mounds
they make in poorly drained areas are too large to
be made with these hoes. To make these mounds, the
Abia farmers hire farm laborers from Afikpo and
Abakaliki Divisions, since they have larger hoes.
When the Abia farmers were asked why they did not
buy larger hoes so that they could make the mounds
themselves, they answered that they could not use
these big hoes because their forefathers had never
used them, and so big hoes were "not for them."
Moreover, since they consider the Afikpo and Abakali¹
people to be inferior, they were not prepared to
adopt their tools.

In the discussion of traditional farming practices earlier in this chapter, the consistency of farming practices within particular communities but the variations found in intercommunity comparisons was emphasized. The intracommunity consistency is supported by the conviction that the methods used are the best ones. Farmers may have no explanation to offer as to why they do something in a particular fashion or they may disagree among themselves over the reason, but this does not alter the conviction that their methods are the proper way to farm. Unlike what is done in many other parts of the region, farmers in the village of Affa in Udi Division plant their cocoyams in plots close to their compounds. When asked why they did this rather than planting cocoyams in open fields, they offered several explanations. Some insisted that cocoyams grow better in the shade, and the compound gardens are better shaded. Others said that they grow better in unshaded areas, but crops near the compound are more likely to be damaged by children and domestic animals; and, since cocoyams are not a highly valued crop, farmers are less concerned about cocoyams being damaged than other crops. Other farmers had still different explanations to offer. Despite the variety of explanations, no one in Affa had any doubts concerning the wisdom of growing cocoyams close to the compound.[37]

Because of the strength of some traditions, it may be easier to substitute whole new complexes of behavior than to make small changes in individual practices. For instance, it might prove easier to introduce mechanized cultivators in Abia than to introduce larger hoes. This is not only because the mechanized equipment might be more efficient but also because it offers such a revolutionary change the farmers would not associate it with the past. For the same reason, it would probably be simpler to introduce a set of new crops and improved farming practices in Affa than to try convincing the Affa farmers to plant cocoyams in open fields or to alter the height of their cocoyam mounds.

As already mentioned in this chapter, another

pattern deeply rooted in all farming communities is
the agricultural calendar and the daily work schedule
Certain times of the day are for farming and certain
times for rest; certain times of the year are for
intense activity, others for a moderate amount of
activity, and still others are for relaxation. New
crops and new techniques require new schedules, and
these new schedules are usually not warmly embraced.
In localities where community plantations have been
organized, clearing has had to start during a time
of the year normally reserved for relaxation, and
this has been a painful adjustment for the farmers
to make.

One encounters an additional problem related
to the agricultural calendar. Because the calendar
is based on tradition and is not worked out by each
farmer, farmers have had little experience with
planning ahead and scheduling new and diverse activities. Tradition has presented them with a ready-made
schedule that meets their needs, but it has not
encouraged them to have foresight or to be flexible.
For instance, in some community plantation projects
there has been a tendency for participants to finish
completely each phase of the work before starting
the next, instead of perceiving overall requirements
and priorities.

Although the people in most sections of Eastern
Nigeria are willing to undertake any type of work
required of a farmer, in some communities, especially
on the Cross River plains, people refuse to climb
palm trees or undertake particularly onerous tasks.
During the nineteenth century the farmers of these
communities owned many slaves, and the slaves did
the climbing and the heavy work. These farmers came
to consider themselves masters, and even though the
circumstances are drastically altered today, it is
difficult for their descendants to see themselves in
any other light.[38] Because they no longer have slave
and cannot afford to hire laborers, the people of
some of these communities prefer not to grow yams,
rather than doing the hard work that yam growing
entails. To harvest their oil palms, the farmers
of these communities either hire laborers or cut the

palms down, since they are not prepared to climb
them. Cutting down a palm to harvest the fruits or
extract palm wine means that its productivity is
reduced to a small fraction of its potential.

When the farmers in one Ikom community were
asked why they do not climb their palm trees, they
said that it is not because they are afraid to climb
but that it is not their "nature" to be climbers.
It was not the work of their forefathers, so it cannot be their work. In another community people
questioned said that they consider climbing to be a
dirty and unpleasant task and thus beneath their
dignity. People in another village said that they
do not fish in the river flowing past their village
because they are not fishermen, they do not climb
palm trees because they are not climbers, and they
do not do much heavy work on their farms because
they are not laborers.

It is not yet clear how rigid self-definitions
will prove to be in regard to the division of labor
between the sexes. In discussions with villagers
one gets the impression that this division is clear-
cut and unalterable, but this does not necessarily
mean that when increased farm income might result
from one sex or the other crossing this traditional
line that the division will prove to be so rigid.

Superstitions and divinely ordained restrictions
on farming activities do not have a serious impact
on agricultural development in Eastern Nigeria, but
their existence needs to be noted. For instance,
many Ibibio villages have taboos against cultivating
particular crops. The farmers of one Ibo community
we surveyed do not plant or eat cassava because they
had a sign from one of their gods indicating that
it would be dangerous for them to handle cassava.
In other communities one finds restrictions concerning
when farm work can be undertaken. For instance, in
one village it was discovered that the gods do not
permit any farm work to be done on market days, which
occur every fourth day. In another village the
farmers believe that their gods will punish them if
they remain at their distant farm plots for more than

three days at a time. In Abia peculiar beliefs concerning the preparation of the soil would make it
difficult to introduce a system of cultivation that
eliminates burning the underbrush after it has been
cut, since they believe that a very hot fire is a
necessary prerequisite to a successful crop.

                    *   *   *

     The above section and several subsequent chapters
of this book address themselves to the question of
the likely propensity of various individuals and
groups in Eastern Nigeria to be responsive to agricultural development programs. The success of the
community plantation program and of certain types of
settlement schemes are also assessed. Unfortunately,
however, little data exist concerning the actual
responsiveness of farmers to other agricultural programs.[39] It is known that certain programs, such
as the Oil Palm Rehabilitation Scheme and the introduction of new varieties of rice, have met with great
enthusiasm and this response hopefully indicates a
general willingness to accept new technology and
practices. Other programs, such as some of the
early fertilizer promotion schemes, failed to realize
their objectives, but one should not interpret the
unresponsiveness of farmers to a particular scheme
as demonstrating a lack of willingness to experiment
or innovate, or a lack of responsiveness to economic
incentives. Some of these schemes were not well
organized or presented. For instance, early efforts
to introduce improved varieties of oil palms met with
little success, but once the package approach of the
Oil Palm Rehabilitation Scheme was introduced, farmers
were enthusiastic and responsive. Other programs,
such as the early fertilizer schemes, tried to promote
products or approaches that had been inadequately
tested and that were not likely to actually increase
production significantly, contrary to the claims of
the programs' promoters. Hopefully the study presented
in this book will be supplemented before long by
other detailed cases studies of particular agricultural
schemes or extension programs. These could provide

more information regarding the preparedness of Eastern
Nigerians to accept agricultural innovations as well
as information on how agricultural schemes can best
be organized and presented to farmers. Purvis has
gathered some interesting data on the Oil Palm
Rehabilitation Scheme, and the Diffusion of Innovations
Study has added some information,[40] but other detailed
studies are required to supplement these, both in
Eastern Nigeria and elsewhere in Africa.

     As indicated in the first part of this chapter,
agriculture in Eastern Nigeria remains preponderantly
peasant agriculture operated at a subsistence level.
Before significant increases in agricultural productivity and rural incomes can be realized, various
types of research need to be undertaken to solve
the technical, economic, educational, cultural, and
political problems related to agricultural growth.
Despite the enormous tasks remaining to be tackled,
the Ministry of Agriculture, in association with
research institutions and universities in various
parts of Nigeria, launched certain research, educational, and production programs, with emphasis
being on production. The dramatic production increases
still required have not yet been achieved, but by
the outbreak of the war in 1967 modest improvements
and hopeful signs were apparent.

                NOTE ON RECENT DEVELOPMENTS

     In mid-1971 the Ministry of Agriculture of East
Central State was struggling to increase total food
production in the state, to increase the protein
content of the diets of those living in ths state,
and to revive many of its former development projects.
However, these activities were being undertaken within
rather severe financial constraints. To enable
farmers to attain their pre-war levels of productivity,
the Ministry of Agriculture with support from the
national Commission for Rehabilitation and philan-
thropic organizations anticipated distributing farm
implements and seedlings to East Central State farmers
worth £N406,000. Rice seed, maize seed, and yam
seedlings were the principal commodities being

distributed, and in the distribution process community
farms were given priority. Another active effort
was a poultry program, which had distributed 500,000
chicks by early 1971 and enabled poultry farms to
purchase feed at half price. The significance of the
poultry program, as with the emphasis being given
to rice and maize cultivation, is to add protein to
diets currently dominated by cassava. Once funds
become available, assistance is also to be offered
to farmers to establish small-scale irrigated rice
projects, many of which will be organized on a community basis.

The agriculture ministries of both South-East
and East Central States are anxious to revive Eastern
Nigeria's successful tree crop subsidy schemes,
particularly the Oil Palm Rehabilitation Scheme.
Because of the lack of locally generated resources,
however, funds to finance these schemes are being
sought from foreign donors. Most of the settlers
from the region's pre-war farm settlements have returned to their respective settlements, but few funds
have been available to invest in their revival or
development. Moreover, with a new emphasis being
given to the needs of peasant farmers, farm settlement
and other high capital projects will probably be
accorded lower priority even when development resources
expand.

NOTES

1. Barry Floyd, Eastern Nigeria: A Geographic
Review (New York: Frederick A. Praeger, 1969), p.
169.

2. Ibid.

3. Ibid., p. 41.

4. It should be clear from the text that the
term "peasant" is not used in the classical sense
of a small, tenant farmer existing within a feudal

economic structure. By "peasant" is meant a farmer
employing unsophisticated farming methods and earning
a meager income, but producing somewhat above the
subsistence level and playing a limited role in a
moneyed and exchange economy.

5. The data for this section was gathered
through a detailed investigation of agricultural
practices obtaining in various parts of Eastern
Nigeria. The areas surveyed included portions of
Orlu Division, Udi Division, Ikom Division, Bende
Division, Calabar Province, Opobo Division, and Aba
Division. For descriptions of agricultural practices
in other areas see H. A. Oluwasanmi, I. S. Dema,
et al., Uboma: A Socio-Economic and Nutritional
Survey of a Rural Community in Eastern Nigeria (Bude,
Cornwall: Geographical Publications Ltd., 1966);
C. A. P. Takes, "Socio-Economic Factors Affecting
the Productivity of Agriculture in Okigwi Division,"
(Ibadan: Nigerian Institute of Social and Economic
Research, 1963, mimeographed); Olatunde Okoko, "A
Study of Socio-Economic Factors Affecting Agricultural
Productivity in Annang Province, Eastern Nigeria,"
(Ibadan: Nigerian Institute of Social and Economic
Research, n.d., mimeographed).

6. Delane E. Welsch, "Response to Economic
Incentive by Abakaliki Rice Farmers in Eastern
Nigeria," Journal of Farm Economics, 47 (November
1965), 900-914.

7. H. A. Oluwasanmi, Agriculture and Nigerian
Economic Development (London: Oxford University Press,
1966), p. 49.

8. According to the "Agricultural Sample Survey
of 1963-64" (Lagos: Federal Office of Statistics
1965) 85 percent of the farmers in Eastern Nigeria
cultivate less than 2.5 acres in the average year.

9. John C. de Wilde, et al., Agricultural
Development in Tropical Africa, Vol. I (Baltimore:
The Johns Hopkins Press, 1967), p. 20.

10. Joseph R. Ascroft, Niels C. Roling, Graham

B. Kerr, and Gerald D. Hursh, "Patterns of Diffusion
in Rural Eastern Nigeria" (East Lansing: Department
of Communication, Michigan State University, mimeographed), p. 21.

11.   Omer W. Hermann, "Nigerian Agricultural
Research" (East Lansing: Consortium for the Study
of Nigerian Rural Development, Michigan State
University, 1968, mimeographed), p. 37.

12.   Ibid., p. 47.

13.   For a review of research on agricultural
economics in West Africa see Carl K. Eicher, Research
on Agricultural Development in Five English-Speaking
Countries in West Africa (New York: The Agricultural
Development Council, 1970).

14.   For a discussion of the spread of cassava
in Africa, see William O. Jones, "Manioc: An Example
of Innovation in African Economies," Economic Development and Cultural Change, V (April 1957), 97-117.

15.   Eastern Nigeria Development Plan, 1962-68,
Official Document No. 8 of 1962 (Enugu: Government
Printer, 1962), p. 8.

16.   "Eastern Nigeria Farm Settlement Scheme,"
Technical Bulletin No. 6, (Enugu: Ministry of Agriculture, n.d.).

17.   Carl K. Eicher, "Transforming Traditional
Agriculture in Southern Nigeria: The Contemporary
Experience," paper presented at the Annual Meeting
of the African Studies Association, Bloomington,
Indiana, 1966, (mimeographed), p. 9.

18.   Ibid., p. 17.

19.   Ibid.

20.   David L. MacFarlane and Martin A. Oworen,
"Investment in Oil Palm Plantations in Nigeria"
(Enugu: Economic Development Institute, University
of Nigeria, 1965, mimeographed), p. 161.

21. One of the first to offer evidence on this point is C. Davis Fogg, "Economic and Social Factors Affecting the Development of Smallholder Agriculture in Eastern Nigeria," Economic Development and Cultural Change, XIII (April 1965), 278-292.

22. "Agriculture Division Programme of Work, 1966-67," Technical Bulletin No. 12 (Enugu: Ministry of Agriculture, 1966, mimeographed).

23. Two works that maintain contrary points of view are C. F. Spence, The Portuguese Colony of Mocambique: An Economic Survey (Cape Town: A. A. Balkema, 1951), p. 52; and Montague Yudelman, Africans on the Land (Cambridge, Mass.: Harvard University Press, 1964), pp. 96-97.

24. De Wilde, op. cit., pp. 65-66.

25. William O. Jones, "Economic Man in Africa," Food Research Institute Studies, I (May 1960), 107-134. See also Edwin Dean, The Supply Responses of African Farmers (Amsterdam: North-Holland Publishing Company, 1966).

26. Gerald K. Helleiner, Peasant Agriculture, Government and Economic Growth in Nigeria (Homewood, Illinois: Richard D. Irwin, Inc., 1966), p. 59.

27. One of the more balanced views of social factors in rural development can be found in William F. Whyte and Lawrence K. Williams, Toward an Integrated Theory of Development (Ithaca, N.Y.: New York State School of Industrial and Labor Relations, Cornell University, 1968). See also Victor C. Uchendu, "Socioeconomic and Cultural Determinants of Rural Change in East and West Africa," Food Research Institute Studies, VIII (No. 3, 1968), 225-242.

28. John W. Mellor and T. V. Moorti, "Farm Business Analysis of 30 Farms, Midhakur, Agra District, U.P., 1959-1960," Research Bulletin I (Agra: The Balwant Vidyapath, 1961).

29. This point has generally been neglected in

the literature. One exception is Clifford Geertz,
"Religious Belief and Economic Behavior in a Central
Javanese Town," Economic Development and Cultural
Change, IV (January 1956), 134-158.

30. A. I. Richards, Land, Labor, and Diet in
Northern Rhodesia (London: Oxford University Press,
1937), p. 215.

31. Okoko, op. cit., p. 18.

32. Before 1950 in Taiwan a tenant was expected
to give 50 to 70 percent of the main crop yield to
his landlord. In addition, the tenant had to provide
his own fertilizers, farm equipment, and farm buildir
See Hui-Sun Tang, Highlights of Land Reform in Taiwar
(Taipei: Joint Commission on Rural Reconstruction,
1957), p. 13.

33. Everett Hagen, On the Theory of Social Chanc
(Homewood, Illinois: The Dorsey Press, 1962), pp.
55-56.

34. Harold R. Capener, "The Rural People of
Developing Countries: Their Attitudes and Levels
of Education," in Albert H. Moseman, ed., Agricultura
Sciences for the Developing Nations (Washington, D.C.
American Association for the Advancement of Science,
1964), pp. 117-118.

35. See, for instance, Bronislaw Malinowski,
"The Primitive Economics of the Trobriand Islanders,"
The Economic Journal, XXXI (March 1921), pp. 1-16.

36. For instance, John A. Hellen, Rural Economic
Development in Zambia, 1890-1964 (New York: Humani-
ties Press, 1968), pp. 268-270; and J. D. N. Versluys
"The Gezira Scheme in the Sudan and the Russian
Kolkhoz: A Comparison of Two Experiments," Economic
Development and Cultural Change, II (April 1953), p.
44.

37. Until further study is undertaken of agricultural practices in Eastern Nigeria and the ecology
of the region, it will not always be possible to

determine precisely which of these practices are
merely traditional behavior patterns that father has
passed on to son through the ages without reference
to ecological requirements, and which are appropriate
responses to ecological conditions. For instance,
the Hudsons, unlike most others who have written
about the herding societies of East Africa, have
argued that the reluctance of the Karamojong in
Uganda to develop commercial or market-oriented
attitudes toward their livestock does not result so
much from any symbolic value accorded cattle as from
the dictates of the ecological system of which the
Karamojong are a part. See Rada and Neville Dyson-
Hudson, "Subsistence Herding in Uganda," Scientific
American, 220 (February 1969), 76-89. Once further
information has been amassed on the subject, some
of the discussion regarding cultural factors may be
open to new interpretations in ecological terms.
See also Robert Netting, "Household Organization and
Intensive Agriculture," Africa, XXXV (October 1965),
422-429; and Philip W. Porter, "Environmental Poten-
tials and Economic Opportunities--A Background for
Cultural Adaptation," American Anthropologist, 67
(April 1965), 409-420.

38. Hellen, op. cit., p. 263, reports the same
phenomena among certain former slave-owing groups
in Zambia.

39. For an interesting discussion of this subject,
see Helleiner, op. cit., pp. 67-79.

40. Ascroft, Roling, Kerr, and Hursh, op. cit.

5

THE
POLITICAL SYSTEM
AND
RURAL
TRANSFORMATION

In most new states the government serves as the primary agent for development since no independent groups or individuals have the skills or resources to plan, finance, or execute large-scale projects. In such a situation the nature of the political system obviously affects development efforts, especially in rural programs where the government tries to reach large numbers of people. Rural transformation depends to a considerable extent on the ability of the government to formulate progressive and feasible programs designed to improve the economic conditions and the quality of life in predominantly agricultural communities. Before the government can embark on such programs, however, it must develop the capacity to penetrate society in order to reach the people and local communities it seeks to change. Many new states draft elegantly framed development programs that sometimes even focus on the rural sector. Very few new states, though, have the capability to undertake large-scale rural development efforts. Characteristically governmental institutions decline in effectiveness along the structural hierarchy with the local or microlevel institutions functioning the least adequately. Consequently the closer the political system comes to its citizens, the less able it is to direct and effect change.

As hopes for rapid development have been frustrated in one country after another, social scientists have come to realize that economically underdeveloped countries tend to be politically underdeveloped as well, and that the low level of effectiveness of the political system inhibits economic development. Without an effective political vehicle, even the most brilliant development plan cannot be translated into the output of an actual program. An inadequate bureaucracy and extension staff, corrupt politicians and inefficient civil servants, or a hostile and apathetic public can undermine development efforts, perhaps less dramatically than chronic political instability, but just as completely. Hence political development, the process through which political systems become more effective and self-directed, often is a precondition for further economic development. While a greater degree of political development does not necessarily assure a faster rate of economic development, a more effective political system provides the requisite institutional medium through which economic programs can be initiated.

Some recent studies of rural development emphasize the need for taking the political factor into account. One book on the development of agriculture in Japan attributes the success there to the emergence of a strong, progressive government in the latter part of the nineteenth century.[1] Similar studies of land reform and the increase in productivity of agriculture in Taiwan also cite the nature of the political system as a significant element.[2] In his analysis of traditional social structures as barriers to change, John Brewster mentions, "In discussions with able persons in foreign aid programs, this writer has repeatedly asked what is the key requirement for getting agricultural development on the move. Invariably, the answer has been the emergence of a stable, progress-oriented government."[3] George Rosen frames his discussion of economic development in the context of the interrelations between the political and economic systems, and particularly the role of the government.[4] Douglas Ashford suggests that rural mobilization and transformation be regarded as organizational problems for the political system entailing new links

between farmers and political and administrative
authorities, markets, and credit sources.[5]

This chapter seeks to assess some of the ways
in which the nature of the political system in Eastern
Nigeria affected rural development there. It con-
centrates on three dimensions of the political system:
its organization, its effectiveness, and its political
culture. The pattern of organization of a political
system determines the manner in which responsibilities
for functions are distributed and levels are linked
together. Effectiveness refers to the ability of the
political system to perform requisite functions. The
political culture alludes to the attitudes, values,
and orientations of the governors and the governed
toward the political system and particularly what the
role of the political system should be in the development process.

ORGANIZATION

Many different aspects of the organization of
a political system influence its ability to promote
rural transformation. Some recent studies of political
development emphasize the importance of increasing
structural differentiation and specialization resulting
in greater institutional complexity.[6] Like most new
states Nigeria embarked on nationhood with complex
and sophisticated institutional structures on the
central and regional levels modelled on those that
had evolved in Britian. This structural similarity
did not, however, confer effective political performance. Further differentiation would not, therefore,
ensure an improved quality of government. Hence an
evaluation of the degree of institutional specialization attained in Eastern Nigeria would not reveal
much about the adequacy of the Eastern Nigerian political system.

Since most members of a predominantly agricultural
society live in relatively isolated villages, one of
the major organizational challenges developing political systems confront is establishing linkages between
central decision-making institutions and these local

communities. Agricultural innovations must be com-
municated to farmers and technical assistance given
to them before new practices can be adopted. Blue-
prints for restructuring the economic life and social
structure of villages remain proposals and not action
programs unless the government has a network of insti
tutions reaching down into the local communities
through which it can exert pressure for change.

While many developing political systems have
similar goals, the manner in which they organize for
rural development on the central or regional levels
of the political system differs considerably.[7] To
some extent the differing organizational patterns
reflect the way in which the political system has
attempted to reconcile the conflicting needs for
professionalism and specialization with those of coor
dination. The proliferation of diverse functions
within a single ministry often limits the amount of
control that can be exercised over the operation of
programs. By establishing several ministries concern
with rural development, the government encounters a
new set of problems relating to competition between
them for resources, conflicts over priorities and
programs, duplication of staff, and coordination.
In some political systems such interministerial rival
ries have significantly hampered the rural developmen
effort.[8] Interministerial committees composed of
political representatives and/or high-ranking civil
servants rarely act as suitable policy-making, coordinating, or executing instruments because it is
difficult to assemble the members on a regular basis
and because the representatives of the ministries oft
reflect the preferences and prejudices of their
respective ministries. At best such interministerial
committees may formulate broad policy guidelines.

This section will not attempt to undertake an
exhaustive analysis of the organization of the Easter
Nigerian political system. It will concentrate on
the following subjects: the division of functions
relating to rural development among the ministries,
the pattern of linkage between the regional and local
levels of the political system, and the allocation
of responsibilities for development on the local

levels. The reader may want to refer to the outline
of the political structure in Eastern Nigeria in
Chapter 2.

    Prior to 1963 the Eastern Nigeria government had
no well-formulated strategy for the economic development of the region's rural areas. As described in
Chapter 4, the region's agricultural program concentrated on a few capital intensive efforts, particularly
on large ENDC plantations and farm settlements. Some
assistance to small farmers was provided through the
extension services and by means of the rehabilitation
schemes for oil palm, rubber, and cocoa, but these
programs reached only a limited number of farmers.
Another ministry operating in the rural areas was the
Ministry of Internal Affairs, whose Community Development Division had a small budget to assist locally
sponsored efforts to construct health centers, maternities, dispensaries, bridges, and feeder roads. By
1963 it was concentrating primarily upon the construction of bridges for villages prepared to contribute
money and labor to the project. The Cooperative
Division of the Ministry of Commerce was responsible
for organizing and overseeing cooperatives, and this
involved work in rural communities. However, virtually
all of the cooperatives in the region were local thrift
and credit societies and not production or marketing
enterprises. Social services and amenities were also
provided in the rural areas by the Ministry of Works,
the Ministry of Health, and the Ministry of Education.

    Concern regarding the lack of attention to the
economic development of the region's rural areas, as
well as concern over the lack of coordination between
the ministries operating there, led to the issuance
of a government policy paper in 1963 that advocated
a new regional development effort that would be
coordinated through an interministerial committee of
civil servants from the relevant ministries.[9]

        The first priority of the Rural Develop-
    ment Program therefore is to transform
    traditional agriculture into a modern
    system of full-time profitable farm-
    ing. . . . We are not seeking merely to

improve village life with government
assistance: We are seeking to change
and modernize it. We now regard 'community development' as the organizing
of a community for economic development as the essential basis for social
advancement and the growth of the whole
community.[10]

As described in Chapter 7, the focus of the
region's new rural development program became the
establishment of community plantations, first in
pilot villages and then more broadly. Principal
responsibility for the program was given to the Community Development Division of the Ministry of Internal
Affairs. Despite the assistance this Division had
given to village construction projects, it had had
no previous experience with agricultural or other
economic projects. With no expertise in these fields,
and with a very small budget, the Community Development
Division had to depend upon cooperation from the
Ministry of Agriculture both for materials and for
technical supervision of projects. It was probably
fortunate that an agricultural staff, potentially in
competition with the Ministry of Agriculture, was not
established within the Community Development Division,
but this lack of expertise within the Division meant
that success of the Division's projects was almost
totally dependent upon the good will and cooperation
of the Ministry of Agriculture. Cooperation from
the Survey Division of the Ministry of Town Planning
was required to have project land surveyed and registered, and the program was dependent upon the Cooperative Division of the Ministry of Commerce to
organize project cooperatives. Cooperation with the
Cooperative Division and the Community Development
Division proved particularly difficult because each
of these divisions had quite divergent ideas regarding
how community plantations should be organized.
Administrative difficulties were also created by the
fact that in addition to the rural development program
the Ministry of Internal Affairs had responsibility
for such diverse activities as government printing,
processing pardons for criminals, fire services, and
social welfare.

In an effort to rationalize the organization of the rural development program, the new military government created a Ministry of Rural Development in 1966. It was composed of the former Community Development Division of the Ministry of Internal Affairs and the Cooperative Division of the Ministry of Commerce, which were respectively renamed the Rural Services Division and the Cooperative Division. This new ministry was vested with responsibility to coordinate all efforts relating to rural development without duplicating the professional functions already furnished by other ministries.[11] Therefore the staff of the Ministry of Rural Development deliberately avoided impinging on the specialist services of other ministries. The role of the Ministry was to review available resources at the village level, particularly in the agricultural sphere, in order to identify economic projects and then to facilitate the application and extension in these villages of the specialist services provided by other ministries. The training program for the Ministry's Rural Development Officers attempted to impart awareness of the specialist services offered by other ministries rather than to vest them with the skills of multipurpose extension workers, the mainstay of most community development programs. Prior to the outbreak of the war, Rural Development Officers in conjunction with the provincial and divisional administration concentrated on identifying communities that were suitable for the establishment of community plantations or for other community economic projects, and providing the stimulation and coordination necessary to implement the projects.

Theoretically the establishment of a facilitiating or coordinating ministry had many advantages since it regularized the often informal and ad hoc cooperation between ministries on the rural development program. One of the principal advantages of this new organizational arrangement was that with a single permanent secretary directing the work of the former Community Development Division and the Cooperative Division, the earlier conflict and disagreements between them were more easily resolved. On the other hand, this mode of organization also introduced new

difficulties, as well as retaining some of the old
ones. It did not eliminate the need for interministerial coordination, and interministerial committees composed of resspresentatives from the Ministries of Rural Development, Agriculture, and Town
Planning did occasionally meet to discuss policy
issues. Moreover, officials of the Ministry of Rural
Development still had to approach the Ministry of
Agriculture and the Ministry of Town Planning to gain
their cooperation and assistance. To complicate
matters, with the Community Development Division raise
to ministerial level, the high-ranking civil servants
in the Ministry of Agriculture began to perceive the
Ministry of Rural Development as a competitor rather
than as a supplicant. With this changed perception
came a somewhat greater reluctance to assist a
potential rival, especially since the Ministry of
Rural Development was headed by an energetic and
aggressive permanent secretary.

The ministries operating within the rural development program were linked from the regional to the
local level through their respective field staffs,
and the central administration was organized hier-
archically from the Chief Secretary through the
provincial secretaries to the divisional officers.
By 1966 the Ministry of Agriculture was staffed by
1,191 technical and professional workers, which
included administrators and research staff as well
as the extension staff in the field. This number
represented almost a doubling of the size of the
Ministry's staff in four years.[12] At that time the
Ministry of Rural Development fielded a cadre of
only 15 Rural Development Officers and also deployed
some 25 specially trained Peace Corps Volunteers.
The Ministries of Health, Education, Town Planning,
and Works also had inspectors, engineers, surveyors,
and other field staff working in the rural areas.

According to the Local Government Act, the prima
responsibility for rural administration rested with
the 107 elected county councils rather than with
provincial or divisional officials or the staff of th
ministries. This act vested county councils with
responsibility for 96 functions, including local

projects in agriculture, forestry, town planning, trade, and cottage industries. In actual practice most country councils concentrated on providing social services, and a few managed to undertake some public works projects. They usually expended their limited budgets on supporting local authority schools and health centers and on maintaining local courts and, if money was available, on building or improving markets, local roads, and bridges. Although the Local Government Act assigned county councils functions pertaining to economic development, they lacked the resources, staffs, skills, and inclination to undertake such projects. When they sponsored the building of roads and bridges, they usually did so for reasons of political patronage rather than to increase the economic potential of the area.

Throughout its history Eastern Nigeria has lacked strong integrative institutions that linked local communities to higher units of government. As Chapter 3 indicated, the village or village-group generally constituted the perimeters of the precolonial socio-political systems for the various ethnic groups incorporated into Eastern Nigeria. During most of the colonial period, the British attempted to govern Eastern Nigeria through native authorities. Although these native authorities manifested an inability to fulfill the terms of their mandate, British administrative reforms until 1951 merely changed the size and boundaries of the native authority councils rather than reassessing the principle of indirect rule as it applied to the region. In some ways this response set a pattern for future local government reforms in that subsequent local government ordinances modifying the three-tier, English style councils introduced in 1950 altered the territorial jurisdictions of the councils to increasingly smaller units without basically questioning the concepts underlying the organization of the political system. Moreover, by reducing the population base of the apex county councils six-fold between 1950 and 1960, successive local government changes rendered the whole structure less viable in terms of its ability to furnish services and undertake development.

Attempts at local government reform also paid
little attention to the need for creating more
effective links between county and village councils
and the regional level. Eastern Nigeria was therefore governed through a series of relatively autonomous administrative layers. Prior to 1950, district
officers (later to become divisional officers)
exercised some control over native authorities, but
the Local Government Ordinance of 1950 transformed
the district officers into advisers who had no direct
power vis-à-vis the new councils. Subsequent local
government ordinances restored some regional financial
control over the councils by requiring approval of
large expenditures by the Ministry of Local Government and by subjecting the councils to annual audits
but they did not vest divisional officers with any
greater policy-making role. By 1958 the two primary
tiers of government in Eastern Nigeria were the
regional bodies and the 107 county councils with few
links existing between them.

Most divisional officers did not see either
their roles or that of the councils as being directly
concerned with economic development. Although some
divisional officers did promote development efforts,
most were imbued with the old colonial conception
of the role of the administrative officer as responsible for law and order. Moreover, the small number
of administrative officers assigned to rural posts,
approximately the same as during the period of indirect
rule, did not allow the divisional officers sufficient
time to work closely with councils let alone attempting
to encourage them to undertake constructive development projects. A few exceptional administrative
officers did manage to influence some councils by
virtue of their dynamism, prestige, and rapport;
most did not even try. The initial lack of commitment to rural development on the part of provincial
secretaries and divisional officers contributed to
the operational difficulties of the ministries with
rural development programs. In an effort to imbue
administrative officers with more enthusiasm for
rural development, the Chief Secretary, J. O. Udoji,
notified them in 1965 that henceforth their contribution to development programs would be an important
consideration in determining promotions. From that

time the provincial and divisional officers displayed considerably more concern with promoting development.

Given the closeness of county councils to local conditions in the rural areas, as well as their statutory responsibility for some aspects of rural development, it had been hoped that county councils might be drawn into the new rural development program. To achieve this, the Community Development Division envisaged the creation of rural development committees at both county and provincial levels. The county committees, which could include representatives of voluntary agencies and ethnic unions as well as members of the county council, were to assist the divisional officer and the rural development officer in selecting viable economic projects within the area. It was also hoped that county councils might be prepared to make financial contributions to projects within their counties. In general, however, the planners of the rural development effort did not view councils as suitable agencies for the initiation or management of projects.[13] Provincial development committees, which consisted of civil servants, were to have the final decision on which projects would comprise the provincial development plan sent to the Community Development Secretary. Although some provincial committees met, at neither provincial nor county levels did rural development committees become fully operational by the time the war broke out in 1967.[14]

As is apparent from the foregoing, the Eastern Nigerian political system did not have an institutionalized means of coordinating rural development efforts at the local level. Since no agency became the czar of rural development, every project required the painstaking coordination of the ministries and administrators working in the area. Officials from the Ministry of Rural Development, for instance, could only tour a locality to evaluate communities for participation in their programs if they were accompanied by the appropriate administrative officer. When rural development officers were posted to the divisions, they were responsible both to the Community Development Secretary and to the local divisional

officer. Project selection procedures as outlined
by the program planners involved the recommendation
of the divisional officer and the field staffs of
the relevant ministries, consultations with the
development committees of the county councils, and
the evaluation of the provincial secretaries and
provincial committees before reaching the Ministry
of Rural Development headquarters staff. The work
of the Ministry of Rural Development was dependent
upon the schedule and free time of the provincial
and divisional administration. The execution of
rural development projects also required extensive
advance preparations in order to have rural development officers, extension workers, surveyors from the
Ministry of Town Planning, and supplies from the
Ministry of Agriculture arrive when needed. Despite
the difficulties and delicacy of coordination involved,
the alternatives of having a single ministry with all
the personnel and control of supplies required by the
program or of having the program directed and coordinated from the Premier's or Chief Secretary's office
would probably have been equally unwieldy.

EFFECTIVENESS OF THE
POLITICAL SYSTEM

The effectiveness of the political system refers
to the manner in which it performs. It is a less
technical and more inclusive term for what some
political scientists call the capabilities of the
political system.[15] Every political system attempts
to fulfill certain functions in order to maintain
itself in being. These functions include decision-
making, extraction of resources, communication,
implementation of policies, application of legitimate
coercion to enforce decisions, allocation of goods
and services, recruitment, provisions for participation, and promotion of social and economic well-
being. However, political systems vary greatly in
how well they are able to perform any one of these
functions or generally respond to needs and crises.
Or to put it in another way, the degree of effectiveness of political systems in fulfilling these functions
varies from the very inadequate to the relatively

adequate. While the degree of effectiveness of a
political system in performing various functions
differs somewhat, developing political systems generally manifest an inability to fulfill most functions
satisfactorily and more developed political systems
exhibit a more adequate operational profile. In
fact, political underdevelopment is by definition
virtually synonymous with operational inadequacy.

Although the effectiveness of political systems
is sometimes related to aspects of organization, two
very similar systems or institutions frequently operate
quite differently. After all, most new states have
patterned their organizational structures and institutions on those existing in more economically and
politically developed countries without as yet
achieving the same results. Hence factors other than
organization, some of which are not yet known, determine the effectiveness of a particular institution
or entire political system. The absolute amount of
resources and the manner in which available resources
are distributed, the size and competence of the
administrative bureaucracies, the honesty or corruption
of participants, and the nature of the culture influence the way in which the political system operates.
The first three of these factors will be discussed
in this section and the fourth in the following one.

All developing political systems suffer from an
inadequate resource base, that is, they do not raise
revenues that are commensurate with their needs. The
relative proverty of their people, reflecting the low
level of economic development attained, obviously
circumscribes the absolute amount of resources the
government can extract. The weakness of the administrative apparatus further reduces the proportion of
the total national product, relative to more politically developed systems, that the government can
acquire through taxation. To complicate financial
affairs even more, developing political systems
frequently maintain, because of the rising expectations
of their citizens and the sophisticated governmental
structure they inherited at independence, far more
social welfare services and a larger administrative
apparatus than more advanced political systems did

at a comparable stage of economic development. In
addition to sustaining this overhead, recent re-
ductions in foreign aid and loans have forced most
new states to rely primarily on their own revenues
to finance their own economic development.

To state, therefore, that the resources available
to the prewar Eastern Nigeria government were
insufficient for promoting economic and political
development would be repeating the obvious. As
Chapter 3 indicated, the discovery and export of oil
in commercial quantities augmented the resource base
of the East in the sixties. The amount of oil revenues
received by the Eastern Treasury prior to 1967 did
not yet drastically transform the economic picture
as it has in other oil-rich states, like Libya and
Saudia Arabia. Per capita revenue was only slightly
higher than in the Western Region. If the political
situation had remained stable and the rate of oil
production increase continued, perhaps in another
ten years oil revenues would have provided the
resources for financing a bolder economic development
program. It seems unlikely, however, that the other
regional components of Nigeria would have allowed
the federal revenue allocation formula based on the
principle of origin rather than on need to remain
unchanged in such a situation, even if the cataclysmic
events after 1966 had been avoided.

In circumstances of relative economic scarcity
the manner in which priorities are set and available
resources distributed assume an overwhelming importance. After 1956 the Eastern Region allocated some
40 percent of its operating budget for education.
While this expenditure on education could be considered a long-term economic investment, it did not
bring immediate economic benefits. Most of the money
went for primary education and therefore directly
contributed to the problem of the unemployment of
primary school leavers, who emigrated from their
rural homes in search of more dignified and pleasant
jobs in the cities without having the requisite skills
to find them. Politicians routinely voted funds for
educational expansion in response to popular demands
for access to schools as a vehicle for economic

self-improvement largely oblivious to the concomitant economic liabilities and the potential political hazards.[16] This massive expenditure on education obviously limited the revenues available for improving communications, extension services, and other programs that could have had more direct pay-offs economically.

As indicated in Chapter 4, according to the stated objectives of the Eastern Development Plan for 1962-68, agriculture had the highest priority followed by manufacturing and processing industries and then technical training and education.[17] The projected pattern of expenditure reflected a major shift in the government's emphasis with respect to agriculture. From 1958 through 1962 only 4 percent of capital and recurrent-expenditure went to primary production, whereas during the 1962-68 plan period primary production was to receive 34 percent of all revenues. During the 1962-68 plan period, education was to constitute 28 percent, trade and industry 12 percent, water 9 percent, and health, planning, and social welfare together 7 percent.[18]

Despite this new emphasis on agriculture, government activity in the agricultural sphere during the plan period focussed upon such large-scale projects as farm settlements and ENDC plantations. This pattern of expenditure prevented the government from significantly expanding the developmental and extension services that could potentially reach large numbers of smallholder farmers, and in the process improve the effectiveness of the political system as an agent of development. By 1966 the Ministry of Rural Development had assisted the establishment and development of some 220 projects: 133 based on oil palm, 31 on rubber, 20 on rice, 8 on cocoa, 5 on fish ponds, and 3 on vegetable gardening.[19] While this list is impressive considering that the Ministry of Rural Development began with 15 pilot projects in 1964, it meant that only a relatively small portion of the population had participated in any of their schemes. The work of the Ministry of Rural Development was hampered by several restrictions, among which were money, staff, and the difficulty of devising a range of suitable projects. For the 1966/67 financial year

the Ministry of Rural Development had a budgetary
allocation of only £N350,000.[20]

The Ministry of Agriculture had the largest staff
of any governmental agency promoting rural development. Its extension workers were supposed to demonstrate new agricultural practices, instruct farmers
in new methods, advise farmers of program requirements
and available supplies, and provide agricultural
supplies. In 1962 the Ministry of Agriculture had a
total staff of 670 persons. According to the goals
prescribed by the 1962-68 development plan, the ministry of Agriculture would expand to a staff of 5,049 by
the end of 1967.[21] By 1966 the Ministry of Agriculture
had a staff of 1,191, less than a fourth of the
objective that had been set for 1967. One study of
the agricultural program in Eastern Nigeria calculated
that in 1966 the ratio of extension workers to farmers
was one extension worker for every 1,750 farmers, or
one for every 38 square miles of densely populated
country.[22] Actually, as the authors of the study
acknowledge, this figure did not accurately represent
the true situation since many staff members of the
Ministry of Agriculture were not engaged in extension
work. Of the 1,191 people employed by the Ministry
of Agriculture, only 569 spent all of their time in
the field demonstrating new techniques and working
with the farmers. Hence the true ratio of extension
workers to farmers in 1966 was about one extension
worker for every 3,585 adult male farmers.[23] Obviously
with this ratio most farmers never met any extension
workers and therefore never learned about new techniques and available assistance. The failure of the
Ministry of Agriculture to recruit more extension
workers in part reflected the relatively low priority
accorded to this part of the Ministry of Agriculture's
responsibilities.

One of the reasons that the county councils never
became more effective units of government and never
undertook many economic projects was budgetary
restrictions. Of the 107 county councils, perhaps
35 had sufficient resources to be viable. In the
early sixties the rural councils spent a total of
about £N4 million a year, 36 percent of which went to

education, 24 percent to public works, 12 percent to health services, and 10 percent for courts. The county and urban councils in 1964 maintained 14 teacher training colleges, 16 secondary schools, 1,800 primary schools, 63 general health centers, 146 maternity centers, and 278 dispensaries. They had also constructed by this time 963 bridges and 15,000 miles of roads.[24] In many cases the county councils had little choice about assuming responsibility for maintaining schools in their jurisdiction since no other agency could provide the operating funds. Moreover, few of the councils had sufficient resources to hire competent professional staff. Even if more councils had been interested in sponsoring economic projects, they would not have had the requisite funds or skills to do so.

Developing political systems characteristically have fewer well-trained, experienced, and competent administrators than the more developed systems. The low level of educational development in most colonial territories, the difficulties Africans and Asians encountered in joining the colonial services, and the rapid pace of decolonization combined to leave most new states at independence with a rapidly recruited and inexperienced bureaucracy. In 1961, shortly after independence, the median age of admini- strative officers in Eastern Nigeria was 33. The average officer had only 3.5 years of government experience. Only 13 administrative officers, most of whom were expatriates, had been in government service for more than 10 years.[25]

Relative to most other states in Africa, though, the Eastern Region was better endowed with adminis- trators. In the early sixties only Ghana and Western Nigeria probably had indigenous civil servants with better paper qualifications than in Eastern Nigeria. In his comparative evaluation of the regional and federal public services in Nigeria, as they operated subsequent to independence, I. Nicolson reserved his highest accolades for the Eastern Nigerian civil service. According to Nicholson, "It is in the Eastern Region at the present time that the gap between the theoretical and the actual is at its

narrowest, requiring only a period of consolidation
of the present pattern of public service, without
further upheaval, to complete the alignment."[26]
Furthermore, in the East "the stage has been reached
when the political leaders can now show complete
confidence in the public service and rely on the
internal leadership in the service to maintain and
improve its own efficiency and responsiveness to the
needs of ministers and of the public."[27] Nicholson
particularly praised Eastern Nigeria for not following
the practice of Western Nigeria and precipitantly
displacing all expatriate personnel and posting new
Nigerian officers to the field before assigning them
to regional ministries.[28]

     However, the organization and ethos of the
Eastern Nigerian bureaucracy reflected the colonial
past more than the contemporary requirements for
development. Individuals were recruited into the
administrative class of the civil service on the
basis of a general university degree. Usually these
recruits had studied humanities or history and therefore lacked any training relevant for administration
or development. Eastern Nigeria did not have a
separate service for economists,as do some other
African political systems. Many administrators were
reluctant to deviate from the roles assumed by their
counterparts during the colonial period despite the
supposed change from a law and order to a developmental orientation. It should be noted, however,
that few new states have had any more success in
making their bureaucracies instruments of development.
Even efforts to define the components of development
administration have met with difficulty.[29]

     On the regional level the permanent secretaries
were the most important shapers of ministerial policy
and operations. As in every other political system,
whether developing or developed, the quality of these
civil servants varied from extremely competent to
mediocre. Many of the permanent secretaries, as well
as other high-level administrators in the government
and the regional corporations and boards, compared
favorably with the occupants of similar positions in
more developed political systems.

Personnel working for the Eastern political system at lower levels, however, who came into more frequent contact with the population, often lacked the requisite education and skills for the positions they filled. Intermediary cadres in the bureaucracy often were less skilled for their positions and did not provide adequate support for high level administrators. While the provincial heads of the agricultural extension bureaucracy usually had a B.S. in agriculture and agricultural superintendents in charge of divisions usually had at least two years of formal agricultural training after secondary school, the agricultural assistant on the county level often had less than a secondary school education and the extension workers under him sometimes had no formal agricultural training whatsoever, and these were the workers who came into primary contact with farmers and their problems. During the 1962-68 plan period, the level of qualification for these positions was not raised, but an effort was made to improve the quality of instruction given in training courses for extension workers.

While the problem of corruption afflicts most societies, developing political systems seem particularly susceptible to this disease of the body politic. The forms and frequency of corruption in any political system are difficult to document. Many observers of Nigerian politics prior to the 1966 military coup, both Nigerian and foreign, believed that the "dash" had become a way of life oiling the governmental machinery at all levels and in all regions.[30] It seems doubtful though that permanent secretaries and/or ministers in the Eastern Nigeria government routinely siphoned off 15 percent or more of the value of all contracts as in Ghana during the Nkrumah regime. However, the ruling party (the NCNC) allegedly received sizable kickbacks from government contracts, and the ethos infusing the political system generated the expectation that "big men" would use their positions both for their own benefit and for the advantage of their communities of origin. Therefore if corruption is defined as "the use of public office or authority for private advantage and gain,"[31] then corruption was endemic, and perhaps a central operating principle,

of the Eastern Nigeria political system. As the
discussion of the ethos of the Eastern political
system in the next section will explore in more
detail, participants viewed politics as a great
marketplace in which one bartered influence for
material assets. These material assets often related
to discretionary development fund allocations.

     Corruption in the commonly accepted use of the
term did plague many, and perhaps most, local councils.
According to Simon Ottenberg, "The most characteristic
feature of corruption in the local government councils
in Southern Nigeria is that it occurs throughout
almost all levels of council activity and is found
a good deal of the time."[32]   (Southern Nigeria would
encompass the Eastern, Western, and Mid-West Regions.)
Furthermore, "very often the reason for becoming a
councillor was not that one had succeeded in life
and wished to offer public services, but that one
had failed in life and needed money."[33] Certainly
the limited resources of many county councils were
squandered or at least partially wasted when councillors or staff members who awarded contracts, hired
personnel,and approved contracts were motivated by
what they would receive in turn. In some cases
council funds probably found their way directly into
the pockets of a few council members.

     Corruption in the local councils inhibited them
from becoming more effective vehicles for administration and development and perhaps constituted the
primary cause for their political decay. The general
dissatisfaction with the way in which councils
operated and particularly the distrust of their
handling of money made the regional government wary
of increasing their funds and probably discouraged
any efforts to transform the county councils into
agents for rural transformation. In fact knowledge
about how the local councils performed in Nigeria
and elsewhere in Africa has stimulated some critics
to question the attempt to transplant the English
system of local government to Africa. One recent
critic categorically stated that "It is now clear
that carbon copies of English local government do
not work in Commonwealth West Africa."[34]

The administrator of the East Central State, Ukpabi
Asika, offered the opinion that in light of the
backlog of historical failures to establish a viable
system of councils the ethnic unions constituted
the real local government of the area.[35]

While R. E. Wraith found evidence that councillors in the Eastern Nigeria did become somewhat
more responsible over time, he believed that the
costs of this education were too high.[36] Perhaps
the greatest casualty of the local councils experiment
was offical and public confidence in one of the key
institutions in the Eastern Nigeria political system.

At the center, Eastern Nigeria had a moderately
effective political system. However, when effectiveness is measured as the ability of the political
system to penetrate society and effect directed
change, Eastern Nigeria had a relatively ineffective
political system. Consequently its political system
could not mobilize population, resources, and personnel for undertaking rural transformation. This
chapter has attempted to delineate some of the factors
contributing to the limited capacity of the political
system to perform functions relating to rural development. The organizational structure of the political
system left the local councils as autonomous units
lacking strong links with regional bodies. Local
councils never became agencies for economic development because their jurisdictions were too small,
their resources were inadequate, their staffs were
poorly trained, their members often were corrupt,
and they conceived their mandate as the provision of
social services. Priorities enunciated by the
regional ministries often channeled scarce resources
into programs and projects that did not have significant economic benefits.

Since the political system encompasses all of
the institutions, organizations, groups, and social,
economic, and cultural factors affecting the political process, the analysis of the organization and
effectiveness of the Eastern Nigerian political system
has thus far omitted one common and significant type
of nongovernmental organization--the ethnic-improvement

unions.   As Chapter 3 indicated, many, and perhaps
most, of the communities in Eastern Nigeria established an ethnic-improvement union.   These ethnic-
improvement unions juxtaposed an ascriptive membership base, which could be defined ethnically or
geographically, with an organizational structure
copied from modern voluntary associations.   Many of
the ethnic-improvement unions collected dues from
members of the community, particularly those employed
in urban centers, and then financed community improvement projects.

The contribution of the ethnic-improvement unions
to development in Eastern Nigeria can be gauged from
the following data.   Some 80 percent of Eastern
Nigeria's primary schools were built and maintained
either entirely or partially by local contributions
In 1966 the government owned less than 1 percent of
the 6,000 primary schools and the local councils operated about 25 percent.   By 1964 most of the 224
secondary schools in the region came into being
through the efforts of local communities, although
they were then usually managed and staffed by missions
While the Eastern government assisted three fourths
of the voluntary agency primary schools and two thirds
of the secondary schools, the impetus for the expansion of education clearly derived from the efforts of
local communities and their ethnic-improvement unions,
and not the government.[37]   Furthermore eight communities constructed their own hospitals.   Local communities also substantially contributed to the construction and operation of at least two thirds of the 500
registered maternities and a slightly lower portion of
the 342 dispensaries and health centers.   According
to the figures supplied by the government in 1962,
local communities built 42 bailey bridges and 11,000
miles of road and contributed toward the construction
of 3,000 waterpoints.[38]

Hence the initiative of communities compensated
to some extent for the inability of the Eastern
Nigeria political system to penetrate down to the
local level and for the lack of effectiveness of
the county councils as autonomous units of government.
This contribution of local communities resulted in

most cases from the existence of an ethnic-improvement
union that was able to channel traditions of self-
help and communal cooperation into constructive
projects. Because the leaders of ethnic unions
were usually some of the most educated members of a
particular community with added experience derived
from living in urban areas, ethnic unions operated
as instruments of modernization and change. However,
the urban character of the leadership of most ethnic
unions generally disinclined them from undertaking
activities related to agriculture. The conception
of moderization or improvement held by the officers
of ethnic unions consisted of bringing urban amenities
and educational facilities to their home village
and not of increasing agricultural production. For
the officers of these unions, agriculture was something for the less-educated and more-traditional
members of the community to concern themselves with.
A very few exceptional ethnic unions did sponsor
projects that directly pertained to economic development. The Itam Clan Union in Itu Division formed a
limited liability company to promote the economic
development of the clan by selling shares to urban
emigrants to start rubber and oil plantations. The
Abiriba Communal Improvement Union in Bende Division,
which was run by professional people and traders
living in urban centers, operated a rubber plantation
as a way to obtain revenue for their other projects.
Most ethnic unions, though, concentrated on the same
kind of projects as the county councils.

THE POLITICAL CULTURE

    Political culture refers to the norms, orien-
tations, and values that influence the operation
and development of the political system, in other
words, the psychological and cultural dimension of
the political order. As it is usually defined, the
political culture also incorporates the symbolic
aspects of the political system.[39] Most developing
political systems have a fragmented political culture
in that different traditional norms, values, and
orientations held by the diverse ethnic, religious,
racial, and linguistic components of the society

have not been replaced by new homogeneous civic
standards. In Eastern Nigeria most of the ethnic
groups shared fairly comparable precolonial political
experiences, and probably for that reason also had
somewhat similar political styles. This section
will attempt to analyze how certain aspects of the
ethos or political culture in Eastern Nigeria
influenced rural development there.

Some attitudes, values, beliefs, and norms
foster the development of the political system more
than others. According to Gabriel Almond and G.
Bingham Powell, Jr., the syndrome of traits intrinsic
to a participant orientation embodies the political
culture most conducive to development. One component
of this type of political culture is an awareness
of the political system as a distinct and specialized
entity, along with this perception of politics as
a distinct sphere, the evolution of a favorable
attitude toward the political system. Then as the
government assumes a wider role, citizens will favor
the performance of new functions. Without such a
positive attitude toward the political system,
Almond and Powell reason that citizens are likely to
reject the conception of the government as the
initiator of change. Another significant component
of the participant orientation is the emergence of
a pragmatic "market place" attitude toward politics.
The participant views the political arena as a place
in which he may gain fairly limited objectives
through compromise and bargaining in much the same
manner as he exchanges economic commodities. This
orientation then promotes an instrumental view of
politics, rather than an ideological one, through
which the individual views ultimate values as being
bound up with political action. The norms of
achievement and of universality underlie this "market
place" attitude toward politics; people judge actors
and actions by their inherent worth and not by their
relation to other factors. In addition, the participant forms attitudes toward the political input
structures consonant with his image of himself as
an actor in the political process. Not only must
the participant know of the existence of parties
and interest groups, he must also be aware of the
role he can play in them.[40]

On the basis of ten case studies, Lucian Pye cites other attitudes as conducive to political development. One such attitude is the general level of trust in the society that determines the willingness of individuals to cooperate for common objectives. The acceptance of the norms of equality emancipates all elements of the population in a universal endeavor to develop the nation. According to Pye, liberty--a central value in the democratic political culture-- often promotes development more than does coercion. Political systems that encourage the evolution of a generalized identification with the nation without undermining parochial units attain the benefits of both integration and pluralism.[41]

Ironically, although the ethos or political culture of Eastern Nigeria embodied many of the attitudes, orientations, and norms identified by political scientists as beneficial for political development, the operating style of Eastern politics often hindered development efforts. Many of the components of the modern or secular or development- promoting political culture, as it is variously termed, characterized the precolonial political systems of the groups incorporated in Eastern Nigeria. Virtually all the traditional sociopolitical systems in the region lacked a rigid hereditary class structure with ascriptively defined leadership positions. Instead, the institutional structure of these societies reflected the egalitarianism embedded in the culture. The central value attached to liberty, or freedom from external constraints, in precolonial Eastern society caused them to forego the benefits of central authority or larger political units in order to retain maximum control over their own affairs in the ordered anarchy of the segmentary systems. Within the bound- aries of the traditional political entities, members assumed communal responsibilities and frequently cooperated for common objectives. While precolonial Easterners probably did not perceive politics as a distinct sphere, since there were not clearly differentiated political institutions, they manifested a great interest in political affairs. Their partic- ipant orientation toward politics and their confidence in their own political competence inhibited them from

delegating authority to any permanent leader. To the
extent that data is available, traditional societies
in Eastern Nigeria incorporated a pragmatic, "market
place" attitude not only in regard to politics, but
also to many other spheres of life.

Many of these precolonial dispositions were
successfully transferred to the conditions of political
life inhering in the larger, more complex colonial
and post-colonial political systems. The wide economic and social chasm separating an illiterate
subsistence farmer from a university trained professional or civil servant was mediated by common ethnic
ties and the continued acceptance of communal obligations. Many of the first generation educated elite
earned their academic credentials through the financial
sponsorship of their local community and its ethnic
unions. Anyone witnessing the dynamics of life could
attest to the manner in which most Eastern Nigerians
fought the encroachment of any controls that would
limit their freedom. The leading positions that
many Easterners assumed in the anticolonial movement
also evinced the continuing attachment to liberty.
Although Easterners embraced more inclusive forms of
identity and more generalized referent groups, they
did not repudiate their primary communal obligations
as shown by the records on the completion of improvement projects by local communities. When, with the
adoption of political reforms after World War II,
Easterners were incorporated into a larger, more
complex political system most communities responded
by accommodating their precolonial style of direct
participation into one more appropriate to the new
representative political institutions. Leadership
still derived from demonstrated skills, but in place
of the concilliator the new political leader secured
support on the basis of his ability to extract benefits
for his constituency from the political system. The
pragmatic, instrumental, exchange characteristics
of the "market place" orientation toward politics
infused and dominated the Eastern political system.

Civil servants, politicans, and citizens over-
whelmingly had an acquistive approach to politics.
One central concern--the benefits that would accrue

individually and/or communally--motivated political
participation and the competition for political
office. Since political participants eagerly sought
the distributive benefits of development allocations,
at all levels of the political system development
was associated almost exclusively with the expansion
of social services and amenities, which often lacked
productive consequences.

In terms of models of types of political systems,
Eastern Nigeria embodied many of the traits of David
Apter's reconciliation system. According to Apter,
the legitimacy of a reconciliation system derives
from the ability of the government to reflect and
actualize existing values and articulated demands.
In contrast to a reconciliation system, a mobilization
system attempts to harness the resources of the society
to restructuring the social and political order in
the image of new values which are expressed in an
ideology.[42] To achieve their respective objectives,
reconciliation systems adopt a loosely structured,
relatively decentralized, institutional structure
that accords much autonomy to its component members,
while the mobilization system incarnates its ethos
in a unitary, centralized, hierachical organization
pattern.[43]

Participants in the Eastern Nigerian political
process perceived the political system as a distributor
of amenities and not as a mobilizer on behalf of
development. To the extent that development entailed
the provision of new social services or the construction of more roads, wells, water pipes, and electrical
facilities in their constituency, people were enthusiastic supporters of development efforts. Few people,
however, embraced a concept of the political system
that defined its role as the initiator of major
economic and social innovations. The same communities
that voluntarily contributed money and labor for the
erection of some locally sponsored project would
have strongly opposed the government's raising taxes
in order to finance a larger agricultural extension
service, especially since benefits from this service
would have accrued to other communities as well.

In the competition for amenities those communiti
with an important politician to represent them or a
high-ranking civil servant to look out for their
interests received much of the available resources.
Cabinet ministers and permanent secretaries particularly had the political capital to exchange for the
distributive commodities available through the political market place. Their success in gaining these
resources for their home communities partially derive
from the direct application of pressure within their
ministries or political barter exchanges between
ministries. In other cases the political notable
was able to inform and prepare his own community to
take part in new programs. When the government, for
example, initiated a water-pipe installation program
that required a substantial deposit from participatin
communities, political notables travelled home to
announce the new opportunity and to stimulate the
collection of funds. After several high-ranking civi
servants became enthused over the community plantatio
scheme, they convinced their home villages that they
should participate in the pilot program. Consequentl
the benefits that accrued to communities supported
by political notables resulted from the greater acces
to information as well as to influence.

What were the consequences of this kind of polit
ical orientation for rural development? Political
considerations often outweighed other factors in
situating projects, making them poor investments.
To enumerate just a few of the politically inspired
mishaps: The malaria control center was put in the
homes villages of the Permanent Secretary of the
Ministry of Health, even though it was in an isolated
place with poor communications and road links, thus
making it almost inoperable. The list of towns in
the Eastern Nigeria Development Plan to be surveyed
for the installation of electricity, while supposedly
based on their suitability for the development of
industry, included several communities whose only
real economic asset was their political representativ
One of the farm settlements eventually had to be
abandoned because its selection was based on politica
rather than economic criteria. Civil servants, feari
the wrath of important politicians, were sometimes

inclined to apportion resources among as many units
as possible rather than concentrating them on the
basis of need or economic potential. Moreover,
designers of new programs often succumbed to political
pressures and expanded too rapidly in order to reach
as many parts of the region as possible. Efforts by
the Ministry of Rural Development to establish community plantations in as many villages as possible
to some extent reflected this kind of political
pressure.

The market-place approach to distribution brought
with it political liabilities as well as economic
casualties. Some 45 percent of the respondents in
the attitude survey thought that the government was
run for the benefit of those in power in comparison
with the approximately 44 percent who answered that
the government was run for the people. The perception
that some communities, those having power through the
aegis of political notables, received a dispropor-
tionate share of the benefits might have provoked
some of the respondents to answer the question in
the manner they did. Certainly when one community--
Mbaise, a county in Owerri Province--raised the
requisite sum of money for the installation of water
pipes and the government first took care of a neighboring minister's village, which did not raise the
necessary money, this did not inspire the confidence
of those involved in the political system. When some
communities received special regional subsidies for
the construction of schools and hospitals and were
the beneficiaries of new tarmac roads while other
communities did not gain anything, the latter could
not be expected to applaud the government for its
fairness and impartiality.

This kind of political orientation typifies
many other political systems, some less and some
more developed than Eastern Nigeria. Frequently the
absence of any strong party discipline in a national
or regional legislature induces legislators to be
motivated primarily by a selfish competitive localism.
In those states characterized by what Myron Weiner
has termed a "politics of scarcity" the knowledge
that there are limited resources to share often

engenders even more intense competition than in a
more affluent system.[44] What made the Eastern
Nigerian situation prior to the military coup in 1966
so unfortunate, therefore, was not its uniqueness
but the inability of the political system to maximize
the exceptional human potential available. The same
cultural dispositions that fueled the innumerable
community improvement projects and that occasioned
the willingness to innovate could have been better
harnassed by a different type of political system
for purposes of economic development. After 1964
serious efforts were made to focus the government
apparatus on the problems of rural economic development, through assistance being given the small farmer
under the Oil Palm Rehabilitation Scheme and by the
establishment of community plantations. The three
years between 1964 and the outbreak of the civil war
in 1967, however, did not offer sufficient time to
test fully either the success of these programs or
the ability of the political system to adapt itself
to the new requirements.

NOTE ON RECENT DEVELOPMENTS

     The division into three states and the reorgan-
ization of the political structure constitute the
most visible modifications of the political landscape.
The Federal Military Government has postponed the
resumption of civilian rule until 1976; in the interi
the states are assuming the functions performed by
the old regions. One dramatic departure from the
past, which gradually is being effected, is the
movement away from revenue allocation on the principl
of derivation.

     During the war, the existing ministerial organ-
ization was abrogated in the former Eastern Region,
government services were suspended, and large section
of the population were displaced from their home
areas. Consequently in 1970 the three states faced
the task of reestablishing civilian political authori
ity in something of a vacuum with regard to modern
governmental institutions. Ukpabi Asika even con-
sciously revived the colonial nomenclature of distric

officers and residents in order to call attention to
the similarity in the types of situations that con-
fronted the first colonial administrators and his
field officers.[45] Both the East Central and South-
East States have also addressed themselves to the
historical failures of local administration in Eastern
Nigeria. In such a situation the reduced effectiveness
of the government was to be expected. It was surprising to discover the degree to which the political
systems had been reconstructed by March 1971, and
the continuity with regard to structure and policy.

In the East Central State the Ministry of Rural
Development has been dismantled, with the Community
Development Division absorbed into the Ministry of
Agriculture and the Cooperative Division reassigned
to the Ministry of Trade and Industry. The Community
Development Division of the Ministry of Agriculture
has 27 Community Development Officers, 22 of whom are
posted in the districts. Following the anticipated
recruitment of 7 additional Community Development
Officers, 29 of the 34 districts in East Central State
will have Community Development Officers assigned to
district headquarters who will be responsible for
assessing new project possibilities and supervising
existing projects. In both of these roles, the Community Development Officer is expected to cooperate
very closely with extension personnel of the Ministry
of Agriculture, with extension personnel from the
Cooperative Division of the Ministry of Trade and
Industry, and with the District Officer and his staff.
The Community Development Division also has 60 Community Development Organizers attached to particular
projects, who are living in project villages. These
Organizers receive supervision from Community Development Officers and are subordinate to them.

Since the abolition of a separate Ministry of
Rural Development does not derive from a reduced
commitment to the kinds of projects that ministry
initiated, it may facilitate policy and operational
coordination. The relocation of the Community
Development Division within the Ministry of Agriculture may reduce the friction and jealousy that sometimes were engendered under the former organizational

pattern. However, if the priorities of future admin-
istrations should change, the absence of a voice in
the cabinet specifically speaking out in favor of
rural development may be an unfortunate aspect of
the present arrangement.

The East Central State has not reestablished
the Ministry of Local Government, but there is a
Divisional Administration Division in the cabinet
office. In place of the suspended county and local
councils, the government is organizing 613 community
councils based on groups of villages within a few
miles radius. The limited geographic jurisdiction
of these community councils reflects Asika's belief
that participation can be meaningful only within
traditional units.[46] Community councils will include
anyone who can make a positive contribution to reconstruction and development. The government expects
these councils to finance local projects, primarily
of an income-generating nature, through contributions
and through organizing voluntary labor.

By establishing community councils to stimulate
and supervise community development projects, the
East Central State Government hopes to replicate
the achievements of the ethnic-improvement unions.
Perhaps under the present circumstances it is not
feasible to institute councils or development committees with a wider jurisdiction. In light, however, of the concern of the incumbent administration
with the historical failure of local administration
in Eastern Nigeria, the affirmation of the traditional
groups of villages as the only suitable units for
participation seems anomalous. As it has been pointed
out in this chapter, the recurrent tendency to frag-
ment local government councils into progressively
smaller units until they have represented individual
traditional communities has been the bane of efforts
to make local administration more effective.

The South-East State has also abrogated old
style local government councils and replaced them
with what it terms "development administration."
The South-East State Government in 1970 created 11
divisional development councils and 140 area

development committees embracing 20 to 40 villages
each to replace the former system of local administration. Very much like the county and provincial
development committees that were proposed for Eastern
Nigeria but never fully implemented before the war,
the development councils and committees will formulate
priorities and will undertake planning with the area
development committees initiating proposals and the
divisional development councils coordinating programs.
To try to assure some control and relative effectiveness, the Military Governor will appoint the chairmen,
who will in most cases be civil servants, and the
divisional agencies of the South-East State Government
will implement the programs.[47] At least as a blueprint, the reconstituted development administration
seems to be a major improvement over what existed in
Nigeria. The absence of professional staff attached
to the committees and councils may hinder planning
efforts though.

The reduced effectiveness of the three state
governments derives from the impoverishment of the
area as well as from the erosion of political authority. Both the reduced tax base and the diminished
capacity of the states to collect taxes severely
circumscribe the operation of the governments. Out
of their meager funds, the governments must also
undertake costly reconstruction projects to restore
the infrastructure. The ability of the Federal
Nigerian Government to subsidize reconstruction is
limited by the need to service the accumulated backlog of short-term overseas liabilities of perhaps
as much as £N2 million[48] As with most ministries
in the East Central State, the Ministry of Agriculture
has very little money for capital expenditure once
it meets the monthly bill for staff salaries. Both
the East Central and South-East States have applied
for foreign assistance to revive rural development
efforts.

There is a potential leadership gap in some of
the ministries in all three states. In many ministries in the East Central State the prewar top
leadership has either reached retirement age or has
been removed. The South-East and Rivers States tend

to have less experienced administrators since relatively fewer top civil servants came from these areas
of Eastern Nigeria. The rural development program
in at least the East Central State should not be very
adversely affected by the departure of the former
leadership since the qualifications of the newly
recruited senior administrators are excellent and
the Ministry of Agriculture is well staffed with
capable people.

After several years of travail, the attitudes
and orientations of the people have undoubtedly been
affected. But while many people in the area are
disheartened, they have not been traumatized. On
the positive side, impoverishment may induce a productionist orientation in place of the consumptionist
one that prevailed prior to the war, and people may
now be more inclined to accept economic and political
innovations.

NOTES

1.   T. Ogura, ed., Agricultural Development in
Modern Japan (Tokoyo: Fugi Publishing Company, 1963).

2.   See Hui-Sun Tang, Land Reform in Free China
(Taipei: Joint Commission on Rural Reconstruction,
1967); S. C. Hien and T. H. Lee, An Analysis and
Review of Agricultural Development in Taiwan: An
Output and Productivity Approach (Taipei: Chinese-
American Joint Committee on Rural Reconstruction,
1958).

3.   John M. Brewster, "Traditional Social Structures as Barriers to Change," in Herman M. Southworth
and Bruce F. Johnston, eds., Agricultural Development
and Economic Growth (Ithaca, N.Y.: Cornell University
Press, 1967), p. 72.

4.   George Rosen, Democracy and Economic Change
in India (Berkeley and Los Angeles: University of
California Press, 1966).

5.   Douglas E. Ashford, "The Politics of Rural

Mobilisation in North Africa," The Journal of Modern African Studies, VII (July 1969), 187-202.

6. See Gabriel A. Almond and G. Bingham Powell, Jr., Comparative Politics: A Developmental Approach (Boston: Little, Brown and Company, 1966); Samuel P. Huntington, Political Order in Changing Societies (New Haven, Conn.: Yale University Press, 1968).

7. For the purposes of this chapter the regional level of the Eastern Nigerian political system will be considered as the central level. The rationale for this is offered in Chapter 2.

8. For a discussion of this problem in Tanzania see Anthony Rweyamu, "Managing Planned Development: The Tanzanian Experience," The Journal of Modern African Studies, IV (May 1966), 1-16.

9. "Policy for Community Development," Official Document No. 27, (Enugu: Ministry of Internal Affairs, 1963).

10. Chief J. O. Udoji, "Objectives and Concepts of the Rural Development Programme," address given to Provincial Secretaries Conference on Rural Development, 1965, (mimeographed) p. 2.

11. For a discussion of why the government decided upon this organizational expedient see R. W. Coatswith, "Establishing a Rural Development Programme in Eastern Nigeria," Administration, III (October 1968), 9-12.

12. Gerald D. Hursh, Niels G. Roling, and Graham B. Kerr, "Innovation in Eastern Nigeria: Success and Failure of Agricultural Programs in 71 Villages of Eastern Nigeria," (East Lansing: Department of Communication, Michigan State University, 1968, mimeographed), p. 202.

13. See N. A. Ndu, Community Development Secretary's statement on "Local Government and Community Development" in "Report of the Seminar on Rural Development for Administrative Officers in Eastern

Nigeria," (Enugu: Community Development Division of
the Ministry of Internal Affairs, 1965, mimeographed),
pp. 57-59.

14.   "Background Brief for District Officers on
the Rural Development Program" (Enugu: Ministry of
Internal Affairs, 1965, mimeographed).

15.   See Almond and Powell, op. cit.

16.   For an excellent study of educational expan-
sion in Eastern Nigeria see David B. A. Abernethy,
The Political Dilemmas of Popular Education: An
African Case (Stanford, Calif.:   Stanford University
Press, 1969).

17.   Eastern Nigeria Development Plan, 1962-68,
Official Document No. 8 of 1962 (Enugu: Government
Printer, 1962), pp. 9-10.

18.   Ibid., p. 12.   This does not include expenditure by local councils on social welfare.

19.   Coatswith, op. cit., p. 15.

20.   Hursh, Roling, and Kerr, op. cit., p. 215.

21.   Eastern Nigeria Development Plan, 1962-68,
p. 19.

22.   Hursh, Roling, and Kerr arrived at this
figure by applying the ratio of agricultural population
to total population as given by the 1953 census to
the total population figures given in the 1963 census
data.   See pp. 21 and 204.

23.   Using the same figures as Hursh, Roling,
and Kerr on the total number of male farmers, it was
then divided by the number of agricultural extension
workers actually engaged in field work most of the
time.

24.   R. E. Wraith, "Local Government," in John
P. Mackintosh, Nigerian Government and Politics
(London: George Allen and Unwin, Ltd., 1966),
pp. 219-221.

25. J. Donald Kingsley, "Bureaucracy and Political Development, With Particular Reference to Nigeria," in Joseph LaPalombara, ed., Bureaucracy and Political Development (Princeton, N.J.: Princeton University Press, 1963), p. 311.

26. I. Nicolson, "The Machinery of the Federal and Regional Government," in Mackintosh, p. 194.

27. Ibid.

28. Ibid., p. 183.

29. See B. B. Schaffer, "The Deadlock in Development Administration," in Colin Leys, ed., Politics and Change in Developing Countries (London: Cambridge University Press, 1969), pp. 177-211.

30. See for example Chinua Achebe's novel based on Nigerian politics, A Man of the People (London: William Heinemann, 1966) and Simon Ottenberg, "Local Government and the Law in Southern Nigeria," Journal of Asian and African Studies, II (January and April 1967), 26-43.

31 This definition is from M. G. Smith, "Historical and Cultural Conditions of Political Corruption among the Hausa," Comparative Studies in Society and History, VI (January 1964), 164.

32. Ottenberg, op. cit., p. 29.

33. "Local Government in West Africa: A Look at the Future," West Africa, March 6-12, 1971, p. 26.

34. Ibid.

35. Ukpabi Asika, "The Structure of the Ibo Community," The Renaissance, March 14, 1971, pp. 3, 12.

36. Wraith, op. cit., p. 260.

37. The figures on the schools are from Hursh, Roling, and Kerr, op. cit., pp. 219-220.

38.   "Community Development in Eastern Nigeria."

39.   See Lucian W. Pye and Sidney Verba, eds.,
Political Culture and Political Development (Princeton,
N.J.: Princeton University Press, 1965), particularly
Pye's "Introduction: Political Culture and Political
Development," pp. 3-26 and Verba's "Conclusion:
Comparative Political Culture," pp. 512-560.

40.   Almond and Powell, op. cit., pp. 57-63.

41.   Pye and Verba, op. cit., pp. 22-24.

42.   One can, of course, question whether a
developing mobilization system could in fact accomplish
its goals.

43.   David E. Apter, The Politics of Modernization
(Chicago: University of Chicago Press, 1965).

44.   For a study of this problem in India see
Myron Weiner, The Politics of Scarcity (Chicago:
University of Chicago Press, 1962).

45.   Asika, op. cit., p. 12.

46.   Ibid., pp. 12 and 16.

47.   "Local Government in West Africa: Nigeria's
Southern States," West Africa, February 20-26, 1971,
pp. 213-214.

48.   "Oiling Nigeria's Works," West Africa, May
1-7, 1971, p. 497.

6

LAND TENURE
AS IT RELATES
TO
AGRICULTURAL
DEVELOPMENT

Throughout the developing world, patterns of land ownership, utilization, and control are critical factors in the development process, having a particular importance for agricultural development. In Asia and Latin America the most significant features of land use and land control relate to the needs for land redistribution, problems of exploitative tenancy arrangements, and the lack of interest in development on the part of many absentee landlords. With some notable exceptions in such countries as Ethiopia[1] and Madagascar,[2] Africa's land tenure problems do not result from a concentration of land ownership or the exploitation of tenants. Africa's land issues more frequently relate to communal versus individual control of land, fragmentation of holdings, lack of land registration, and the absence of a land market.[3] The character and intensity of Africa's land tenure problems vary considerably from country to country and from locality to locality, but almost universally land tenure is a subject worthy of serious attention.

For the most part, African governments have not developed clear-cut policies relating to land use and ownership. However, the lack of activity in this sphere relates more to the emotional fervor that attaches to land issues in Africa than to a lack of concern. Governmental policies in this sphere, or lack of policies, naturally have important

implications for the character of agricultural development in a particular country or locality. Aaron
Segal has pointed out the importance of policies
relating to land use and ownership in Tanzania for
its village settlement program and for foreign-owned
plantation agriculture. Also, according to Segal,
the development in Kenya of a policy of individualized
tenure and land consolidation both reflects and rein-
forces Kenya's effort to encourage single-family
farms.[4]

   It would be misleading to suggest, however, that
land tenure practices will remain rigidly traditional
in those countries that currently assume a laissez-
faire attitude toward land issues. Despite the
propensity of some analysts to imply that land tenure
systems tend to remain static in traditional societies
considerable evidence exists that land tenure practice
do change, and they are particularly prone to change
when agricultural development and increased farm
incomes necessitate change. Polly Hill, for instance,
has persuasively demonstrated the degree to which a
land market has developed in the cocoa-growing areas
of Ghana. She has also shown how Ghanaian cocoa
farmers, most of whom belong to matrilineal societies,
have developed means of assuring that the land they
develop will be inherited not only by their brothers'
and their sisters' sons in accordance with matrilineal
inheritance patterns, but by their own sons as well.[5]
Moreover, land markets are developing slowly in
Western and Northern Nigeria in response to developmental needs.[6]

   Despite the absence in the past of well-formulate
policies relating to land on the part of the Eastern
Nigeria government, evolutionary but nonetheless
significant changes in the land tenure system are
occurring in Eastern Nigeria, as this chapter will
indicate. Before discussing these evolutionary
changes, however, an attempt will be made to assess
the significance of Eastern Nigeria's various traditional land tenure systems for agricultural development. Although the land tenure systems prevailing
in the non-Ibo portions of Eastern Nigeria are not
well documented, aspects of Ibo land tenure practices

are described in several studies.[7] The concern in
this chapter is not to review this literature, but
to confine the discussion to the conclusions drawn
from the authors' research regarding land tenure
as it relates to agricultural development.

SIGNIFICANCE OF TRADITIONAL
LAND TENURE SYSTEMS

Unlike many parts of Africa, in Eastern Nigeria
the largest land-owning unit is the village or the
village-group. Land owned on a communal basis by a
village or a village-group is generally made available
to individual villagers for farming on a year-to-year
basis. In addition to communally controlled land,
land is also controlled on an individual and a family
basis. By individual control is meant the right of
an individual to use the land as he wishes from
year-to-year and to have this land passed on to his
children upon his death. The major portion of
Eastern Nigeria's farm land is controlled in this
fashion. However, within a given community, some
land might be controlled by the village, other land
by family units, and the remaining land by individuals.
Family land might nominally be controlled by the
eldest male in the family, but in fact all the men
in a family usually play a role in decisions relating
to family land.

Within the Eastern Nigerian context, to say
that individuals or families or villages control
pieces of land does not mean that their control is
absolute; they generally do not have the right to
sell the land they control. According to Elias,
"There is perhaps no other principle more fundamental
to the indigenous land tenure system throughout
Nigeria than the theory of inalienability of land."[8]
Two methods exist, however, for temporarily transfer-
ring the usufruct rights to a piece of land: Land
may be leased and land may be pledged. Land that
is leased is given over to someone's use on the basis
of a fixed rent for a fixed period of time. Almost
invariably, land is leased for very limited periods,
in most cases for one or two years. Land rents vary

from locality to locality; as already indicated the
range is from two shillings to £N5 per acre.

Pledging usually occurs when the owner of a
piece of land needs a sum of money for some purpose.
He gives over the use of a piece of his land to
someone in return for an agreed amount. The term of
this loan is not fixed and no yearly rent is paid;
the agreement is that as soon as the land owner has
sufficient funds to pay back the loan, he can do so
and redeem his land. The one using the land has to
accept the funds and return the land to its owner
as soon as the annual crops he has planted there
are harvested. In some cases the amount of money
involved in a pledge is sufficiently high that it
may be tacitly assumed that the pledge will never
be redeemed, but in principle the possibility of
redeeming such a pledge always remains. An individual
who controls a piece of land through a pledge has
the right to repledge the land to another individual,
but when the owner repays the amount of the original
pledge, the land must be returned to him.

Trees and the land upon which the trees are
growing are considered to be separable, and land
may be leased while the owner retains control over
the trees. In pledging, either the land or the trees
can be pledged separately from each other. Because
of this differentiation, complex patterns of land
and tree cultivation frequently develop and can be
quite confusing to a Western observer. The general
outlines of land inheritance patterns vary considerably from one locality to another. In most areas
only men control land, and a man's land is passed
upon his death to his sons. In these patrilineal
areas each of a man's sons usually receives a
share of his father's land. In the matrilineal
areas a man's land is inherited by his brothers,
by his sisters, by his sister's children, or by
some combination of these. In the double descent
areas, such as Ohafia in Bende Division, some land
is inherited according to the rules of the patrilineage and other land according to the rules of
the matrilineage.

Because of the generally accepted rule that
land is inalienable and because of the practice that
all the sons of a man receive shares of his inheritance, the vast majority of village dwellers in
Eastern Nigeria own at least some land; in the
traditional setting no landless class exists. However, because of (1) the subdivisions that occur
from generation to generation and (2) the increasing
population density in Eastern Nigeria, some farmers
only own very small pieces of land. (Examples of
farm sizes in selected parts of the region have
been cited in Chapter 4.)

As can be seen from what has already been said,
the principal means of acquiring land is through
inheritance. Individuals can also be accorded the
right to use portions of family or village-owned
plots, or they can acquire the use of additional
land through leasing or pledging arrangements.
Although the sale of land is usually prohibited,
instances occur in which it is possible for individuals
to buy parcels of land. Although this possibility
usually applies only to small parcels in residential
portions of the village that can be used as building
plots, in some cases farm plots have been purchased
under special conditions. In those areas where
virgin land remains, an individual can also acquire
new land by clearing a portion of this virgin land.
In its virgin state, land is considered village
property, but the village usually allows individuals
to assume control of pieces of this land if they
are prepared to fell the trees and clear the underbrush.

From this brief outline of land tenure practices
in Eastern Nigeria, the implications of land tenure
for agricultural development become evident. One
of the most obstructive barriers the current system
poses to agricultural development is the difficulty
an ambitious farmer faces if he wishes to acquire
additional land. The amount of land a man can
inherit is restricted by the amount his father owned
and the number of children his father had. Although
in some areas new parcels can be acquired by a

farmer's clearing virgin forest, Eastern Nigeria's
virgin land is quickly disappearing and this option
is only open to farmers in a limited number of communities. In no case would a community that has
virgin land allow someone from another community to
assume control of it, except on the basis of a leasing
or pledging arrangement.

   The principal reason that land cannot be purchase
is that the selling of farm land is considered unfair to a man's children and the generations that
will follow him. T. O. Elias quotes a chief in
Western Nigeria as saying, "I conceive that land
belongs to a vast family of which many are dead,
few are living, and countless members are yet
unborn."[9] Comparable explanations were heard from
many of those interviewed in Eastern Nigeria. A
man is reluctant to sell his land because of the
sense of responsibility he feels regarding the well-
being of his descendants. Even if an individual
were willing to sell his land, it is unlikely that
his family would allow him to do so. In one village
people said they would kill any member of their
family who tried to sell farm land. In another
village where a piece of farm land had recently been
sold, the members of the man's family explained that
they only agreed to his selling the land because he
had no children and thus would not be depriving his
descendants of land on which to farm. His relatives
also emphasized that they were only willing to allow
the man to sell his land to someone from their own
village.

   Despite the difficulties for agricultural develo
ment created by the absence of a land market, government encouragement of such a market would not necessa
ily be a wise policy. As the informants indicated,
traditional prohibitions against the sale of land
protect the interests of future farming generations
insofar as it assures them of land ownership. The
absence in Eastern Nigeria, as well as in many other
parts of Africa, of landlessness, absentee landlordis
exploitative tenancy arrangements, and sharp class
divisions in the rural areas results primarily from
traditional attitudes regarding land ownership.

To encourage a land market, unless this market is
carefully controlled and supervised, is to incur
many social and economic risks that Eastern Nigeria
has thus far been able to avoid.

The acquisition of additional farm land on the
basis of a pledging agreement can prove unattractive
to the ambitious farmer for one or both of two reasons.
First, pledging does not offer sufficient security
of tenure, since the owner can redeem the land at
any time. As a consequence a farmer who acquires land
on the basis of a pledge is not likely to want to
make significant investments to improve the land,
because he does not know how long the land will be
under his control. It only makes sense for a farmer
to build access roads to a piece of land, build storage
facilities, set up an irrigation system, or start a
soil improvement program if he knows that he can use
the land for a sufficiently long period to profit
from these investments. He has no assurance of this
for land acquired under pledge. The second barrier
to developing pledged land is that the land owners
do not permit pledgees to plant trees on the land,
thus eliminating investment in oil palms or other
high-potential tree crops. This prohibition arises
from the fact that the planting of trees on a piece
of land usually implies ownership of that land.
Moreover, from the point of view of the pledgee,
investment in tree crops is not sound because the
landowner may redeem his land before the trees have
become profitable, and the landowner is generally
under no obligation to compensate the pledgee for
trees that he might have planted or other improvements
he might have made.

Traditional leasing arrangements do not offer
the farmer satisfactory means of increasing his
acreage either. As with pledging arrangements,
leases do not assure sufficient security of tenure
to justify making permanent improvements to the
land because in most cases the maximum length of
time encompassed by a lease is one or two years.
Moreover, land is usually leased on the understanding
that no trees will be planted, since the leasor
might try to claim ownership of the land if he is
allowed to plant trees on it.

Restrictions against the planting of trees also
usually apply to those who farm on village land,
and in most instances this holds for family land as
well. Usufruct rights to village or family land are
usually granted on a year-by-year basis, so that no
individual can achieve long-term control over the
parcel he is allocated. For a villager to plant
trees on communally controlled land is considered
unfair to the others in the village, since all villagers are supposed to benefit equally from village-
owned land. Occasionally families agree to a member
of the family planting trees on a portion of family
land, and thus the rules governing the use of family
land are in some cases more flexible than those
governing village land. In general, however, the
only land a farmer can plant with trees or make
substantial improvements upon is land he inherits.
A subsequent section of this chapter discusses the
basis upon which land has been made available in
many communities for the planting of tree crops
on community plantations. The novelty and significan
of these arrangements relate to their ability to
provide satisfactory safeguards and assurances such
that land owners have agreed to the planting of
trees on the land they let out on lease and village
elders have permitted communally owned land to be
planted with trees as well. The innovations involved
may appear simple, but their effect on agricultural
development in Eastern Nigeria is potentially dramati
possibly even to the point of being revolutionary.

Traditional attitudes regarding outsiders or
"strangers," although not precisely speaking a
feature of the land tenure system, constitute an
additional factor militating against the rational
and efficient utilization of Eastern Nigeria's
land resources. Because in the precolonial era
the communities of Eastern Nigeria were largely self-
sufficient and essentially isolated from each other,
outsiders generally aroused fear and distrust.
Although as social interaction has broadened over
the past 60 years and these fears have become less
intense, one still finds a reluctance on the part
of many villages to admit strangers into their midst
for extended periods.10 This poses a formidable

obstacle to attempts by the government to encourage
the relocation of villagers from high-population
density to low-density areas, where unused or underutilized land can be found.[11] Some communities
that have an excess of land and want to increase
their populations accept outsiders, but in most
villages there is considerable reluctance to allow
strangers to achieve control of land, whether through
gift, purchase, or pledge. Strangers are usually
only permitted to have access to land if they lease
it on a year-to-year basis. Increasing governmental
attention is likely to be given within the next
few years to means by which greater population balance
can be achieved, so that areas currently being over-
farmed can be cultivated less intensively and other
areas can be more productively exploited. A pilot
project at Ugwuaku in Okigwi Division aimed at
achieving this end is described in Chapter 9.

The fact that land owners generally do not hold
legal and registered titles to their land poses
another problem. The lack of title does not mean
that an individual's traditional rights to a piece
of land are not respected, but the absence of title
and land registration does mean that land disputes
occur frequently. At times large tracts of land
are rendered temporarily unusable because their
ownership is under dispute. The frequency of land
disputes is exemplified by the fact that in three
of the fifteen pilot community plantation projects,
ownership of project land was under dispute and in
one case the project had to be abandoned for this
reason. When land disputes are taken to court they
often require the expenditure of large sums of
money on court and lawyers' fees, and peasant farmers
can ill afford to spend what little money they have
in such unproductive fashion. The absence of land
registration and titles also means that farmers are
usually unable to use their land as collateral for
farm improvement loans. When a farmer cannot produce
a title to a piece of land, banks and other lending
agencies hesitate to accept a piece of land as
security for a loan.

Thus far this chapter has discussed the following

barriers to agricultural development posed by the
land tenure system: the difficulty involved in
acquiring new land, the inability of a farmer to
make permanent improvements or plant tree crops on
land which is communally owned or on land which he
holds by pledge or short-term lease, and the absence
of land registration. Probably the most important
and difficult of Eastern Nigeria's land problems--
fragmentation of holdings--will be discussed in the
following section.

FRAGMENTATION OF HOLDINGS

The term "fragmentation" when used in reference
to land has two meanings, and both meanings apply
to the land tenure situation in Eastern Nigeria.
Land can be fragmented in the sense that as land is
passed from father to sons, total holding becomes
increasingly smaller in size,* and the smallness of
land holdings in many parts of Eastern Nigeria does
inhibit agricultural development. Another meaning
of fragmentation is that a man's land holding is
composed of several small and scattered parcels.
It is this sort of fragmentation that will be focussed
upon, as well as a consideration of the possibility
of consolidating fragmented landholdings.

In those sections of Eastern Nigeria where
land is scarce, fragmentation constitutes a serious
problem. As indicated in Chapter 4, it is not
unusual to find farmers with farms totaling 3-5
areas in size but divided into 20 or 30 fragments.
A 100-acre piece of land surveyed in Bende Division
was found to be divided into 900 fragments owned by
400 different farmers. Mention has also been made
of the fact that a farmer's land parcels can be
scattered at considerable distances from each other.
As might be evident from this description of the
situation, land fragmentation poses several serious

_____

*The term "fractionalization" can also be
applied to this type of fragmentation.

barriers to agricultural development. In the first
place, when someone farms plots that lie at considerable distance from one another, he wastes time and
energy, which could be devoted to more productive
activity, walking from one plot to another. Fragmentation can also cause land to lie idle, as was discovered in a village in Udi Division where the farmers
use only part of their land because the remaining
parcels are too widely scattered. Fragmentation also
makes mechanization impractical, because of the
difficulties involved in moving machinery from one
plot to another and in maneuvering equipment within
such a small space. To lay out a road system in
such manner that each of a farmer's scattered plots
lies on a road is practically impossible; to do so
would necessitate covering a large proportion of a
farmer's land area with roads. Even if a road system
were laid out, the delivery of farm supplies, such
as seedlings and fertilizers, and the collection of
farm produce would be tedious and inefficient.
Moreover, the introduction of land conservation
measures and such other improvements as systems of
irrigation, drainage, and terracing is prohibitively
expensive when one has to deal with such small units.
Fragmentation of holdings is not a problem unique
to Eastern Nigeria or even to the developing world,
since such countries as France, Greece, and Japan
have grappled with this problem for generations.[12]
However, it seems to be generally agreed that where-
ever fragmentation has occurred, it has posed troublesome barriers to agricultural development that have
only been overcome by some kind of consolidation
of holdings. Studies in France, for example, indicate
30 percent decreases in farm costs and production
increases of up to 15 percent resulting from land
consolidation.[13]

Because fragmentation occurs over a period of
generations, farmers are generally unaware of how
they each contribute to the fragmentation process.
Each farmer's contribution is small, but the end
result is disastrous. Among the ways in which
fragmentation has occurred in Eastern Nigeria are
the following:

1. A man with one piece of land may feel that

this piece is too small to satisfy his needs, and
so he acquires additional land, either by clearing
a piece or virgin land, or through pledge or purchase
An ambitious farmer, particularly where land is
plentiful, might acquire several new pieces of land
during the course of his life, but these pieces are
generally not contiguous. This begins the process
of fragmentation.

2.   When a man distributes his land among his
sons, or when the sons divide up their father's
land, they usually attempt to see that each son
receives an equitable share of both good and bad
land, if the land varies in quality. This means
that if the father's several pieces of land vary in
fertility, he will probably give a fraction of each
piece of land to each son. This problem is compounde
by the fact that not merely gross differentiations
in soil types are made; distinctions are also made
between soils on the basis of which soils are good
for different crops. If a farmer has a piece of
land that is good for maize and another that is
good for yams, he would normally like each of his
sons to have a piece of each type of land.

3.   What P. C. Lloyd refers to as "the gradual
manner by which sons succeed a father" also contribu
to fragmentation.[14] When a boy becomes old enough
to start farming, his father assigns him a piece of
land that he can use. When other sons mature the
father allocates more pieces. As the father becomes
older and the sons become capable of handling larger
farms, the sons are then given additional pieces of
the father's land. However, the pieces of land they
are given gradually are usually not contiguous.

4.   In places like Afikpo and Ohafia, which
have systems of double descent and where land is
passed through both patrilineal and matrilineal line
a farmer gets land from two sources. This means
that at the very minimum he has his farm land in
two sections, and where normal fragmentation occurs,
these farmers experience it in double quantity. In
places where land is normally passed matrilineally,
a man may give a piece to his son so that on his dea

his land will not all go to his brothers and his
sister's sons, which serves as an additional source
of fragmentation.

In sections of Bende Devision, parents often
give parcels of farm land to their daughters at the
time they marry, which means that they farm partly
on their own land and partly on their husbands' land.
This sort of fragmentation proves particularly troublesome if the girl marries a man from another village,
for this means that she farms in two different villages.

EFFORTS TOWARD LAND CONSOLIDATION

Land consolidation in Africa has had its only
significant success in Kenya. Systematic efforts
toward land consolidation started in 1955 under the
colonial government, and by 1961 over 2 million
acres (or 3,000 square miles) of land had been consolidated.[15] The revised five-year development plan
for Kenya published in 1966 gave the backing of
the independent Kenya government to land consolidation
as a national policy.[16] Since the early land consolidation efforts were undertaken during the Emergency
in the 1950's, some observers maintain that the consolidation program owed its success to the ability
of officials to employ the emergency regulations.
According to Sorrenson, "Although there was no overwhelming tide of Kikuyu pressure forcing government
to rush ahead with consolidation, . . .there was
also no attempt by government to force it through
at the point of a bayonet, or even by widespread
use of Emergency regulation."[17] However, "if the
Kikuyu did not and could not resist consolidation
they did not heartily approve it. . . .Indeed it
was probably the Kikuyu enthusiasm to stake claims
to land that officials mistook for enthusiasm for
consolidation itself."[18] Since consolidation was
accompanied by land registration, participation in
the consolidation scheme assured legal title to one's
holdings, which would be an appealing component of
any land reform scheme in Africa. Despite the early
ambivalence of Kenyan villagers toward the program,

the Kenya government currently can not satisfy the
demand for consolidation and land registration,
despite the fact that fees are charged for surveying
and titling.[19] The chief benefits deriving from
Kenya's land consolidation program are greater
efficiency of farming operations, increased individualized tenure with a resultant reduction in community control over land, and a decrease in the
number of land disputes.

     Despite the prospect of similar benefits accruing
to agricultural development in Eastern Nigeria, land
consolidation faces formidable obstacles. One of
the principal obstacles to effective action in
this sphere is the hesitance on the part of the
government to grapple with the problem because of
the intense emotions aroused by any discussion of
issues relating to land. It is significant, however,
that Nigeria's Second National Development Plan
(1970-74) points out the necessity for land consolidation in Southern Nigeria.[20] Fear of the
government's taking land away from individual farmers
surrounds any government involvement in land reform.
Another obstacle derives from the fact that people
develop sentimental attachments to particular pieces
of land, especially when these pieces have belonged
to a family for generations. However, in Eastern
Nigeria the drive toward economic advancement is
sufficiently great that where a clear conflict exists
between sentimental attachment to land and economic
advantage, sentiment will likely prove the weaker
force; the difficulty lies in assuring farmers that
land consolidation is economically advantageous.

     Earlier in this chapter mention was made of
the fact that farmers try to assure that their sons
inherit a variety of soil types. The eagerness of
farmers to control a variety of soil types poses
another obstacle to consolidation. If, as a result
of consolidation, a farmer is given a single plot
of land, he may not be satisfied with the uniformity
of its soil. In localities with a variety of soil
types it may be necessary to give each farmer two
or three plots instead of one. Although a situation
in which each farmer has 2 or 3 plots is not ideal,

it is a substantial improvement over his having 20
to 30. In parts of France where efforts at consolidation have met with considerable success, the
average number of holdings is still 2.25.[21] Where
significant variations in soil fertility exist, the
same approach might have to be taken, in that each
farmer may have to be given a piece of land in the
more fertile portion and another piece in the less
fertile section. Alternatively, those receiving
land less fertile than what they are giving up might
be given larger portions. However, with the introduction of fertilizer, soil conservation, and other
improved techniques, land thought to be infertile
might be made quite productive. If improved techniques
of land management can be introduced in conjunction
with consolidation, differences in soils may not
prove to be an insuperable barrier.

The presence of permanent buildings scattered
over a community's land poses another obstacle to
land consolidation. Houses made of mud are sufficiently inexpensive that they could be destroyed
and rebuilt on a man's new landholding, but cement-
block houses represent a sizable investment and
those owning such houses could constitute a serious
source of opposition to any redistribution of land
holdings. Where settlement areas are compact, this
is not a problem, because the residential area can
be left intact; but where houses are scattered, it
would not be possible to assure each house owner
that the land upon which his house stands will still
be his following consolidation. On the other hand,
the very existence of this problem provides an
argument in favor of consolidation being undertaken
as soon as possible. The longer the delay, the more
permanent houses will be constructed, and the
problem will only increase in magnitude.

When the possibility of land consolidation was
discussed with Eastern Nigerian villagers, misgivings
also arose from the fact that land is thought to
belong not just to the current generation but also
to those members of the family who have died and those
yet to be born. Thus, they argue, the current generation has no right to make adjustments in landowning

patterns. However, a peasant family in Eastern
Nigeria is generally sufficiently concerned about
the welfare of the family's future generations that
if the economic advantages of consolidation can be
demonstrated, they will probably be prepared to
risk offending some of their ancestors.

Those living in villages that operate a community-wide land rotation system, such that everyone
in the community farms in one section one year and
in another the next (as described in Chapter 4),
expressed fears that consolidation would disrupt
their pattern, since no longer would a farmer have
plots of land within each of the community's rotation
blocks. However, since each farmer usually has
several small plots within each of these sections,
if consolidation were only to be undertaken within
each rotation block so that a farmer would then have
a single plot within each block, this would represent
an improvement over the current pattern of excessive
fragmentation. Alternatively, it might be possible
to convince these villagers that the advantages of
consolidation outweight the advantages of their land
rotation system and that they would be well advised
to accept the abandonment of this system as the
price for consolidation. If some of these communitie
were unwilling to agree to any type of consolidation,
mechanized farming might still be feasible through
the cooperative utilization of farm machinery.
Since everyone is planting the same crop at the same
time in a single section, a tractor operated on a
cooperative basis could work all the land in the
section, disregarding the boundaries of individual
plots within the section.

Despite the cultural, social, and attitudinal
obstacles a land consolidation program would face in
Eastern Nigeria, the authors are convinced that the
government should be more active in this field than
it has been in the past. Only limited progress can
be achieved, however, without the enactment of some
enabling legislation. Because of the patchwork
character of landholding, a land consolidation
project requires the participation and cooperation
of virtually all the villagers in a particular

community if it is to succeed. Without legislative
mechanisms that permit land to be consolidated if a
majority of the land owners in a village desire it,
unanimous consent within a community is a prerequisite
to consolidation: Since everyone's land will be
affected, everyone must agree to the new patterns of
land ownership. Even if unanimity is achieved in
the initial stages, if one person refuses to accept
the land allocated to him, the other villagers have
no way of forcing him to cooperate unless legislative
backing exists to force his cooperation. A variety
of provisions to assure cooperation have been included
in land consolidation legislation in different
countries. In some European countries if more than
half of the landowners in a particular locality agree
to the consolidation of their respective holdings,
the other landowners are required by law to have
their holdings consolidated as well. In India 75
percent of the landowners in a community must agree,
and in Kenya a "general demand" for consolidation
is required.

In arguing for enabling legislation it is not
meant to imply, however, that no progress is possible
before such legislation is enacted. In fact, it is
unlikely that enabling legislation will ever be
enacted unless pilot land consolidation projects
are undertaken on a voluntary basis to demonstrate
the feasibility and economic benefits of consolidation.
Because of the almost revolutionary implications of
consolidation for rural Eastern Nigeria and the
many delicate issues inherent in any project relating
to land ownership, it seems advisable for initial
pilot projects to attempt consolidating only one
portion of a community's land. In 1965 such an
approach was attempted in Abaja-Umukabia in Okigwi
Division. Various landowners in that community had
set aside a 500-acre piece of land that they wished
to develop as a community oil palm plantation. At
the suggestion of the senior author, the Divisional
Officer for Okigwi Division recommended to the
villagers that they permit the government to measure
the plots of land each man owned in the area, calculate
his total holdings there, and then give each man a
single, consolidated piece of land of equivalent

size to his portion of the community plantation.
Each landowner would have just as much land as
previously, but it would be in one piece, rather
than in scattered parcels. The hope was that people
of Abaja-Umukabia would discover the advantages of
consolidation once they had participated in this
initial experiment, and then in time agree to have
all their landholdings consolidated. The villagers
did agree to the initial pilot effort and seemed
receptive to the idea of consolidation in general.
Before much progress could be made, however, factionalism and local politics disrupted the project and
it had to be abandoned. It is unfortunate that this
pilot project did not progress further, because
such a project could demonstrate the advantages
of land consolidation and assist the government in
discovering how the problem might best be approached.

Another partial approach to land consolidation
worth encouraging on a pilot basis is the voluntary
exchange of land parcels. Although selecting equivalent parcels that can be exchanged would obviously
be difficult, a farmer in Mbawsi in Aba Division
built up a farm of 400 acres largely through exchanging
scattered pieces of land for other pieces that lay
adjacent to his original holding.[22] Moreover, some
of the informants indicated that the exchange of
residential plots for building purposes is not uncom-
mon. The Luo of Kenya have generally resisted land
consolidation of the kind undertaken in Kikuyu
country, but they have effected a degree of consolidation through the voluntary exchange of farming
plots.[23]

The most important precondition for a successful
program of land consolidation is that participation
by a farmer in the scheme must turn out to be economically advantageous to him. The popularity of
land consolidation among the Kikuyu seems to result
largely from the increased income to be earned on
consolidated holdings from such crops as tea, coffee,
and pyrethrum, as well as the increased security of
tenure, which results from land registration. Given
the current state of peasant agriculture in Eastern
Nigeria, a land consolidation program would probably

not prove very popular unless it were accompanied
by an innovative scheme like the Oil Palm Rehabilitation Scheme or the community plantations scheme.
Ideally, land consolidation should be introduced in
conjunction with new crops and new techniques that
will be economically beneficial but which will only
be beneficial in significant measure if the farmers'
plots are consolidated.

The importance of economic considerations becomes
apparent when one traces the progress of land consolidation in Europe. Movement toward consolidation
has been considerably more rapid since tractors and
other mechanized farm implements have been introduced,
because the economic benefits deriving from consolidation are most dramatic when farm work is mechanized.
In Eastern Nigeria consolidation should become more
appealing to farmers as land rotation (or the bush-
fallow system) is eliminated and permanent or semi-
permanent cropping becomes possible. Fragmentation
is not such a great burden when a farmer is only
utilizing one third to one fifth of his parcels
each year. However, as scientific understanding
of tropical soils advances and as fertilizers, new
crops, and an improved system of crop rotation are
introduced, a farmer ought to be able to farm every
plot every year, and when he does the inefficiency
caused by fragmentation will be multiplied several
fold.

Several means of encouraging villages to agree
to land consolidation are open to the government.
For instance, farmers in communities without sufficient
land to grow many cash crops could be offered a
"package" of new crops, better varieties of existing
crops, fertilizers, and new techniques that would
enable them to satisfy their food needs on a portion
of land smaller than that normally required. Land
would thereby be released for cultivation of cash
crops, which might be either tree crops or arables.
The government could make such assistance conditional
upon agreement by the farmers in the community to
permit their land to be consolidated. Such an approach would not merely be a gimmick or means of
coercion: The new crops and techniques can be much

more profitably utilized if a farmer's land is in a
single consolidated piece.

Economic benefits deriving from consolidation
can be enticing whether these benefits are inherent
in consolidation itself or are offered as inducements
by the government. Some European countries have
stimulated consolidation by offering tax concessions
to farmers who have agreed to cooperate with the
program. Impressive results might also be achieved
if the government were to offer to help construct a
road network or provide some other amenity if the
farmers in the community agree to consolidate their
farm lands.

Consistent with the importance of economic
pay-off in any land consolidation program, it is
possible that in some parts of Eastern Nigeria
total landholdings may be so small that even with
consolidation farmers may not end up with economic
farming units. Given the sorts of farming techniques
that will be employed in the forseeable future in
Eastern Nigeria, farms in such high-population densit
areas as Owerri Province will probably remain margina
whether holdings are consolidated or not. Sorrenson
argues that consolidation in Kikuyu country in Kenya
might have provided a basis for a genuine agricultura
revolution if the consolidated farming units were
not so small that most farming of necessity remained
at a subsistence level. His contention is that
consolidation should have been undertaken in conjunction with resettlement and population redistribution if its full potential were to be realized.[2]

INNOVATIVE LAND CONSOLIDATION
PROJECTS

Despite the lack of a government-sponsored
program in Eastern Nigeria to encourage land consolidation or other types of land reform, reforms of an
evolutionary character have been occuring as a by-
product of other agricultural programs, particularly
the Oil Palm Rehabilitation Scheme and the community
plantations program. For instance, in one village

that established a community plantation, the plantation
project resulted in the consolidation of 900 tiny
parcels of land into 100 farming units. Land consolidation per se was rarely mentioned in discussions
with the villagers involved, but since the consolidation
of land was just one aspect of an agricultural venture
that the villagers were convinced would benefit them,
they accepted consolidation along with the rest of
the project. To indicate the sorts of innovative
land arrangements that have been devised for community
plantations, examples are cited below from 4 of the
origional 15 pilot community plantation projects.
In some cases scattered parcels were consolidated,
in others communally controlled land was used for
tree crops, and in others long-term leases enabled
farmers to plant tree crops on family or individually
controlled land that had never before been used for
that purpose. Chapter 7 relates the details of how
these and other community plantations were organized;
the discussion below is confined to the arrangements
by which land was made available for plantation
development. Although some might view these examples
as merely isolated cases of innovative land arrangements, the popularity of the community plantation
program suggests that the sorts of land arrangements
devised in these pilot projects might provide the
basis for widespread land reform in Eastern Nigeria
of great significance to agricultural development.

Akwete, Aba Division

Until about 1960 most of the men of Akwete were
middlemen in the trade of plam oil and palm kernels.
As the volume of their trade declined, they needed a
new source of income. They owned ample farm land,
but since they had not been using it farmers from
nearby villages started farming it without permission.
In some cases these squatters subsequently claimed
the land to be their own. As a result, much of
Akwete's land was under dispute and therefore could
not be developed. However, one large piece of about
330 acres, whose ownership was under dispute, was
declared in a 1964 court judgement to be Akwete's
land. Prior to the dispute over ownership, most of

this land was owned by one family, but since the
whole town contributed to the costs of adjudicating
the land dispute, the land was proclaimed to be
communal and controlled by the whole village.
Subsequently, partly as a means of increasing their
incomes and partly as a means of assuring that their
ownership rights were not infringed again, the Akwete
people decided to develop this land as a community
oil palm plantation. Thus the community resolved
for the first time in its history that a piece of
communal land could be planted with tree crops.
There were two reasons for the Akwete people embarkin
on this major departure from village tradition. In
the first place, the Eastern Nigeria government was
prepared to send surveyors to survey the land and to
record its location and ownership by the village,
which meant that no subsequent dispute could arise
concerning community ownership, even if individual
farmers planted trees there. Secondly, since the
94 farmers chosen to participate in the plantation
project were broadly representative of the families
living in Akwete and constituted a majority of
Akwete's farmers, the community as a whole expected
to benefit from the development of this land as a
community plantation. The terms controlling use of
the land were set down in a long-term lease worked
out between the farmers and the village's governing
assembly. In order to constitute themselves into
a body legally competent to sign such a lease, the
farmers organized themselves into a corperative,
which was registered by the Cooperative Division
of the Ministry of Commerce.

The lease signed by the cooperative covered a
period of 99 years, with a grace period on the
payment of rent for 3 years, followed by per-acre
rates that were to be determined later, but would
be between 2 and 5 shillings per acre. The heads
of Akwete's 20 patrilineages signed the lease on
behalf of the community, and these lineage heads
will have the right to determine how much of the
rent money should be allocated to such community
projects as the school or the market, and how much
to the various lineages of Akwete.

Akoliufu Alayi, Bende Division

The 100 acres of land designated to be developed
as a community plantation had previously been divided
into individually controlled parcels of land and
farmed by over 400 farmers. The farmers who had been
farming here had other pieces of land elsewhere in
the community, but the total amount of land available
for arable crops was reduced as a result of the
establishment of the plantation project and thus the
fallow cycle on the remaining land had to be shortened
to maintain the level of food production. The farmers who gave up their land for the project were
willing to do so both because they knew they would
collect some rent from those participating in the
plantation scheme and because they believed that
the plantation would enrich the community. Moreover,
some of the landowners participated in the plantation
project as farmers, so they did not really lose any
farm land.

The lease governing use of the land covered a
period of 99 years and was the first long-term lease
ever signed in Akoliufu, as well as being the first
lease agreement that ever permitted the planting of
trees. As in Akwete, the people of Akoliufu were
willing to permit the planting of trees on this
land because the land had been surveyed by the
government and the individual owners had had their
land claims registered in the lease agreement, which
was witnessed by government representatives and was
filed in government offices in Enugu. Moreover,
participation in the scheme was sufficiently wide
that a broad cross section of Akoliufu would benefit
from the project. The lease was signed on one side
by the officers of the farmers' cooperative, and on
the other by the heads of Akoliufu's 16 lineages,
along with the government-appointed chief of the
area and members of the Akoliufu Local Council. It
is apparent, by comparing those who signed the
respective leases in Akwete and Akoliufu, that each
village determined for itself who the rightful sig-
natories were. Even though the land used for the

plantation in Akoliufu was individually controlled
by 400 farmers, the lineage heads signed on behalf
of the individual landowners, each of whom belonged
to one of Akoliufu's 16 lineages. Since originally
there were 900 small parcels of land on the 100 acres
and since there were 100 participants in the plantati
project each of whom would receive a 1-acre piece of
land upon which to plant oil palms, this project had
the effect of consolidating land in the ratio of
approximately 9 to 1. However, it was not a conven-
tional approach to land consolidation, in that consolidation was effected on the basis of a long-term
lease rather than on the basis of transferred ownership. Moreover, each participant had 1 acre under
his control, regardless of what portion of the 100
acres he may have owned. Payment for use of the
land is determined and divided on the following
basis: 10 percent of the profits the cooperative
makes from the plantation are paid over to the community; one third of this amount (i.e., 3 1/3 percent) is divided among the various land owners as
compensation for use of their land, and the remaining
two thirds (i.e., 6 2/3 percent) is used for communit
projects. Since it was too difficult to survey each
individual's parcels, the amount of rent to go to
each land owner is calculated on the basis of how
many yam mounds each owner had previously been able
to plant on his parcels.

Ikwa and Ikot Ita, Opobo Division

The 700 acres being developed as a community
plantation in Ikwa is communal land controlled jointl
by these two small villages. Before the community
plantation project began, anyone from either village
could farm on this land on a year-to-year basis, but
much of the land remained virgin and uncleared.
More extensive use had not been made of this land
previously because until the community project
started individual farmers had not been allowed to
plant tree crops on it, in line with traditional
prohibitions. However, as a community project in
which 86 men participated, the villagers agreed
that tree crops could be planted on the basis of a

government survey of the land and a long-term lease.
Officers of the farmers' cooperative and the heads
of the seven patrilineages in the two villages
signed the lease. Despite the fact that some of
the farmers in the two villages have less land for
their food crops now that this piece of communal
land is no longer available for that purpose, the
community plantation enables the community as a
whole to make more profitable use of the land.

Abia Ohafia, Bende Division

Over 1,000 acres of land have been set aside
in Abia for development as a community plantation.
Approximately half of this land had previously been
used as farm land, while the remainder was virgin
forest. The forest portion is owned communally by
the whole village, while ownership of the remaining
half is divided among 15 patrilineages and 8 matrilineages. This configuration results from the fact
that in Abia, as in the rest of Ohafia, land is
controlled by both patrilineages and matrilineages
and reflects a system of double descent characteristic
of the Ohafia villages. The amount of land owned
by each lineage was determined by a land survey, and
each lineage receives rent payment from the farmers
cooperative at the rate of 2 shillings per acre.
Each of the landowning lineages sent one representative
on its behalf to sign the 99-year lease. The officers
of the cooperative represented the 170 farmers participating in the project in signing the lease. Although
the involvement of so much land and so many farmers
in a single economic venture is unique in Abia's
history, two Abia farmers had previously leased 15-
and 30-acre plots on a long-term basis to plant oil
palms.

*   *   *

The willingness of these four communities and
many others to agree under certain conditions to
the utilization of land for tree crops on the basis

of a long-term lease once the land had been surveyed
and registered suggests an approach that might be
successfully employed to achieve land consolidation
in Eastern Nigeria. Using an approach similar to
that used in organizing community plantations, everyone in a village might lease their scattered parcels
of land to a cooperative composed of all the people
in the village. The cooperative, in turn, could
lease consolidated plots of equivalent size back to
its members, i.e., the villagers. Members given land
of comparable value and fertility to what they gave
up would be required to pay only nominal rents.
However, if the land varies in fertility and soil
types so that one could not be assured of receiving
land exactly equivalent in value to what he gave up,
then a system of rent payments could be devised so
that a farmer would pay rent for the land he is
assigned and receive rent payments for the land he
contributed. The lease arrangement would assure
landowners that they still retain ultimate control
of their land, even though they agree to reassign
usufruct rights to the land for a long period of
time. To the Western observer, the difference
between giving up ownership of one's land and giving
up control of it for a period of 99 years may seem
trivial, but to villagers of Eastern Nigeria it
could well make the difference between a successful
and unsuccessful program of land consolidation. The
mere fact that they knew that their ancestral land
still belonged to them and to their descendents
would be reassuring.

      Through a system of rent payments it would also
be possible for the land-controlling cooperative to
lease land in terms of a farmer's ability to use it,
instead of simply in terms of the size of his previous
holdings. Thus a landowner who could not make effective use of all his land could be compensated
through rent payments for the amount of land he has
given up for others to use, but he would only receive
as much land in the redistribution process as he
could effectively farm. The difficulties a village
would face in attempting to inaugurate such a scheme
might warrant the involvement of the government as
an intermediary. The government could lease the

land from the landowners and then redistribute it in
consolidated pieces on the basis of long-term leases.
Although in some parts of the region government
involvement would arouse hostility and suspicion,
elsewhere administration of the program by the government would create greater confidence in the scheme.
The successful operation of this scheme, or any
other approach to land consolidation, would also
require that controls be placed on the redivision
of land so that fragmentation does not recur. The
Kenya approach to land consolidation, for example,
includes controls over land inheritance and the sale
or leasing of landholdings to avoid recurrence of
fragmentation.

As mentioned earlier in this chapter, the Oil
Palm Rehabilitation Scheme, like the community plantation scheme, has apparently had as one of its by-
products the consolidation of fragmented land on a
limited scale. The scheme encourages consolidation
through the requirement that to participate a farmer
must have a plot of land at least five acres in
size. Despite the small size of most farms in
Eastern Nigeria, the average farm under this scheme
is 15 acres.[25] The scheme has also encouraged the
development of a limited land market, as evidenced
by the fact that 28 percent of a sample of participants
indicated that they acquired the land they have
planted with oil palms through purchase.[26] In
considering the portion of participants who managed
to purchase land and the size of their plantations,
it should be stressed that those participating
represent the elite of Eastern Nigeria's farming
population.

SUMMARY

In this chapter the following barriers that the
land tenure system in Eastern Nigeria poses for
agricultural development have been discussed:

1. the difficulty involved in acquiring new
land because of the prevailing belief that land
should not be sold;

2.   the unwillingness of villagers to lease
or pledge excess land to outsiders, which results in
some sections of Eastern Nigeria being overpopulated
and others underpopulated;

3.   the refusal of communities to allow individuals to plant economic trees on land owned communally
by the village;

4.   the prohibition usually placed on the planti
of economic trees on land that is leased;

5.   the way in which the system of inheritance
contributes to fragmentation of land into tiny,
scattered parcels, which are difficult to farm efficiently; and

6.   the complexity of the land tenure system and
and the absence of land registration, which means
that land disputes frequently occur and land has to
lie idle until disputes are settle.

The final portion of the chapter discussed
possible approaches to land consolidation in Eastern
Nigeria and the beneficial impact the community
plantation scheme and the Oil Palm Rehabilitation
Scheme are having on the land tenure system.

Some observers argue that land tenure problems
need not be tackled by the government in any comprehensive fashion, and that the obstacles posed by the
land tenure system tend to dissolve when profitable
investment opportunities develop.[27]   Although it has
been maintained in this chapter that land reform
must be undertaken within the context of agricultural
development projects that promise economic benefit
to the farmer, it is not felt that a laissez-faire
approach to the problems of land tenure will prove
adequate.   If serious thought is not given to how
the difficulties posed by the land tenure system
can be overcome, the consequences to Eastern Nigeria'
long-term agricultural development could be close
to disastrous.

NOTES

1.   H. S. Mann, Land Tenure in Chore (Addis
Ababa: Haile Sellassie I. University Press, 1965),
p. 47.

2.   Rene Dumont, False Start in Africa (New York: Frederick A. Praeger, 1966), p. 131.

3.   For a general discussion of land tenure in Africa, see John C. de Wilde, et al., Agricultural Development in Tropical Africa, Vol. I (Baltimore: The Johns Hopkins Press, 1967), pp. 132-156.

4.   Aaron Segal, "The Politics of Land in East Africa," Economic Development and Cultural Change, XVI (January 1968), 275-295.

5.   Polly Hill, The Migrant Cocoa Farmers of Southern Ghana (Cambridge: Cambridge University Press, 1963), pp. 75-86.

6.   Godwil Okurume, "The Food Crop Economy in Nigerian Agricultural Policy" (East Lansing: Consortium for the Study of Nigerian Rural Development, Michigan State University, 1967, mimeographed); Kenneth Anthony and Bruce F. Johnston, "Field Study of Agricultural Change: Northern Katsina, Nigeria" (Stanford, Calif.: Food Research Institute, Stanford University, 1963, mimeographed). Significantly, however, Anthony and Johnston maintain that the sale of land in Northern Nigeria has been encouraged by the fact that families in that portion of Nigeria are not bound to particular localities by ties to clans and clan land.

7.   S. N. C. Obi, Ibo Law of Property (London: Butterworths, 1963); L. T. Chubb, Ibo Land Tenure (Ibadan: University of Ibadan Press, 1961); T. O. Elias, Nigerian Land Law and Custom (London: Routledge and Kegan Paul, 1962); H. A. Oluwasanwi, I. S. Dema, et al., Uboma: A Socio-Economic and Nutritional Survey of a Rural Community in Eastern Nigeria (Bude, Cornwall: Geographical Publications Ltd., 1966); R. W. James and A. B. Kasunmu, Alienation of Family Property in Southern Nigeria (Ibadan: Ibadan University Press, 1966); C. K. Meek, Land Tenure and Land Administration in Nigeria and the Cameroons, Colonial Research Studies, No. 22 (London, HMSO, 1957); and William P. Huth, "Traditional Institutions and Land Tenure as Related to Agricultural

Development Among the Ibo of Eastern Nigeria," Research
Paper No. 36 (Madison: Land Tenure Center, University
of Wisconsin, 1969, mimeographed).

8. Elias, op. cit., p. 181.

9. Ibid., p. 182.

10. Although his description of this distrust
of outsiders is too sharply drawn to apply to Eastern
Nigeria, John M. Brewster, "Traditional Social
Structures as Barriers to Change," in Herman M.
Southworth and Bruce F. Johnston, eds., Agricultural
Development and Economic Growth (Ithaca, N.Y.: Cornell
University Press, 1967), pp. 79-80 presents an
interesting discussion of this fear as a widespread
phenomenon in developing countries.

11. Another obstacle to relocation is that
localistic orientations on the part of prospective
settlers often make them hesitate to migrate from
their home villages. However, the eagerness of
many young men in Eastern Nigeria to participate in
farm settlements indicates that many farmers are
prepared to migrate to other areas if the economic
prospects for them there are good.

12. Jean Roche, "Important Aspects of Consolida-
tion in France," in K. H. Parsons, F. J. Penn, and
Philip Raup, eds., Land Tenure (Madison: University
of Wisconsin Press, 1956), pp. 536-543; Euthymois
Papageorigiou, "Fragmentation of Land Holdings and
Measures for Consolidation in Greece," in Parsons,
Penn, and Raup, pp. 543-548; and Setsuro Hyodo,
"Aspects of Land Consolidation in Japan," in Parsons,
Penn, and Raup, pp. 558-559.

13. Roche, op. cit.

14. P. C. Lloyd, Yoruba Land Law (London:
Oxford University Press, 1962), p. 285.

15. F. D. Homan, "Consolidation, Enclosure and
Registration of Title in Kenya," Journal of Local
Administration Overseas, I (January 1962), 8.

16. Kenya Development Plan 1966-1970 (Nairobi: Government Printer, 1966).

17. M. P. K. Sorrenson, Land Reform in the Kikuyu Country (Nairobi: Oxford University Press, 1967), p. 241. See also de Wilde, op. cit., Vol. II, Part I.

18. Sorrenson, op, cit., p. 243.

19. Segal, op. cit., p. 286.

20. Second National Development Plan (1970-74) (Lagos: Federal Ministry of Information, 1970), p. 110.

21. Roche, op. cit., pp. 542-543.

22. Chubb, op. cit., p. 20.

23. Sorrenson, op. cit., pp. 251-252.

24. Ibid., pp. 220-236.

25. Malcolm J. Purvis, "Report on a Survey of the Oil Palm Rehabilitation Scheme in Eastern Nigeria-1967" (East Lansing: Consortium for the Study of Nigerian Rural Development, Michigan State University, 1968, mimeographed), p. 21.

26. Ibid., p. 23.

27. For instance, Carl K. Eicher, "Reflections on West Africa's Rural Development Problems of the 1970's," a paper presented at the Symposium on Africa in the 1980's, Adlai Stevenson Institute of International Affairs, Chicago, 1969 (mimeographed), pp. 10-11; and Glenn L. Johnson, Orlin J. Scoville, George K. Dike, and Carl K. Eicher, Strategies and Recommendations for Nigerian Rural Development 1969/1985 (East Lansing: Consortium for the Study of Nigerian Rural Development, Michigan State University, 1969), pp. 27-29.

7

A NEW APPROACH
TO
RURAL TRANSFORMATION:
COMMUNITY
PLANTATIONS

In 1963 the Eastern Nigeria government came to
the conclusion that a new approach to the development
of rural areas was urgently required. The shortcomings
of the farm settlement program referred to in Chapter
4 were becoming painfully obvious. The capital costs
per settler of establishing a farm settlement were
so high that the government's development resources
could be stretched to include only a very small
proportion of the region's farming population in the
settlement program. Moreover, the economic viability
of the settlements was in question; it was not at
all clear that the settlers would be able to pay
back the large debts the settlements were incurring
on their behalves during the development phase of
the project.

By 1963 it was becoming more widely accepted
within the government that agricultural development
efforts in Eastern Nigeria had to concentrate on the
peasant farmers, who made up the vast majority of
the farming population and produced the bulk of the
region's agricultural output. The revolutionary
transformation of agriculture sought in the establishment of farm settlements and the commercial plantations
of the Eastern Nigeria Development Corporation had
to be replaced or at least supplemented by programs
of an evolutionary nature aimed at assisting the
smallholder. The potential pay-off of the Oil Palm

Rehabilitation Scheme and the parallel programs for
rubber and cocoa was becoming increasingly apparent.

The principal shortcoming of the tree crop
programs aimed at the peasant farmer was that participation was confined to relatively few farmers. In
part this resulted from the difficulties the government had in providing technical supervision as well
as the planting material and fertilizer that were
required. A more significant limiting factor was
the government's requirement that a farmer had to
devote a minimum of five acres of land in one solid
piece to the scheme before he was allowed to participate. This requirement was understandable in terms
of the government's desire to make efficient use of
extension service manpower and of available agricultural materials, but it meant that the average
farmer, who did not have five acres in excess of the
land that was required for growing crops to feed his
family, could not participate. Those who had a
total of five acres available in several small
fragmented parcels were also ineligible. The obstacle
involved in a farmer's acquiring new land have been
enumerated in Chapter 6.

A consultant's report by Arthur Gaitskell to
the Eastern Nigeria government in 1962 stated:

> The greatest difficulty facing the exten-
> sion of service in implementing the (Oil
> Palm Rehabilitation Scheme) is undoubtedly
> the prevailing system of land tenure.
> The existing ownership of land, and of
> individual palm trees, is extremely frag-
> mented and quite small parcels of land
> are frequently subject to claims of owner-
> ship by different members of a family
> group and often by different family
> groups. Even to acquire the one-acre
> plots used by the West African Institute
> for Oil Palm Research for demonstration
> experiments has been quite a task.[1]

Alongside the growing realization that agricultural assistance needed to be directed to the

smallholders, a reassessment of the government's
community development program took place. By 1963
Eastern Nigeria's considerable achievements in the
field of community development had received wide
recognition. A large portion of the roads in Eastern
Nigeria have been constructed by voluntary village
labor; innumerable maternities, dispensaries, schools,
village meeting halls, markets, and churches have
been constructed by community effort as well. In
the past the government had encouraged this activity
by making financial contributions to projects, but
as the self-help movement gained momentum, these
contributions involved the government in burdensome
expenditures. By 1963 it had become increasingly
clear that the greatest bottleneck to village
improvement was not a lack of interest in development
activity or a lack of willingness on the part of villagers to contribute their labor, but a lack of money.
It had become difficult to find the money to pay for
materials, and more importantly, difficult to find
the money to pay for upkeep and operating costs.
Thus, the real barrier to village development was
financial, rather than motivational. When this was
recognized the government decided to shift its
emphasis in the field of community development from
social service projects to economic projects. The
new objective became that of increasing village
income, and doing this by capitalizing on the tradition
of self-help and community effort. With increased
income, the government thought that villagers could
enjoy a higher standard of living as well as finance
their own village development.

In late 1963 and early 1964 officials of the
Community Development Division of the Ministry of
Internal Affairs (it later became a division within
the Ministry of Rural Development) assisted by
members of a Ford Foundation advisory team, toured
all the provinces of Eastern Nigeria meeting with
government officials and village leaders in an effort
to determine what types of community-based economic
ventures could usefully be encouraged and assisted.[2]

By September 1964, 15 pilot communities had been
selected as project sites. In each of these villages

plans were devised with the villagers to establish
community-based agriculture projects which, it was
hoped, would increase the level of income within
the village. In one locality officials decided that
assistance should be given to an oil palm and rubber
plantation that was to be organized as a limited-
liability company whose purpose was to finance the
economic and social development of the area. The
local shareholders of the company purchased land for
the plantation and local villagers were hired as paid
laborers to do the work, while the profits were
divided between, on the one hand, those who had
orginally provided share capital, and the villages
of the area on the other hand. The portion of the
profits going to the villages was to be used to
maintain the secondary school serving the area plus
providing other services and amenities.

Elsewhere support was given to projects whose
sole purpose was to provide the village with funds
for development projects. In some of these a
cooperative served the same purpose as the limited-
liability company in the first community, with the
cooperative hiring laborers to do the work and then
allocating profits to community projects. Elsewhere
work on the plantations was performed by all the
villagers on a voluntary and communal basis. These
plantations were generally located on village land,
and the profits went to village development projects.

The approach found to be most workable and the
most popular in the region as a whole, though, was
organized somewhat differently. The prototype of
what was later to be termed a "community plantation"
was worked out in Abia Ohafia, the home village of
the Community Development Secretary, N. A. Ndu.
To establish a community plantation, the men of
the community are expected to release a sizable
portion of land (usually a minimum of 100 acres) for
development as a plantation, which is then surveyed
by the Surveys Division of the Ministry of Town
Planning. The farmers who will work on the plantation are selected from the village, and they form
themselves into a farmers' cooperative. A lease
agreement is then worked out between the cooperative

and the community, if it is village land, or with
the landlords, if it is family or individually owned
land, by means of which the cooperative is granted
use of the land for a period ranging from 60 to 99
years. The deed resulting from this agreement is
registered with the Lands Division of the Ministry
of Town Planning to assure that it is honored.

During the initial year of operation, a portion
of the total land area is cleared and each member
of the cooperative is given control over a piece
that he will plant, care for, and eventually harvest.
The vast majority of the community plantations planted
thus far have been devoted to oil palms, but cocoa
and rubber provide alternatives. After the land has
been fully planted, each farmer has between four and
ten acres, depending upon how much land is available
for development. The farmers pay between two and
five shillings per acre rent either to the landlords
or to the community for use of the land, but aside
from this all the money a farmer realizes from his
efforts is his own. In addition to clearing, planting,
and caring for his part of the plantation, each
farmer also plants his usual food crops so that he
can feed himself and his family. Thus the plantation
is expected to supplement his normal farming operation,
rather than supplant it. Evidence of the popularity
of the community plantation concept is seen in the
fact that over 100 community plantations were established between 1964 and 1967, when the civil war
broke out.

The participants in community plantation schemes
are eligible for assistance under the oil palm,
rubber, and cocoa rehabilitation schemes, and thus
they received seedlings and fertilizer free, plus a
small cash subsidy during the five years it takes
the trees to begin to bear. These subsidy payments
constitute the only direct financial assistance the
farmers receive from the government, in contrast
to farm settlements where houses, schools, roads,
and other public facilities are initially provided
at government expense.

The government also provides technical assistance

in the form of agricultural extension personnel and
rural development officers. In most cases the
extension agent assigned responsibility for a large
community plantation is expected to spend between
one third and one half of his time working on that
project, while spending the remainder of his time
performing his normal extension activities. In
the first year of operation a Rural Development
Officer (RDO) from the Community Development Division
and a Peace Corps Volunteer (PCV) were assigned
to each pilot project. Later a given RDO assumed
responsibility for several projects. His responsibilities complemented those of the extension agent,
consisted of supervising the work, assisting in
the organization of the cooperative, assisting in
the preparation of the lease, dividing the land
into equal-sized plots for the individual farmers,
and serving as a communication link between the
village and the government.

One of the principal advantages of the community
plantation scheme as an approach to rural transformation in Eastern Nigeria is its low cost.[3] As
mentioned above, expenditure by the government on
the scheme consists of the normal costs of financing
the Oil Palm Rehabilitation Scheme or one of the
other tree-crop rehabilitation schemes, i.e., seedlings, fertilizer, a cash subsidy amounting to
£N18 per acre, plus technical supervision provided
by the agricultural extension service and an RDO.
Because the participants remain in their home villages
this approach eliminated the costs of resettlement
and the establishment of new villages--two elements
that usually make plantation schemes expensive. Also,
the farmers continue to feed themselves through growing
their own food crops. Thus, aside from the small
subsidy payments, the cost of maintaining the
farmers before the trees start to bear does not have
to be covered by the government. Much of the work
required by the plantation can be done at times that
are normally slack work periods, so that a farmer's
total productivity is substantially increased.

Another advantage of the community plantation
approach is that it permits the efficient use of a
limited number of technical specialists. On a

particular community plantation an extension worker
can give technical supervision to as many as 175
farmers, while still having time to attend to the
needs of other farmers in the area not participating
in the community plantation. Normally, extension
agents working at village level, who have only
bicycles or motorcycles for transportation, would
not be able to assist nearly that many farmers.
Also, since so many farmers are planting the same
crop at the same time on adjacent plots, the agent
can supervise them more closely than he is able to
when he has to assist farmers working on scattered
plots in several localities and needing supervision
with a variety of new crops and farming practices.

The community plantation approach also enables
peasant farmers to overcome the land tenure barriers
that in the past have kept so many of them from
participating in the Oil Palm Rehabilitation Scheme
or comparable development programs. As described
in detail in Chapter 6, participation by a broad
cross section of the community in the project means
that villages are prepared to permit the utilization
of communally owned land that might not otherwise
be exploited. Because the land is accurately surveyed
and a long-term lease is prepared and is registered
with the Ministry of Town Planning, landowners,
whether they are individual landlords or those who
control the use of community land, also permit the
participants in the project to plant tree crops
instead of restricting use of the land to annual
crops, which is the traditional limitation. Since
the total size of the project land exceeds five acres,
the Ministry of Agriculture permits entrance into
the Oil Palm Rehabilitation Scheme, even if the
land controlled by individual project participants
does not fulfil that requirement. Thus, the community plantation approach enables new land to be
put into production, enables farmers to plant trees
on land where it would not normally be permitted,
and brings government assistance to the participants
even when they control less than the normal minimum
of five acres of land. Moreover, as described in
Chapter 6, community plantations often bring about
the consolidation of fragmented holdings that had
previously been less efficiently utilized.

Even if new land were available within particular
communities for exploitation by the peasant farmers,
an effort to induce farmers on an individual basis
to plant the improved oil palms or other cash crops
would generally not generate as dramatic a response
as the community approach. When the whole community
is involved in the project, individuals tend to
overcome the doubts and fears they might have if it
were merely an individual enterprise. It is difficult
to imagine how long it might take an extension worker
to induce the 175 farmers participating in some
community plantations to engage in such a venture and
to adopt the innovations required on an individual
basis. Moreover, even though each man controls an
individual parcel of land, community work groups--
buoyed by a sense of community pride and group
solidarity--build the access roads, prepare the
nursery for planting, and in some cases clear the
project land prior to division into individual plots.
Okediji reports that a basic cause of the desertion
of settlers from farm settlements in Western Nigeria,
and in turn a fundamental reason for the lack of
success of settlement schemes in general, is the
lack of social homogeneity within the settler population.[4] When an agricultural project is based upon
an existing community that has a sense of indentity
and unity, the participants stimulate each other to
greater productivity.

Despite the success of the community plantation
program during the first three years of its existence
and the advantages this approach represents over
most other avenues to economic development in rural
Eastern Nigeria, community plantations do not provide
a panacea to Eastern Nigeria's rural economic problems
The most heavily populated portions of Eastern
Nigeria do not contain any unused or underutilized
land that can be devoted to new plantings of oil
palms on a plantation scale: All available land is
already intensively cultivated to satisfy the food
needs of the residents. There is even some question
as to whether the community plantation scheme should
have been introduced into some of the more heavily
populated areas where some of the projects are
located. Without detailed economic appraisals it is

impossible to determine whether the food crop land
that has been given over in some of these projects
to oil palms would have been more efficiently and
profitably used if it had remained under food crop
production. Community-based agricultural projects
utilizing crops that can be more intensively cultivated, such as tomatoes, onions, and rice, have been
experimented with and appear to hold some potential
for these areas. A more radical approach to these
high density areas, involving an attempt to resettle
persons in other locations where more land is
available, is described in Chapter 9.

The community plantation approach to agricultural
development also necessitates a level of village
esprit de corps and of village leadership that is
lacking in many of Eastern Nigeria's villages.
Although leadership and group spirit can sometimes
be nurtured and developed, in many localities one
has to recognize the futility of attempting community
projects and instead rely upon individual effort and
innovation. Other communities possess the requisite
preparedness for cooperative effort, but are unwilling
to engage in the strenuous labor that plantation
agriculture requires. In these localities development
of commercial agriculture may depend upon hired labor
rather than upon self-help.

Despite the fact that the community plantation
approach is not universally applicable in Eastern
Nigeria, we estimate that community plantations,
or some variation on the community plantation theme,
could be successfully and profitably introduced into
approximately 25 percent of the villages in Eastern
Nigeria. If this estimation is accurate, community
plantations hold the potential for making a very
important contribution to increased agricultural
production and higher farm incomes in Eastern Nigeria.

SOCIAL, CULTURAL, AND PSYCHOLOGICAL
FACTORS IN THE ESTABLISHMENT
OF COMMUNITY PLANTATIONS

Social, cultural, and psychological factors
have proved to be of considerable significance in

both the selection of suitable project sites and in
the successful implementation by the village of the
project plan. For instance, issues relating to land
tenure often prove to be of critical importance in
determining whether a proposed project could be
successfully launched. In many cases the sites
that villages propose for community plantations turn
out to be areas of disputed land ownership, and in
several of these cases the project proposers have
hoped to secure their claim on the disputed area by
having the government assist them in starting a
project there. It has proved necessary to have the
villagers cut a boundary trace around the proposed
area at any early stage of project consideration in
order to determine whether ownership rights are in
fact secure. If a trace can be successfully cut
without another village or another group of landlords protesting that their rights are being infringed
then one has reasonable assurance that those proposing
the project hold undisputed rights to the land.
Because commitments by a village of land and manpower
often turn out to be exaggerated, it has also become
necessary for the government to offer assistance to
a project on a tentative and contingent basis until
it is clear that the village can in fact produce
the men and land it has pledged.

     The question of whether the villagers are
prepared to devote the physical energy to the project
that is required also presents problems in the site
selection process. Of the original set of 15 pilot
projects, three happened to be in places where the
people hire laborers to do most of their farming.
The residents of these villages conceive of themselves as landlords, rather than as workers. At
one time they depended upon slaves to do their work
for them, and now they rely on hired laborers. Two
of these three projects ended up as failures for
precisely this reason. Although the villagers told
the government officials who did the selection that
they were willing to do the work required, when the
hard work started they drew back. In dealing with
villages where the residents are not accustomed to
doing hard farm work the wisest policy has been

either to exclude them from the scheme, or to
organize a different type of project, based upon
the use of hired laborers.

Attention needs to be given in the selection
process to what social or geographical unit constitutes an appropriate basis for a project. Eastern
Nigeria's villages have very clear ideas about whom
they can work with and whom they can not. In some
areas the original selection team discovered that a
village chosen for a project was insistent that an
adjacent village be included as well, since they
traditionally cooperate in development activities.
Elsewhere, particular portions of a village-group
refused to cooperate with other portions of the same
village-group in any joint undertaking. In another
case where two villages had successfully launched
a community plantation on a cooperative basis, work
came to a halt at one point for several weeks while
the two villages argued over which name should come
first in the plantation's title.

One of the most critical issues involved in the
successful establishment of a community plantation
concerns decision-making and power. One of the most
important questions the project organizer needs to
ask is: With what individual or group should one
work in a particular community to assure that things
get done and that effective decisions are made?
The critical nature of this question became apparent
when it was realized that in no two of the pilot project communities were exactly the same type of power
structure being dealt with. Some indication of the
variations in the traditional political organization
found in different parts of Eastern Nigeria was given
in Chapter 3. The following examples illustrate the
variety of contemporary patterns found in the pilot
project communities.

The most important decision-making body in one
pilot village (Akwete, Aba Division) is the village
meeting. Village meetings are held whenever important
issues arise and are attended by most of the men in
the village. These meetings are chaired by one or
the other of the community's two most influential

people, one of whom is a member of the county council
and the other is chairman of the local council. A
decade ago most of the important decisions for this
village were made by a group composed of the head
of the village's 20 patrilineages. Although on
some issues this group must still be consulted, it
has lost much of its influence, partly because it is
divided into factions and is unable to select a head.
Moreover, the younger residents of the village consider this group too conservative and unsophisticated
to deal with the problems encountered in the modern
world. The young men living in the village, along
with those born in the village but currently residing
in some urban area, have organized themselves into
a group called the Citizen's Union, and this has
become an influential organization that concerns
itself with many village issues. The village's age-
grades meet regularly as well and concern themselves
with any project which involves voluntary cooperative
effort. Thus, the village meeting constitutes the
most important decision-making body, but various
other groups must be consulted about issues which
affect the success of Akwete's community plantation.

     In another project village (Oban, Calabar
Province) power and authority rest firmly in the hands
of a traditional ruler. In most of the decision-making
done in the village, this ruler's will almost inevita-
bly prevails. When government representatives called
meetings to discuss the proposed project, they ended
up carrying on a dialogue with the chief, in the
presence of the other villagers. After he had spoken
he would turn to the others and they would nod their
approval. If someone disagreed with the chief in
these sessions, his views were heard but they rarely
had much influence. Unlike most villages in Eastern
Nigeria, the women here attend all village meetings
as full participants, and a woman chief sits next to
the head chief on these occasions.

     At another project site (Umuogbo Nkwerre, Orlu
Division) no decisions of any importance can be
taken without consulting the "sons abroad," i.e.,
those from the village who are resident in urban
areas. Minor issues can be handled by the village

elders in consultation with a teacher who is very influential in village affairs, but important decisions have to wait until Christmas time when the sons abroad return home to dispose of issues that have accumulated during the past year. The Christmas meeting in 1964 made certain decisions concerning the village's community plantation with which the Rural Development Officer disagreed. When he explained to those participating in the project that he believed the decisions taken were unwise, they told him that they saw his point but that no changes in village policy or plans could be effected until the following Christmas when the sons abroad would return home for another meeting.

Two other project villages (Affa in Udi Division and Akoliufu in Bende Division), are typical of large portions of Eastern Nigeria, in that power is very broadly distributed among various village organizations. Family meetings, lineage meetings, village meetings, age-grade meetings, and meetings of various special interest groups all have an opportunity to influence the village's decision-making. In these localities, disapproval by any significant minority within the community of an idea involving the project constitutes an effective veto.

In this citation of various patterns of political organization the emphasis has been on the diversity found in various project villages, but one general principle can be stated that holds for all but one or two of the original 15 pilot villages. An important issue that affects the whole community can only be disposed of by consulting all the adult men of the village, and in a few cases the women as well. Although this consultation may be achieved by holding a series of meetings with different sections or lineage segments of the village, the most effective means is through the holding of village meetings.

The political organization and processes of most villages in Eastern Nigeria is understandably, but regrettably, adapted to the requirements of a slowly changing society in which speed in reaching decisions is not critical to the successful conduct of village

affairs. The complexity of the system and the requirement in most communities that near unanimity be
achieved before action can be taken, do not permit
efficient planning and operation of development
projects that are dependent upon precise timing and
efficient decision-making. One of the most important
tasks facing RDO's in project villages is the encourage
ment of new political forms, usually involving
representative bodies, that can dispose of village
and project problems with dispatch. However, it is
not always easy for those accustomed to participating
in all village decision-making to agree that someone
should be deputized to handle issues on their behalves
nor is it easy to instill in the representatives the
notion that they have to consult their constituents
on major issues, as well as report the conclusions
reached to those whom they represent. Moreover, in
most villages the organization of a representative
body to handle the everyday business of the project
does not, and should not, completely replace the
village meeting or meetings for all the project
participants when important issues have to be settled.

     Another task that has fallen to the RDO's is
that of trying to introduce orderly procedures into
village or project meetings, both to quicken the
pace of decision-making and to assure that everyone's
views are heard rather than being lost as they are
on occasion in a din of uncontrolled discussion.
Some efforts are also being made to gain acceptance
of the notion of majority rule as the basis for
reaching decisions rather than waiting for near
unanimity to be reached. Although on some major
issues the attempt to reach unanimity usefully
protects minority views, it also makes village
decision-making a laborious process. The residents
of one project village argued among themselves for
months over which piece of land should be assigned
for project use; by the time unanimity was reached,
it was too late in the growing season to prepare
and plant much of the selected area.

     Project organizers continually face the perplexi
issue of what type of village leadership to look
for and encourage. The presence of a strong,

charismatic leader in a potential project village has
its obvious advantages. Such an individual can assume
responsibility for organized village meetings, for
seeing that decisions are reached, and for guiding
project planning. Moreover, he can effectively
explain needs and desires of his village to the
government, and he can interpret the government to
his village. However, despite the advantages of
this sort of leadership, strong village leaders have
not turned out to be an unmixed blessing to the
government's rural development program. Two of the
least successful pilot projects are located in villages that are under the influence of strong and
sophisticated leaders. These leaders, however, have
tended to work at cross purposes with the RDO's
assigned to the projects, and to use their influence
over the villagers to have them disregard the guidelines for the rural development program laid down by
the government.

On the other hand, two other villages that have
strong leadership have been among the most successful
projects. The principal difference between the
leadership of these villages and that of the unsuccessful project villages mentioned above is that the
leaders of these two villages have a dual loyalty--to
their villages and to the government. Both of these
leaders are highly placed civil servants, and they
are able to appreciate the interests of their home
village as well as those of the government, and to
assure that a project is established that will satisfy
both.

Another danger of sophisticated and persuasive
village leadership arises from the naivete and
gullibility of many villagers concerning development
projects. It is both frightening and encouraging to
ponder the statement made by one village leader to
the effect that the people of his village were willing to assign a piece of village land for development
as a community plantation simply because he told
them to do it. It is a hopeful sign when villagers
are prepared to accept an innovation and to deviate
from traditional patterns. On the other hand, it is
somewhat frightening to realize how little the

people of this village probably comprehended what
they had committed themselves to.

The government has faced one major issue, and
two minor issues, relating to participation in community plantation projects. The major issue is
whether "sons abroad" are eligible for participation.
As indicated in Chapter 3, in Eastern Nigeria probabl
more than in any other part of Africa, sons abroad
continue to play an active role in village affairs
and are usually prepared not only to contribute ideas
at village meetings but also to donate money to village development projects. Because sons abroad usual
consider themselves full-fledged members of their
home villages, they also tend to believe they have
an equal right to participate in village projects,
especially when these involve the exploitation of
village-owned land. Some villages depend so heavily
upon sons abroad for ideas and leadership that their
participation in the community plantation has proved
essential. However, we found that where it is
possible to organize a viable project and still
confine participation to those resident in the
village, the project has tended to be more successful. It is difficult for the project participants
to plan and coordinate project activities when some
members live considerable distances away from the
village and are unable to attend project meetings
on a regular basis. Moreover, those resident outside the village have to hire laborers to perform
most of the work on their project plots, and it is
difficult for the work of these laborers to be
adequately supervised or controlled when their
employer is so distant from the place of work. Sons
abroad are also not able to contribute their full
share when voluntary cooperative work has to be
performed, for instance when access roads are constructed by the project participants.

In a part of the world where women play such
a prominent role in agricultural production, it is
natural that the issue should arise as to whether
women should be admitted to community plantation
project as full participants. In most of the pilot
areas the women of the community have not requested

a chance to join, and the men have not invited their
participation, both because they do not want to
accord women the prestige of participating on an
equal basis and because some of the work required
is thought to be too heavy for women. However, in
one project village 8 of the 94 original participants
were women.[5] In this project some aspects of the
work have proved to be too burdensome for the women,
and they hire laborers to do it for them. In those
projects where women are not full participants, they
frequently assist their husbands in the project by
cutting shrubs and grass on the project land, for
which they usually receive a portion of the subsidy
money as recompense. Elsewhere women interplant
maize and cassava between the rows of the newly
planted oil palms. The project in which women have
played the largest role is one in Udi Division based
upon the growing of vegetables for sale in Enugu.
Women predominate in this project, since the work
is light and vegetable growing is traditionally
the province of women in this locality.

Given the problem of unemployment among young
men who have recently finished primary school,
some government officials have argued that participation in community plantations should be confined
to these young "school leavers." In the pilot areas,
however, it was discovered that the most successful
arrangement was for there to be a mixture of older
and younger men, and of literates and illiterates.
The younger, educated men are better able than the
others to perform such tasks as the simple calculations required to space the trees properly, but the
older established farmers are able to set an example
for the younger men both in terms of general knowledge
of farming and in terms of preparedness to work hard
and steadily. Judging from the difficulties faced
by school leavers' farm projects in Mid-West Nigeria
and by farm settlements in Western Nigeria, whose
settlers are mostly school leavers, the community
plantation projects are fortunate to have such a
high proportion of established farmers. Many school
leavers have been unwilling to participate in community plantation projects because they feel that
farming does not offer adequate prestige as an

occupation and is not sufficiently remunerative.
Hopefully, if community plantations and other agricultural projects can convince these young men that
they can earn a good living as farmers, farming will
become a more attractive occupation to them.

During the formative stages of the community
plantation program the question of whether work on
the plantations should be planned on an individual
or a communal basis generated more controversy than
any other issue. Disagreement on this point came
both among the government officials responsible for
administrating the program and among the farmers whose
villages had been selected as potential project sites.
Some of those arguing for a communal pattern cited
the precedent of the communal labor approach taken
in clearing village paths and building village roads,
as well as the reciprocal work agreements between
individual farmers in many parts of Eastern Nigeria.
While, as already noted, construction projects based
on voluntary communal labor have played an important
role in rural Eastern Nigeria, these projects require
only occasional communal labor and short bursts of
sustained effort and enthusiasm. An economic project
however, operated completely on a communal basis
always faced the basic difficulty of insuring that
the work gets done. Although, as will be discussed
more fully later in this chapter, discipline is
generally difficult to impose in all village projects
without the appeal to self-interest the problem
becomes even greater.

Experience with community plantations indicates
that when a farmer knows that his future earnings
depend on the regularity and productivity of his
labor, he is prepared to exert himself. Although
in projects operated individually, gross neglect
or incompetence by a participant has to be spotted
and checked by the cooperative, the individual who
does not plant carefully or care for his trees
adequately is imposing his own punishment on himself
since his eventual income from his plot will be
reduced. In those projects where a forest has been
cleared communally or access roads have been built
communally, these aspects were consistently more

difficult to organize than those portions of the
project undertaken on an individual basis, when
each participant was working on his assigned parcel
of land. Furthermore, communal economic projects
are particularly vulnerable when participants continue
to plant and produce food crops individually on
other parcels of land since they are more likely to
spend time on their own parcels than to turn up for
communal work. The amount of supervision that is
required to make sure that each person contributes
his fair share in a communal project also contributes
to higher project costs. For instance, careful
records have to be maintained of how much work each
person does, and checks have to be imposed to
ascertain whether he is working sufficiently hard.
Although the fact that community plantations represent
community effort assists in arousing initial enthusiasm for the project and in overcoming the fears and
hesitations that might make individuals hesitant to
innovate, the elements of self-interest still need
to be given as much prominence as possible in the
design of the project.

     For these reasons the Community Development
Division adamantly maintained in the early stages
that no project could be established with government
support unless the farm work was planned and undertaken on an individual basis. Later this position
was modified when it was realized that it was very
difficult to divide up a piece of forest land into
individual parcels until after the clearing of the
land had been completed. In some cases the government
has also supported projects even when they are
organized completely on a communal basis. In the
vast majority of projects, however, the principle of
individual control of plots has been a basic element
in the design. In most cases the villagers themselves
have preferred this approach, and in some other cases
where they have proposed communal work and equal
distribution of profits, the RDO's and other supervisory officials were able to persuade them to adopt the
division of the land in individual parcels.

     With regard to communal versus individual labor,
the Eastern Nigeria experience of community

plantations has certainly not been atypical. Philip
Leis reports that in the Niger Delta area the difficulties involved in cooperative work arrangements led
many villagers to change occupations.[6] J. S. Boston
cites the failure of an attempt in the Igala area of
Nigeria to impose communal oil palm plantations on
a people who have traditionally organized their oil
palm industry individualistically.[7] After discussing
the difficulties faced by communally organized agricultural projects in Tanzania, Ruthenberg states:

> Cooperative actions on the level of
> production usually lack the direct
> relation between the individual's
> efforts and the gain to which small-
> holders are accustomed. Farmers all
> over the world are distrustful people,
> all the more so if they are in an
> early stage of commercialization. One
> always fears that the other one might
> work less. The participants rarely
> feel themselves responsible for the
> success of the cooperative action which
> has been initiated by outside institutions
> anyway. The individual's field comes
> first, and there is nobody who is willing
> or able to press the participants into
> working efficiently.[8]

Regrettably two factors seem to be particularly
prominent in the thinking of those in Eastern Nigeria
and in Africa as a whole, who propose communal
farming projects. One is the erroneous notion that
undeveloped and unsophisticated rural economies are
basically communal in nature, and therefore that
the communal approach is a natural one for farmers
at the level of development found in most parts of
rural Africa. But the nuclear family rather than
the community constitutes the basic economic unit
in the villages of Eastern Nigeria and it probably
has been so ever since farming began. Another
unfortunate influence is the model provided by the
kibbutzim in Israel. Realization of the inappropri-
ateness of this model for Eastern Nigeria has been
slow in coming. It is clear to most observers by

this time, however, that the ethnic-national spirit
and idealistic fervor that sustain these communal
economic ventures in Israel are not present in sufficient quantity in Eastern Nigeria to enable similar
projects to thrive there. Even in Israel the significance of kibbutzim in the agricultural economy is
steadily declining.

The final operational problem of community
plantations worthy of discussion is that of discipline within the project. Even when work is organized
individually and each participant is allocated his
own plot, there have been instances in which members
have been so negligent of their work that the supervising RDO felt they needed to be expelled and their
parcels of land reallocated to farmers who would
take their work more seriously and would make more
productive use of the land. Cases of less importance,
such as failure by an individual to participate in
such communal work projects as the building of an
access road, arise with regularity. The progress of
projects requires some form of discipline and social
control, but this poses one of the greatest problems
not only for community plantations but for village
organizations in Eastern Nigeria generally. It is
generally very difficult for Eastern Nigeria's
village organizations to control their members or
to punish those who violate organizational rules.

Some community plantation projects have been
able to fine those members who fail to appear for
communal work projects. In most project villages,
however, attempts by the project cooperative to
impose fines on those who fail to attend meetings
or appear for communal work have failed. Those
villages that succeed in collecting fines appear to
be able to do so for one or both of two reasons.
Members of these particular projects take sufficient
pride in the project and have developed sufficient
loyalty to it that they feel compelled to succumb to
the cooperative's directives and discipline. Also,
if the project includes virtually all of the farmers
living in the project village, it is difficult for
a participant to find people in the village to support him if he attempts to defy the project's norms
and regulations.

Although the participants in most projects
agree to the desirability of imposing fines on
persons not adhering to rules and requirements laid
down by the cooperative, most project cooperatives
have not accepted the notion that participants
should be expelled from the project, even if they
seriously neglect their duties and responsibilities.
In one project the members did agree to expel a
member, but only because the RDO and the PCV attached
to the project virtually demanded that the person be
expelled. Even then, the final date of expulsion
was extended several times in hopes that the individual would do sufficient work in the interim to
continue to qualify for membership. In two other
projects, after considerable prodding by the RDO and
PCV, the project cooperative decided to expel some
members, but subsequently both cooperatives rescinded
their actions and readmitted the expelled members.
In one case those who had been expelled never
recognized their expulsion and continued to attend
work days and meetings. Deadlines and rules are
easy to formulate, but when their consequences
begin to affect particular individuals it is difficult to impose them.

In trying to comprehend the difficulties such
village organizations as the cooperatives managing
community plantations have in establishing social
control, one must remember that most of the members
of a particular project cooperative are related to
each other. Family relationships and personal ties
have governed their interactions heretofore. To
expel a member from such a cooperative is, to the
Western mind, comparable to firing an employee or
withdrawing someone's club membership. However, to
the farmers in these community plantations expelling
a participant from the project is analogous to
disowing someone from the family.[9]

Despite the considerable operational problems
facing the community plantation program, this approach to the development of large parts of Eastern
Nigeria's rural areas holds enormous potential. It
is based upon technology, which promises substantial
economic rewards to farmers. Moreover, this program

has overcome many of the difficulties encountered
in previous attempts in assisting large numbers of
farmers to increase their incomes. Given the limited
resources available for assistance to these projects,
however, the government must assure that the best
project sites are selected. This is necessitated
both by the widespread demand by villages to obtain
government assistance in establishing community
plantations and by the need for the government to
invest in those villages from which the greatest
return in rural incomes will be forthcoming. A
discussion of one effort to devise a technique for
selecting those project sites with the greatest
chance of success, and in turn the greatest likelihood
of achieving the government's objectives, provides
the subject of Chapter 8.

NOTE ON RECENT DEVELOPMENTS

Of the 85 community plantations successfully
established in the prewar area now constituting
East Central State, 15 survived the war and many of
these are now producing palm oil on a commercial
scale. One of these plantations has 275 acres of
palms in production and another one 330 acres.
Even where communities' plantations were either
burned or became overgrown during the war, most of
these communities are anxious to reestablish them.
However, both because of the need for increased
food production and because of the lack of funds
currently available to revive the Oil Palm Rehabilitation Scheme, the Community Development Division
of East Central State's Ministry of Agriculture has
been encouraging the establishment of community food
farms rather than new community oil palm plantations.
The community approach to food farming permits the
equitable distribution of limited supplies of improved seed and fertilizer, more productive utilization of community-owned land, more efficient utilization of agricultural extension personnel in
promoting improved agricultural practices, and an
opportunity to capitalize on community esprit de corps
for productive purposes--many of the same advantages
accruing from the community plantations. Despite

the present emphasis on food production, the government's intention is to assist with the revival of old community plantations and the organization of new community plantations as soon as this is feasible An experimental effort is being exerted to organize community fishing projects, in which community members would organize themselves into cooperatives and share fishing equipment and undertake smoking and marketing on a cooperative basis. Community works projects to repair damaged roads, bridges, and community buildings are being undertaken by communities as part of the Food for Work Program that distributes food provided by the Rehabilitation Commission to communities engaged in such self-help activities.

NOTES

1.   Arthur Gaitskell, "Observations on Agricultural Development Plans in Eastern Nigeria," 1962 mimeographed, p.14

2.   For a detailed discussion of how the new rural development program was conceived and organize in administrative terms, see R. W. Coatswith, "Establishing a Rural Development Programme in Eastern Nigeria," Administration, III (October 1968) 9-12.

3.   Jerome C. Wells emphasizes this point in "Government Agricultural Investment in Nigeria: 1962-67," (Ann Arbor: Center for Research on Econom Development, University of Michigan, 1968, mimeographed), p. 229.

4.   Oladejo O. Okediji, "The Role of Rational Planning in Economic Development: A Nigerian Example," Human Organization, 28 (Spring 1969), 42-4

5.   The participation of women in this project is partially a function of the unusual pattern followed by many families in this village of forbidding their eldest daughters to marry. These women are still encouraged to have children and they become

heads of their families, and thus assume many of the responsibilities of a man. Several of the female participants in this project are unmarried eldest daughters.

6. Phillip E. Leis, "Palm Oil, Illicit Gin, and the Moral Order of the Ijaw," American Anthropologist, 66 (August 1964), 828-838.

7. J. S. Boston, "The Igala Oil-Palm Industry," Nigerian Institute of Social and Economic Research, Conference Proceedings, March 1962 (Ibadan: 1963, mimeographed), pp. 100-110.

8. Hans Ruthenberg, "Some Characteristics of Smallholder Farming in Tanzania," in Ruthenberg, ed., Smallholder Farming and Smallholder Development in Tanzania (London: C. Hurst and Co., 1968), p. 351.

9. For an enlightening account of the difficulties created when a tribal society has a system imposed upon it whereby relations are governed by impersonal rules and bureaucratic procedures, see Lloyd Fallers, Bantu Bureaucracy: A Century of Political Evolution among the Basoga of Uganda (Cambridge: W. Heffer and Sons, Ltd., 1956).

CHAPTER

8

PREDICTING

SUCCESS

IN

RURAL

DEVELOPMENT

In a developing country like Nigeria where resources are scarce, development projects cannot be
located in every rural community. A careful process
of selection must be undertaken to determine where
limited resources can best be invested. In determining where the greatest potential lies, the development agency must be concerned with both physical
and human resources. If the program is agricultural,
climate and soil must be evaluated, along with the
availability of manpower, land, and markets.
Transportation, processing, and storage facilities
must also be investigated.

In addition to these physical and economic
evaluations, human variables are also critically
important. Considerable advantage could be gained
if one could predict how responsive particular individuals and particular communities would be to a
project and how successfully they would manage it.
This part of the evaluation and selection process
is generally the most difficult because few means
exist by which one can predict responsiveness and
success. Considerable research has been conducted
in the U.S. and abroad on the adoption of innovations
by individual farmers,[1] but practically nothing is
known about what differentiates communities that
are responsive to community project ideas and those
that are not.[2] Valuable resources are often wasted

on communities that end up not being enthusiastic
about the project or not able to cope with it.

Some analysts argue that a development agency
should not confine its attention to potentially
responsive communities, for the agency's task is not
only to establish projects but also to motivate the
unmotivated. This may be a valid approach where
motivation is the greatest obstacle to development
and where one encounters relatively few highly motivated communities, but in places like Eastern Nigeria
where a sufficient number of highly motivated communities do exist, the development agency would do
well to concentrate on these. The best way to stimulate communities that hesitate is to have them wit-
ness the rewards reaped by those that respond.

As a first step in attempting to predict where
development projects can be most successfully established, two aspects of success must be distinguished.
The successful village is one that indicates an interest in launching the project and makes an effort
to do so. In addition to being responsive, the successful village also establishes a viable project.
Although a device that can predict which villages
are likely to be responsive initially may have some
validity in predicting which villages will be able
to carry a project through to the end, the two are
not the same. To be able to predict, however, which
villages will be responsive is of considerable value
in itself. It usually takes several visits to a
community and a succession of village meetings to
explain a project and ascertain whether the villagers
are sincerely interested. To be able to predict
which villages are likely to be responsive and which
are not can permit considerably greater efficiency
in the use of agency personnel, as well as the more
rapid establishment of projects.

In Eastern Nigeria's community plantation
program (described in Chapter 7), the Divisional
Officer, with the assistance of a Rural Development
Officer, is responsible for evaluating prospective
sites for community plantations within his administrative division and then with the assistance of

the RDO supervising their establishment. This involves
his touring extensively and assessing the physical,
economic, and human potential of each village he
visits. (He is assisted in his technical evaluation
by a representative of the Ministry of Agriculture.)
Before he can complete his evaluation and solicit a
definitive response from the community as to whether
they are sincerely interested in establishing a
project, he may have to visit a village 10 to 20
times.

This chapter discusses the development of a
device for predicting which villages in Eastern
Nigeria are likely to be responsive to the community
plantation program. The purpose of this predictive
device is to assist the Divisional Officer and the
RDO in focusing their attention from the outset on
communities that are likely to be responsive, so
that the evaluation, explanation, and response process will be brief, and so they will not waste their
efforts on communities that eventually turn out not
to be interested. After the projects have been in
existence long enough to judge how well they have
been instituted, the same methodological approach
might be used to develop a device to predict longer-
term project success. Thus far only prediction of
initial responsiveness has been worked on.

DEVELOPING THE DEVICE

In developing the device the authors' approach
was to take matched pairs of villages that had proven
in the program to be either responsive or unresponsive, administer a questionnaire in each village,
(see Appendix and Chapter 10), look for significant
differences in community structure and attitudes
held by the people in responsive and unresponsive
villages as revealed by responses to the questionnaire, and then develop a short list of questions
that might be used to predict which newly approached
villages would be responsive and which ones would
not be, or at least which villages would tend to be
more responsive and which ones less responsive. To
find matched pairs of responsive and unresponsive

villages, the authors wrote to all 29 Divisional
Officers in Eastern Nigeria, asking them to send the
names of two communities in their division that fit
the following categories:

1. a community that has accepted the idea of
establishing a community plantation and has made
substantial progress towards establishing such a
plantation;

2. a community that has sufficient land and
population to establish a community farm, but when
the idea was presented to them, they did not turn
out to be interested.

By selecting pairs of villages within particular
divisions there was assurance that the villages were
reasonably well matched in terms of ethnic composition
as well as certain physical characteristics. On the
basis of the responses from the divisional officers, 8
matched pairs were selected, 16 villages in all. Four
pairs were Ibo villages and the other 4 pairs were
Ibibio villages (the Ibos and Ibibios being the two
major ethnic groups in Eastern Nigeria).

The survey was conducted in these 16 villages
by 4 different interviewers. Two Ibo interviewers
handled the Ibo villages and 2 Ibibio interviewers
handled the Ibibio villages. It was made sure that
a single interviewer handled both members of the
pair, so that there was not any interviewer bias in
the comparison of responsive and unresponsive
villages. The interviews with Ibo informants were
conducted in Ibo and those with Ibibios were conducted
in Ibibio. In each village 20 adult males were interviewed, giving a total of 160 persons from responsive villages and 160 persons from unresponsive
villages. (The selection technique is the same as
that described in Chapter 9.) The interviews involved
67 questions, some of which gathered information on
community structure, but most of which were questions
concerning attitudes.[3]

To determine what significant differences existed
in the answers given to the survey questions by
responsive and unresponsive villages, the totals on

responsive and unresponsive villages, the totals on
each question for the responsive group of villages
were contrasted by means of chi-square tests with
the totals for the unresponsive group of villages.
Where differences at the .01 level of significance
were found between the two groups, a further type
of analysis was done. The purpose of this analysis
was to make sure that the differences that were found
were not merely the result of differences between
one or two pairs of villages, because the interest
was in finding questions that consistently (or at
least in most cases) differentiated responsive and
unresponsive villages. In the final designation of
questions that fairly consistently differentiated
responsive and unresponsive villages, those questions
for which (1) the total responses given by the two
sets of villages differed at the .01 level of significance, and (2) the responses given by each matched
pair of villages differed in the expected direction
in at least 5 out of the 8 cases and varied in the
unexpected direction in a maximum of 2 cases were
taken. In other words, the minimal difference that
was acceptable was 5 pairs differing in the expected
direction, 2 differing in the unexpected direction,
and 1 pair identical.

The approach was ex post facto, in that the
villages surveyed had already been approached concerning the establishment of projects before the
authors came to measure attitudes and investigate
community structure. However, in no case had the
initial approach to the village been made more than
24 months before the survey was conducted, and in
most cases the time gap was on the order of 12 months.
Given the basic stability of the attitudes that were
being measured, it seems reasonable to assume that
the measurement gave a fairly accurate indication of
what attitudes prevailed at the time the projects
were initially proposed. The survey itself was
completed within a period of four months, which means
that at the time the villages were surveyed they
were all existing in basically the same political
and economic milieu. Moreover, the survey was completed before August 1966, when Eastern Nigeria began
undergoing so many rapid social, economic, and political changes as a result of the influx of refugees.

DIFFERENCES BETWEEN RESPONSIVE
AND UNRESPONSIVE COMMUNITIES

When the responses to the questionnaires were
tabulated and the results obtained from responsive
and unresponsive villages were compared, the following
differences were found between the two sets of
villages:

1.   responsive villages tend to be more integrated and cohesive with less migration to urban
areas than unresponsive villages;
2.   they also tend to be somewhat more folk-
like;[4]
3.   their inhabitants tend to be more optimistic
about their economic futures,
4.   to be more likely to believe that by working
hard they can improve their position,
5.   to have a more positive attitude toward the
government,
6.   to be more self-reliant, and
7.   to be more fully imbued with (a) the puritan
ethic and (b) the entrepreneurial spirit.[5]

Probably the most interesting difference between
the responsive and unresponsive villages is that
responsive villages tend to be the more traditional
and folk-like. For instance, more people in responsive
communities still hold to the traditional religion
(28 percent in responsive communities compared to
16 percent in unresponsive communities), and they
believe that there is less conflict within their
villages between those who want to do things in modern
and traditional ways. Fewer persons from the responsive villages have migrated to urban areas, and there
is less tendency on the part of those who remain to
ever think of migrating (14 percent and 29 percent).
There also tends to be greater trust of one another
within the responsive villages, in that those in
responsive villages are more likely to say that they
can find someone in their village who can be trusted
to handle large sums of the community's money without
taking any for himself (85 percent and 74 percent).

There also seems to be greater harmony within
the responsive villages, since those coming from
responsive villages are more likely to say that in
the past they have gotten whole-hearted cooperation
on community projects (98 percent and 79 percent).
In line with the more traditional outlook, there is
also a difference in literacy levels. In the responsive villages 28 percent of those interviewed are
literate, while 41 percent in the unresponsive
villages are literate. However, this difference
does not occur in enough of the pairs of villages to
meet the standard set for significance. Overall, the
responsive villages offer a picture of somewhat
greater isolation and traditionalism, plus greater
homogeneity and integration.[6]

This picture stands in sharp contrast to conven-
tional ideas of what sorts of communities "choose
progress." In selecting a community for a development
project one would ordinarily be inclined to look for
a community with a high literacy rate, extensive
urban contact, and as little traditionalism as possible. The authors' findings are just the opposite.
In understanding these results, however, it is important to keep in mind the nature of the development
project being introduced: It is an agricultural
project and it is a community project. It is quite
possible that a project that does not depend upon
community-wide cooperation would find fertile ground
in some of the villages that are not responsive to
this project.[7] In similar fashion, maybe a cottage
industry project would be more appealing to the
communities that reject the agricultural project.
Education and urban contact often turn people against
farming as an occupation, and this is very likely
one force at work in those communities that did not
respond to the community plantation scheme, even
though the vast majority of residents in all the
villages surveyed are farmers. Consistent with this
line of reasoning, as mentioned in Chapter 7 it was
found that where projects are established, young
men who have recently left school are on the whole
less enthusiastic and less conscientious in their
work than are those who are illiterate.

Another difference between responsive and unresponsive communities is that those from responsive
villages tend to be more optimistic. They are more
likely to believe that their village is progressing
rapidly (34 percent and 17 percent) and to think that
in five years time their village will be better off
economically than it is today (84 percent and 69
percent). From the observations there is no objective
basis for thinking that one set of villages would be
able to progress faster than the other set. The
reason for differing responses being given to these
questions seems to be simply a difference in outlook
and attitude.

This positive outlook finds expression in two
other areas as well. The informants from responsive
villages are more likely to believe in the possibility
of improving their economic situation, in that they
are more likely to say that one can improve his
economic position through hard work (78 percent and
63 percent). Also, they have a more positive attitude
toward the government, in that they are more inclined
to believe that the government is trying to help
them (87 percent and 67 percent). Those from unresponsive villages are more likely to believe that
the government is being run just for the benefit of
those who are doing the governing.

A final set of differences between those interviewed in responsive and unresponsive villages relates to achievement motivation.[8] Those from responsive villages tend to be more self-reliant, and
to be more imbued with the puritan ethic and the
entrepreneurial spirit. Self-reliance is implied
in a question that asks whether the construction of
a new village school should be the responsibility
of the villagers themselves or the government.
Those from unresponsive villages are more likely
than those from responsive villages to say it is
the government's responsibility (30 percent and 14
percent), while those from responsive villages are
more likely to say it is the villagers' responsibility. The puritan ethic is revealed in a question
that asks whether they think it is advisable to
forego immediate pleasures in order to achieve more

lasting satisfactions in the future. Those from
responsive villages are more likely to believe one
should forego immediate pleasures (92 percent and
79 percent).

The entrepreneurial spirit is evident in a question that asks whether they would prefer to be employed
by another person, employed by a company, or be self-
employed. Of all the questions asked, this question
produced the greatest difference between the two sets
of communities. Those from responsive communities
are much more likely to prefer to run their own business. Of those in responsive communities, 70 percent
said they would prefer to start their own business,
compared with 39 percent in unresponsive communities.
From unresponsive communities, 60 percent said they
would like to be employed by somebody, compared to
29 percent in the responsive communities.

THE PREDICTIVE DEVICE

The main purpose of determining which questionnaire items differentiate responsive and unresponsive
communities was to enable us to compile a list of
questions that could be used to predict which communities would be likely to be responsive and which
ones unresponsive. The following questions are the
ones that, on the basis of our analysis, should have
the best predictive value:

1. How many members of your family (mother,
father, children, uncles, aunts, and first cousins)
have migrated away from this village and are currently
living in an urban area?
2. Do you ever think seriously about moving
away and living in another village or a city?
3. When it comes to cooperating on some community project, how well do the people of this village
cooperate?
4. Is there much conflict in this village
between people who want to do things in the old ways
and people who want to do things in the new ways?
5. Are there any people in this village whom
you would trust to be treasurer of a cooperative

and to handle hundreds of pounds without taking any
for himself?

6. What would you say about the progress of
this village? Would you say it is progressing rapidly,
progressing slowly, or not progressing at all?

7. Some people say that through working harder,
you will attain a higher standard of living. What
would you say?

8. Some people say the government is run just
for the benefit of those in power. Others say that
the government is run to benefit the people. What
do you say?

9. Suppose this village wanted a new school
built. Who should be mainly responsible for this
sort of project--the government, the villagers, or
both together?

10. If you could choose, would you rather be
employed by somebody or start your own business?

11. Do you agree, partly agree, or disagree
with the following statement: It is a wise man who
learns to forego immediate pleasures in order to
achieve more lasting satisfactions sometime in the
future.

12. (To be answered by the interviewer) How
cooperative was the informant in answering your
questions?

Not only did these questions provoke significantly different answers from responsive and unresponsive villages in the test interviews, but their
inclusion can be defended on logical grounds as well,
since the answer to each of these questions reveals
something that has a direct bearing on the establishment of a community plantation. Questions 1, 2, 3,
and 4 are important for the following reason: For
a community to be responsive to the idea of a community plantation and for such a plantation to be
successfully established, it is important that the
community be cohesive, that personal relations be
harmonious, and that the villagers' principal loyalty
be to the village rather than to some other group or
locality. If the villagers are contemplating migrating, then they will not be interested in making
a long-term investment in the village. Village
integration and harmony are particularly important

in community activities in Eastern Nigeria, because of the nature of traditional political organization there. The absence of centralized control within most Eastern Nigerian villages means that there is generally no authority within a village that can command support or coerce people to cooperate. For a community project to be established, the whole community has to be supportive.

Question 5 is not only of value in helping reveal the degree of integration and harmony within a village; it is also of value in a more specific way. A community plantation is run by a cooperative, which has a treasury, and such a cooperative can only operate successfully if the people in the community trust one another sufficiently to be able to select a man to handle the cooperative's funds. Answers to question 6 help reveal the extent to which the villagers think it is worthwhile investing in their village. They also reflect more general attitudes concerning the extent to which it is worthwhile investing in anything or hoping for a better life. Question 7 indicates whether they think the economic, social, political, and supernatural forces impinging on them are such that through their own effort they can get ahead in life or not. If no amount of hard work can improve someone's position, then there is little point in his trying a new economic experiment or adding a new responsibility to those he already bears.

The community plantation scheme involves government assistance and government supervision being given to those who start plantations, and responses to question 8 are important indicators of how much the villagers trust the government's good intentions. Some communities that do not exhibit an interest in establishing community plantations believe the scheme is an attempt on the government's part to steal their land or to make them labor on something from which only the government will benefit.

The willingness of villagers to take initiative and assume responsibility is reflected in answers given to question 9. Many villagers believe that

initiative for any project should come from the
government rather than from themselves. Since a
community plantation requires considerable local
initiative with little government assistance, a community that looks to the government to push it along
will not be the sort of community that can establish
a successful community plantation. Question 10 also
relates to self-reliance and is a key question in
determining whether a village would be a good prospect
The reason given most frequently by villagers for not
wanting to start plantations is that they do not
want to assume responsibility for the project. They
would prefer to have the government organize the
project and hire them as laborers, which would assure
them a steady income and would let the government
assume the risks. These are the sorts of individuals
who would answer question 10 by saying they would
like to be employed by somebody. Individuals who
are prepared to start their own business, however,
prefer to work on their own and are prepared to assume
risks in the hopes of realizing a higher return on
their investment of land and labor. Such individuals
are the ones who are more likely to start successful
community plantations.

    Aside from subsidy payments by the government,
a participant in a community plantation project does
not begin to realize a return from his investment
for about six years, which is the period required
for oil palm trees to start producing. This means
that participants must be prepared to have their
rewards delayed for a considerable period, and this
is what makes question 11 relevant. Unless someone
is prepared to forego immediate pleasures for the
sake of larger rewards in the future, then the community plantation concept will not be attractive.

    In the attitude survey, responsive and unre-
sponsive villages differed sharply in terms of how
cooperative the informants were with the interviewer,
and this is the reason for including question 12.
Unless a village is prepared to cooperate with outside
agents, and particularly agents of government, then
it would be very difficult to work with them in
establishing a community plantation. A lack of

cooperation with the interviewer most likely results
from a suspiciousness of outsiders in general and of
agents of government in particular.

APPLICATION AND CONDITIONS FOR USE

It needs to be reemphasized that the predictive
device discussed here was developed for use in a
specific locality and for a specific type of development project. At this point it is impossible to
claim any wider applicability. Moreover, the authors
can only claim it to be of value in predicting a
community's responsiveness to the project proposal;
it does not differentiate between responsive villages
whose projects turn out to be long-term successes,
and those that do not.

In order for this device to be used to assist
officials to site community plantations in the best
locations, they could interview 20 adult males in
each prospective village. Some method of selection
needs to be employed to choose the 20 persons to be
interviewed, and since census lists are generally
not available, it probably will be necessary to use
some type of systematic sampling, taking one informant from every fifth house, or some comparable
formula. Each interview should take only 10 to 15
minutes, and the whole selection and interviewing
process for 20 informants in a village should not
exceed 4 hours.

The following system could be used to give each
of the villages surveyed a score for potential responsiveness: After all the villages in an area have
been surveyed, the responses for each question can
be totaled. The percentage breakdown of these totals
can be used as a norm against which to judge whether
each individual village deviates on a particular
question in the direction of potential responsiveness
or unresponsiveness. A village can be given a plus
for each question on which it deviates from the norm
in the direction of responsiveness, and a minus for
each time it deviates toward unresponsiveness.
After the pluses and minuses are totaled, each village

TABLE 4

Results of Initial Questionnaire Survey

Question	Totals for All 16 Villages A	Responsive Villages B (in percents)	Unresponsive Villages C
1. How many members of your family (mother, father, children, uncles, aunts, and first cousins) have migrated away from this village and are currently living in an urban area?			
a. 0-2	62	72	52
b. 3-5	22	17	26
c. 6 or more	15	10	21
d. no answer	1	1	1
2. Do you ever think seriously about moving away and living in another village or a city?			
a. often	11	5	16
b. sometimes	11	9	13
c. never or hardly ever	78	86	70
d. no answer	0	0	1
3. When it comes to cooperating on some community project, how well do the people of this village cooperate?			
a. much cooperation	88	98	79
b. fair cooperation	7	2	12
c. poor cooperation	3	1	6
d. no answer	2	0	3
4. Is there much conflict in this village between people who want to do things in the old ways and people who want to do things in the new ways?			
a. much conflict	4	1	7
b. some conflict	39	36	42
c. hardly any or no conflict	57	62	51
d. no answer	1	1	1
5. Are there any people in this village whom you would trust to be treasurer of a cooperative and to handle hundreds of pounds without taking any for himself?			
a. yes	80	85	74
b. no	18	14	21
c. no answer	3	1	5
6. What would you say about the progress of this village? Would you say it is progressing rapidly, progressing slowly, or not progressing at all?			
a. progressing rapidly	26	34	17
b. progressing slowly	58	59	58
c. not progressing	14	6	22
d. no answer	2	1	2

Question	Totals for All 16 Villages A	Responsive Villages B	Unresponsive Villages C
		(in percents)	
Some people say that through working harder, you will attain a higher standard of living. What would you say?			
a. I don't believe it	10	3	17
b. it would help a little, but not enough to be worth the effort	18	19	18
c. yes, it would definitely help	71	78	63
d. no answer	1	0	2
Some people say the government is run just for the benefit of those in power. Others say that the government is run to benefit the people. What do you say?			
a. only for those in power	14	10	18
b. for the people	77	87	67
c. no answer	9	3	16
Suppose this village wanted a new school built. Who should be mainly responsible for this sort of project--the government, the villagers, or both together?			
a. government	22	14	30
b. villagers	43	49	37
c. both together	35	37	32
d. no answer	0	0	1
If you could choose, would you rather be employed by somebody or start your own business?			
a. by another person or a company	45	29	60
b. start my own business	54	70	39
c. no answer	1	1	1
Do you agree, partly agree, or disagree with the following statement: It is a wise man who learns to forego immediate pleasures in order to achieve more lasting satisfactions sometime in the future.			
a. agree	86	92	79
b. partly agree	5	2	9
c. disagree	8	6	11
d. no answer	1	0	2
(To be answered by the interviewer) How cooperative was the informant in answering your questions?			
a. very good	45	52	38
b. good	25	23	26
c. fair	24	18	30
d. poor	4	4	3
e. very poor	1	1	1
f. no answer	1	1	1

can be given a score, and the villages can be ranked.
Assuming other factors being approximately equal,
those villages that are at the top of the list should
be the best prospects for projects.

This device is still too crude to be able to
suggest a cut-off score, with those villages scoring
above tending to be responsive and those below tending
to be unresponsive. The best one can do at this
stage is to rank a group of villages in terms of how
responsive they are likely to be.

Column A in Table 4 gives the gross totals for
all the villages surveyed in the initial survey, and
if one wanted to score each village in that survey,
this is the norm against which one would judge responses by each village. From columns B and C one
can see the direction in which the responsive and
unresponsive villages surveyed tend to deviate from
this norm.

The instrument discussed in this chapter was
developed at the request of the Eastern Nigerian
government because government officials realized
the difficulties involved in selecting the best
possible villages for siting community plantations.
Although such factors as the availability and suitability of land and the availability of manpower are
also seen to be important, the potential responsiveness of the villagers in a particular locality is
of critical significance to the government in determining where it should invest its scarce resources.
The technique used in developing the instrument was
the following: By means of a questionnaire differences were discovered in attitudes and community
structure between pilot villages that were responsive
to the idea of community plantations and those that
were unresponsive. These differences were then used
as a basis for developing a short list of questions
that can be used elsewhere as predictor of responsive
ness in potential project areas.

The approach used recognizes the significance
of cultural, social, and psychological factors in
economic development, and enables project planners

and organizers to take these factors into account
when instituting a development program. Although
this instrument was developed for use in Eastern
Nigeria in siting a particular type of development
project, the technique utilized in developing the
instrument ought to have wider applicability. It
also suggests an avenue for making the field of rural
development somewhat more scientific and the results
deriving from a rural development program somewhat
more predictable, since it illustrates that more
scientific means can be employed to determine where
rural development projects should be sited.

NOTES

1. See, for instance, Everett Rogers, Diffusion
of Innovations (New York: The Free Press of Glencoe,
1962); J. P. Hrabovszky and T. D. Moulik, "Economic
and Social Factors Associated with the Adoption of
an Improved Implement: A Study of the Olpad Thresher
in India," Agricultural Development Council Paper,
1967; Robert C. Clark and I. A. Akinbode, "Factors
Associated with the Adoption of Three Farm Practices
in Western Nigeria," n.p. 1967, mimeographed; and
Joseph R. Ascroft, Niels G. Roling, Graham B. Kerr,
and Gerald D. Hursh, "Patterns of Diffusion in
Eastern Nigeria" (East Lansing: Department of Communication, Michigan State University, 1969, mimeographed).

2. Howard Schuman conducted a psychological
survey of a set of villages participating in the
Comilla program in Pakistan and a set of control
villages. However, his interest was not in predicting
responsiveness but in analyzing the kind of psychological impact the Comilla program had upon its participants. Howard Schuman, "Economic Development
and Individual Change: A Social-Psychological Study
of the Comilla Experiment in Pakistan," Occasional
Papers in International Affairs, No. 15 (Cambridge,
Mass.: Harvard University Center for International
Affairs, 1967). Hursh, Roling, and Kerr studied
characteristics of villages whose individual residents had adopted or had not adopted particular

agricultural innovations being offered by the Ministr
of Agriculture. This was primarily a study of individual responsiveness rather than village responsiveness. Gerald D. Hursh, Niels G. Roling, and Graham
B. Kerr, "Innovation in Eastern Nigeria: Success
and Failure of Agricultural Programs in 71 Villages
of Eastern Nigeria" (East Lansing: Department of
Communication, Michigan State University, 1968,
mimeographed).

3. The questionnaire employed in this analysis
was also used for the rural attitude survey discusse
in Chapters 10 and 11. See Chapter 10 for a discussion of the questionnaire and the Appendix for a
copy of it. Some of the questions used were adapted
from a questionnaire prepared by William F. Whyte
and Lawrence Williams for their study of rural devel
opment in the highlands of Peru, and the authors
are indebted to Whyte for permitting them to use
the questions.

4. Robert Redfield, "The Folk Society," The
American Journal of Sociology, LII (January 1947),
293-308.

5. There was also a significant difference in
the average age of the informants from the two sets
of communities, but internal checks indicated that
this was a sampling bias, rather than a real difference. However, this difference in age did pose the
possibility that the other differences found betwee
the two sets of communities might be because of
differences in the ages of the informants rather
than anything relating to responsiveness. To test
this, the two samples were adjusted statistically
until they contained approximately the same age
distributions. When the two sets of communities
were compared again, significant differences were
found on the same questionnaire items as were found
originally. This indicated that age was not the
cause of the differences.

6. This term is being used here as it is in
Alexander Leighton, et al., Psychiatric Disorder
Among the Yourba (Ithaca, N.Y.: Cornell University
Press, 1963), pp. 203-240.

7. The importance of the community aspect of
the project in understanding our findings is suggested
by the fact that Hursh, Roling, and Kerr (pp. 78 and
115) claim to have found, although their findings
were not conclusive, that villages in Eastern Nigeria
with higher levels of education and greater exposure
to urban influences tend to have more individual
agricultural innovators. On the other hand, Anthony
and Johnston found the farmers of Northern Katsina
to have very little interest in western education
and yet to be quite responsive to agricultural innovations. Kenneth Anthony and Bruce F. Johnston,
"Field Study of Agricultural Change: Northern
Katsina, Nigeria" (Stanford, Calif.: Food Research
Institute, Stanford University, 1968, mimeographed),
p. 67.

8. David C. McClelland, "The Achievement Motive
in Economic Growth," in B. F. Hoselitz and W. E.
Moore, eds., Industrialization and Society (The
Hague: UNESCO-Mouton, 1963), pp. 74-96.

9

SETTLEMENT
SCHEMES
AS AN APPROACH
TO
RURAL DEVELOPMENT

It has been estimated that since 1955 1 percent of the entire population of Africa has been moved from its traditional homesteads to new areas by government-sponsored development projects.[1] In most of these cases resettlement has been necessitated by such projects as the construction of dams and the creation of man-made lakes. In these instances people are resettled because they happen to be where they are not wanted; their resettlement is not for the purpose of improving their economic position.[2] Some dam projects, such as the Volta project, have attempted to improve the economic opportunities of those relocated, but these efforts have not thus far been uniformly successful.[3]

Despite the fact that most resettlement projects in Africa have paid relatively little attention to the social and economic betterment of those being resettled, some resettlement schemes have had this as their principal purpose. The best documented cases of such projects include the Niger project,[4] the land settlement schemes in Kenya, the Mwea project,[5] and the villagization scheme in Tanzania, all of which involve voluntary resettlement, and the Zande Scheme, where relocation was forced.[6] In the Kenya scheme 35,000 families (180,000 individuals) have been settled in the former White Highlands on land previously farmed by Europeans.[7] According to

de Wilde, the basic concern of this Million Acre
Settlement Scheme in Kenya "was not with the maxi-
mization of output, but with the accommodation of
more Africans on the land that was previously owned
by Europeans."[8] In general, the scheme has involved
little experimentation with new methods of production
or with new settlement patterns; for example, no
attempt has been made to cluster the settlers into
village units as an alternative to the traditional
Kikuyu pattern of living in scattered homesteads.[9]

The Village Settlement Scheme in Tanzania
emphasized the grouping together of peasant farmers
into nucleated villages to provide a basis for the
provision of amenities and educational facilities.
Once the farm families were gathered into village
communities, the government attempted to introduce
new communally operated and mechanized farming
systems. Aaron Segal characterizes the Tanzanian
scheme in the following fashion:

>The village settlements are much more
>important as social than as economic
>experiments. Economically, they are
>capital-intensive mechanized farms
>managed by expatriate technical experts
>until and when they are turned over to
>African cooperators. Socially, they are
>the first attempt to deliberately produce
>in East Africa organized multitribal
>village life based on modernized farming
>and communal tenure.[10]

The current effort in Tanzania to create Ujamma
villages is a modification of the village settlement
approach. Families form Ujamma villages by voluntari
deciding to farm cooperatively and by moving their
homesteads into a centralized area to facilitate
this new economic arrangement.

The farm settlement scheme of Eastern Nigeria
discussed in Chapters 4 and 7 provides an example
of a comprehensive but costly approach to agricultura
settlement. The farm settlements of Western Nigeria,
although predating the Eastern Nigeria scheme by a

few years, are based on a similar approach in that
both programs are largely modeled after the Israeli
Moshav.[11]

RESETTLEMENT TO ACHIEVE MORE
ECONOMIC UTILIZATION OF LAND:
THE UGWUAKU SCHEME

It is apparent that settlement schemes in Africa
have had a variety of economic, social, and political
purposes, and that even when the purposes of two
schemes have been approximately the same, the means
employed to achieve this end have often differed.
The Ugwuaku project in Okigwi Division of Eastern
Nigeria (see Map 2, p. 228) seeks to achieve a more
economic utilization of land in that part of the
region, through moving farm families from densely
populated areas where land is scarce to sections
where farm land is more abundantly available.

A glance at the census figures for Eastern Nigeria
quickly reveals the unevenness of population distribution. Sections of Onitsha and Owerri Provinces
have population densities in excess of 1,600 persons
per square mile, while the Calabar, Cross River, and
delta areas, which together constitute approximately
one third of Eastern Nigeria's land area, have less
than 100 persons per square mile. In some places,
such as portions of Udi and Nsukka Divisions, low
population density is related to low soil fertility,
but in general the relationship between population
density and soil fertility is inverse. In high-
population areas land has been overused and soils
depleted, while in most low-population areas soil
fertility remains high. If the farming population
could be more evenly distributed, total productivity
could be substantially increased; some areas are
underproductive because of overuse and other areas
are underproductive because of underuse. While
farmers in some areas are trying to eke out an
existence on farms of less than one acre, virgin
lands lie untouched elsewhere.

After commenting on the important role settlement

MAP 2

RESETTLEMENT SCHEMES: UGWUAKU AND ABAKALIKI

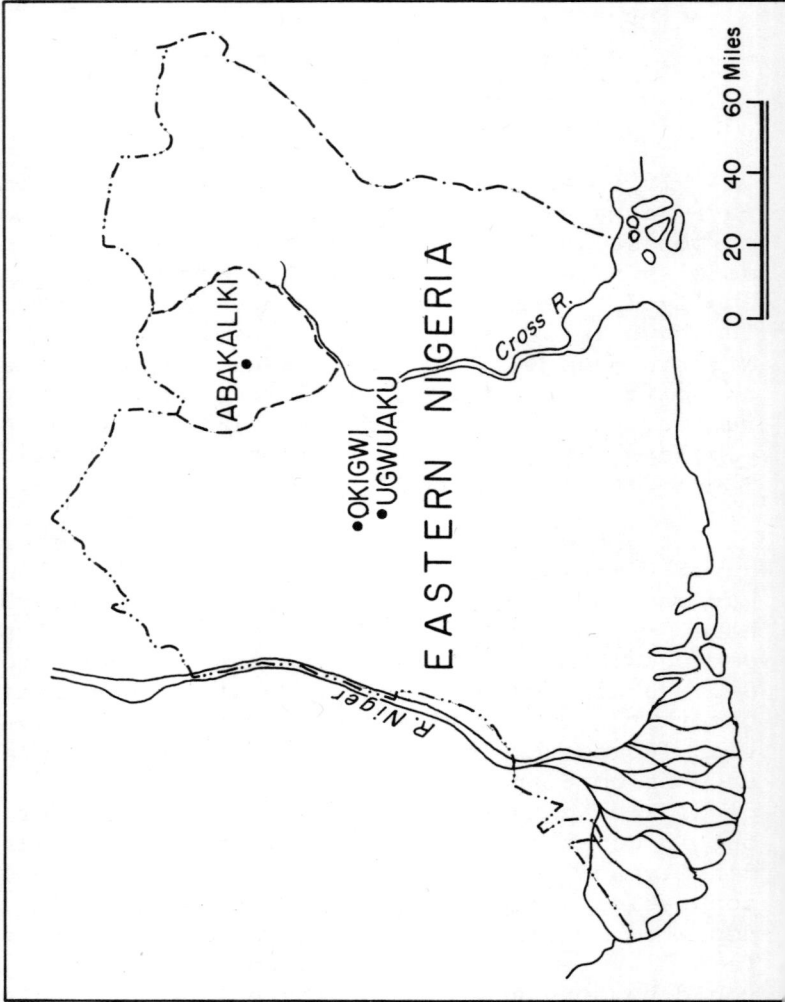

of virgin areas played during the nineteenth century in the United States in preventing the build-up of excessive population pressure, F. F. Hill of the Ford Foundation states:

> The moral of the U.S. story--if there is one--is that a country such as Nigeria which has undeveloped lands ought to pursue a vigorous policy of settlement in new areas as part of its total develop-ment program. I should think it highly improbable that business and industry can be developed fast enough during, say the next 50 years to prevent substantial pressure of population on the land in the old settled areas. If this develops, fragmentation of land (or farm incomes) can easily lead to a sub-stantial degree of rural stagnation.[12]

Unfortunately, this sort of stagnation already prevails in the most densely populated portions of Eastern Nigeria, but it could be stemmed or reversed at least in part by population redistribution.

Some population redistribution occurs spontane-ously at the present time, but not on the scale that Hill is advocating. Wealthy farmers acquire pieces of land in places like Calabar and Ogoja to develop plantations, and relatively large numbers of small farmers migrate on an annual basis to localities where land can be leased.[13] Despite the number of farmers involved in these migratory movements, they provide no real solution to the problem. Even with these migrations, excessive variations in the intensity of land use still prevail. Moreover, these migratory tenant farmers are usually given use of land on a year-to-year basis, which means that they tend to exploit the land with little concern for its future productivity. They also have little incentive for investing in permanent improvements such as drainage or irrigation systems, and they are not permitted to plant tree crops, which currently offer the greatest potential return in most portions of the region.

Settlement of virgin land in a manner comparable to American homesteading has occurred in some parts of Africa. For instance, such migration and settlement of virgin areas has taken place since World War I in the Sukumuland section of Tanzania with a minimum of government encouragement and assistance.[14] Daryll Forde and Richenda Scott have advocated "a general 'creep' of population into under-settled areas" in Eastern Nigeria.[15] What should not be forgotten in the Eastern Nigerian situation, however, is that all the virgin areas in the region are owned by particular communities or lineages. Homesteading or "creeping" can only be encouraged if the landowners agree to make their land available to the settlers, or are forced to do so. As described in the next section of this chapter, the people of Abakaliki have a history of encroaching on the land of neighboring groups and slowly expanding the boundaries of their farming communities, and this was a pattern followed by other groups in Eastern Nigeria in earlier times. However, the Eastern Nigeria government can neither encourage nor condone migratory movements that involve the stealing of land by the migrants.

The unwillingness of most landowners to sell land has been discussed in Chapter 6, as has the reluctance on the part of landlords to allow tenants to plant tree crops or to agree to tenancy arrangements beyond a single season. In addition to these barriers posed by land tenure patterns, ethnic and cultural differences between tenants and landlords often give rise to suspicion and hostility, and as a result there is considerable reluctance in many land-plentiful localities to permit outsiders to settle. This tendency is accentuated by the fact that the land-scarce areas are generally populated by Ibos and Ibibios, while the land-plentiful areas of Calabar and the Cross River plains are populated by smaller ethnic groups with distinctive cultural traditions and fears of being engulfed by the larger ethnic groups who need room for expansion. Furthermore, among potential tenants there is sometimes a reluctance to break ties with their home village and settle among people they do not know and may not trust.[16]

In attempting to effect a redistribution of population in order to increase agricultural productivity,
two general approaches suggest themselves. The first
involves moving people from the densely populated
areas to the virtually unpopulated portions of Calabar
Province and the Cross River plain. Although this
approach theoretically holds the greatest potential,
the cultural diversity and traditional hostilities
between potential settlers and landlords make this
approach of doubtful feasibility. It is probably
best for the present to encourage immigration and
the leasing or sale of land in these areas on an
individual basis rather than organizing a government
program. One possible means of encouraging the
leasing, sale, and productive exploitation of land
in these places is to impose a land tax on land which
is unused or underutilized.[17]

A second, somewhat more modest approach to the
redistribution of the farming population is to
resettle people close to their home villages where
underutilized land can be found. With surprising
frequency one encounters communities with an abundance
of land and communities with a scarcity of land in
close proximity to each other. Many such areas are
currently farmed by tenant farmers who lease the
land on a seasonal basis, and permanent settlement
of such places might in the first instance be by
these migratory tenants. Where there are no such
tenants or where the tenants are unwilling to settle
or are not acceptable to the landowners, other farmers
from nearby densely populated areas could be encouraged to settle there.

A resettlement scheme of this type has several
potential beneficial consequences. Unused or underutilized land can be more fully exploited, agricultural productivity can be increased, the farm
incomes of the settlers can be improved, and the
landowners can profit more fully from their previously
unused or underutilized land. Moreover, the influx
of settlers into an underpopulated area can aid the
residents of that area in financing the construction
and maintenance of schools, health facilities, and
other amenities.

TABLE 5

Population of Umuagwu Ugwuaku

Married men resident at home	26	
Unmarried men resident at home	5	
Married men resident "abroad," i.e., living in urban areas	2	
Unmarried men resident abroad	4	
Total number of men		37
Married women	39	
Unmarried women (including widows)	10	
Total number of women		49
Total number of children		128
Total population		214

When the possibility of such a pilot resettlemen
project in Eastern Nigeria was posed in 1965, government officials generally recognized the potential
payoff, but were skeptical of the project's feasibility. They expressed doubts that potential settler
would be willing to be uprooted from their villages
and settle in an alien environment. Of even greater
concern, however, was whether villages with surplus
land could be found that would be prepared to accept
strangers into their community and make land availabl
on a permanent or long-term basis.

The pilot project site selected was Umuagwu
Ugwuaku, one of the four subdivisions of Ugwuaku,
which lies in the Northern Okigwi County Council area
in Okigwi Division. Despite the fact that portions
of Okigwi Division have densities exceeding 1,200
persons per square mile, many communities have sizabl
pieces of unused or underused land. Ugwuaku is such
a place. Table 5 indicates the composition of the
small pilot project community of Umuagwu Ugwuaku.

All the Ugwuaku men who are resident at home are
farmers, although some are also part-time petty trade
or fishermen. All the women also farm, and have full
responsibility for processing palm products, as well
as cultivating and processing cassava and all other
vegetables except yams. In 1965 all the houses were

were of mud with thatched roofs, except for one house
made of cement blocks. These houses were situated on
both sides of a road that passed through the center
of the village. Until 1964 this road was merely a
footpath, but it was then improved so that trucks
could drive into the village to collect farm produce.

Agriculture in Ugwuaku is strictly traditional
in character, in that the palms are wild, cultivation
of crops is done by hoe, no fertilizer is used, etc.
The only exception to this lies in the community oil
palm plantation started in 1965 with the assistance
of the Ministry of Rural Development and the Ministry
of Agriculture. On this plantation, which is organized
along the lines described in Chapter 7, 23 acres of
oil palm were planted in 1965 and an additional 15
acres were planted in 1966. All the able-bodied
farmers of the village participated in the project.

The land of Umuagwu Ugwuaku is divided into three
categories: The land along either side of the road
running through the village has been used for the
construction of houses, and the plots upon which
houses stand are owned by the individuals who own
the houses; the land surrounding the residential area
is owned by the various extended families of the
village, and is devoted to food production; a small
river serves as one outer boundary of the farming
area and divides land used for food crops and unused
land that is communally owned by the whole village
and which in 1965 was designated as the site for the
community plantation.

Because Umuagwu Ugwuaku has more land than its
farmers can effectively utilize, between 10 and 20
tenant farmers from nearby villages lease land here
each year. These tenants come from villages where
land is either not as fertile or not as abundant as
it is in Ugwuaku. Since the tenants are usually
relatives or friends of the landowners, no rent is
charged, but they are expected to make a gift of palm
wine and yams to the landowners at the time of harvest.
To safeguard against these tenants ever claiming
ownership of the land they farm in Ugwuaku, landlords
only permit them to use a particular piece of land

for a single growing season. For the same reason
they are not allowed to plant tree crops on their
leased plots, even though Ugwuaku's land is ideal
for both cocoa and oil palms. Since these tenant
farmers come from nearby villages, they never put up
houses in Ugwuaku or remain overnight; they come to
Ugwuaku for a day at a time and return to their home
villages at night.

     At various times in the past individual families
from outside have been allowed to settle in Ugwuaku
on a permanent basis, not unlike many other villages
in Eastern Nigeria that on occasion accept families
prepared to break all links with their place of birth
Five of the 31 households in Ugwuagwu Ugwuaku are
composed of strangers, some of whom settled there as
long ago as 1935. No new families had been permitted
to settle in Ugwuaku since 1960; infact, Ugwuaku neve
has actively encouraged outsiders to settle there.
The integration of these stranger families into the
community has involved the stranger's attaching
himself to an Ugwuaku family, which provided him with
shelter and land to farm. If he proved to be of good
character, he was permitted to plant crops on some
of the community's communal farm land. After a
probationary period he was assigned a piece of land
upon which he could build a house. After 20 or 30
years he may eventually be accorded some more owner-
like control over the land he has been farming. To
become fully accepted by the Ugwuaku community he
had to swear an oath that he would cause no trouble.
He also had to take full part in community activities
and pay his share when collections were taken up for
community projects.

     Several elements distinguish the settlement
scheme initiated in Ugwuaku in 1966 from the traditional method of integrating strangers into the
community. In contrast to the new scheme, the traditional method involved small numbers of settlers,
a lengthy period of testing and integration, a
prohibition against strangers planting tree crops
for many years, and a very slow process of land
acquisition. The people of Ugwuaku were prepared to
modify radically their attitudes toward settlers

partly because the government was involved in this scheme, and partly because they felt the government would protect them against any attempts by the settlers to steal their land or to cause any other kind of damage or disturbance. When the government surveyed the land and worked out a registered lease agreement with the settlers, it both assured the settlers of long-term use of the land and guaranteed the Ugwuaku people that the settlers could never claim full owner-ship of the land even though they planted trees on it. The Ugwuaku people also see the settlers con-tributing in important measure to the development of their community. They realize that unlike larger communities they will never be able to finance the construction and maintenance of schools, churches, maternity centers, markets, water systems, and health centers unless their population grows. Their hope is that with an increased population and increased farm incomes, these village amenities will be within their grasp. Ugwuaku has a primary school, but its most consuming ambition is to provide secondary school and university scholarships to children from the community, and eventually to build its own secondary school.

The plan for the Ugwuaku settlement scheme, which later became known as a "village farm settlement," was predicated upon certain key principles: (1) The project had to be economically attractive to both Ugwuaku and the settlers; (2) it had to strive for the successful integration of the settlers, in the hopes that the community would remain unified; (3) the interests of both landowners and settlers in regard to leasing and land tenure arrangements had to be adequately protected; and (4) the project had to keep its capital costs as low as possible to avoid the pitfall into which Eastern Nigeria's farm settle-ments and most other settlement schemes in Africa have fallen. The details of the plan were worked out jointly by representatives of government and the Ugwuaku villagers. As with community plantations, the government officials involved included represen-tatives of the Divisional Office for Okigwi, the Ministry of Rural Development, and the Ministry of Agriculture. Assistance was also given by members

of the Ford Foundation advisory team and two Peace
Corps Volunteers. Despite the fact that relatively
small numbers of people were to be resettled in this
project, the plan was devised with considerable care
since it was hoped that it could serve as a prototype
for comparable projects elsewhere in Eastern Nigeria.

Although the preliminary estimates of Ugwuaku's
surplus land were larger, once a survey had been
completed it was ascertained that 216 acres were
available. The responsible officials decided that
this would provide sufficient plantation land for
the farmers of Ugwuaku plus 20 settlers. To relieve
the Ugwuaku people's apprehensions vis-à-vis settlers
who might come from distant and culturally dissimilar
localities, applications for these 20 places were
solicited only from farmers coming from the land-
starved portions of Okigwi Division. Again at the
request of the Ugwuaku people, the Divisional Officer
for Okigwi was made responsible for selection of the
settlers from among the applicants. With 20 settlers
and 23 active farmers from Ugwuaku, there was sufficient land for each participant in the expanded oil
palm community plantation to have five acres under
his control. In addition, half-acre plots within
the existing food-crop area were assigned to each
villager and each settler to enable them to plant
food crops and build a house. Rent was initially
set at five shillings per acre for both residential
and development plots, and this money went to the
farm cooperative society of which both farmers from
Ugwuaku and settlers were members. The cooperative
agreed to give one third of these rent payments to
the landowners, and the remaining two thirds to the
Town Fund to finance such village development projects
as the construction of a medical dispensary.

Since a large portion of the rent money is to
be used for village improvement, the settlers benefit
along with the landowners from the rent they pay for
the project land. The lease assures use of the land
by all members of the cooperative for a period of
99 years. Given this security of land tenure, the
permission granted to plant tree crops on their leased
land, and the fact that the five and one half acres

each settler has for his farm and residence is considerably more land than he had in his home village, the project has proven very attractive in economic terms to the settlers. By the time the civil war started in July 1967, only 1 of the 20 settlers had dropped out of the project, and he did so because he was offered a good job. One other settler had died.

One of the most attractive features of the Ugwuaku plan for a government anxious to stimulate the development of its rural areas but starved for development funds is that the Ugwuaku project has cost the government relatively little, and certainly far less than it spends on farm settlements. The Works Unit of the Ministry of Rural Development built a bridge across the river and provided culverts and other types of assistance in the building of an access road to the project area. The costs incurred in providing this assistance were debited as a recoverable advance against the cooperative society. In addition, building materials and artisan assistance worth approximately £N70 were provided as a loan to those settlers who wished to build a house meeting certain minimum specifications. Those who opted to build such houses were expected to repay the loan from the proceeds of the maize and cassava they interplanted with oil palms in the community plantation. Those who repaid this initial loan were eligible for further advances to expand and improve their houses. The government also provided the usual assistance with seedlings, fertilizers, and technical supervision offered under the Oil Palm Rehabilitation Scheme. Unlike what is provided to the settlers on farm settlements, the government did not pay a subsistence allowance or offer additional amenities. The fact that only one settler was enticed away from the project during the first 12 months of operation indicates that the settlers were prepared to live with these conditions. By timing the move to the new settlement so that the settlers were able to harvest their food crops on their old farms and carry this produce with them when they moved to Ugwuaku, the settlers were able to feed themselves throughout the transition period. They were able to get settled in Ugwuaku during the

dry season, and then plant their next crop in Ugwuaku
without missing a growing season.

One of the most important elements in the Ugwuaku
plan was the notion that every effort should be made
to see that the settlers were fully integrated into
the Ugwuaku community as quickly as possible. If the
landlord-tenant distinction had been rigidly maintained, then the project's long-term viability would
have been doubtful and it would have had only limited
value as a model for moving other people from one area
to another. Although Ugwuaku had traditional mechanisms for integrating strangers into the community,
the processes involved were too tedious to permit the
rapid and effective incorporation of the relatively
large number of settlers who came in this instance.

Preliminary sociological investigations revealed
that Ugwuaku had no organizations, societies, or clubs
from which settlers would be excluded. Moreover, the
Ugwuaku elders were prepared to permit children of
settlers to be initiated into Ugwuaku age sets along
with Ugwuaku children. Since all the adults of
Ugwuaku are at least nominally Christian, there were
no religious societies from which the settlers would
be excluded either. In the plan drawn up by the
project organizers for the development of Ugwuaku,
a portion of land was set aside as a residential
area where both settlers and Ugwuaku people were
assigned building plots. (Even though the residents
of Ugwuaku already had houses, most of these structure
were sufficiently dilapidated that they hoped to
build new houses.) Plots were assigned in such a
manner that the settlers and the landowners were
thoroughly integrated and no geographical division
existed to distinguish the two groups. Both settlers
and Ugwuaku farmers were members of the same project
cooperative and paid identical rent for use of the
project land, although in recognition of the landowners' continuing special rights to the land, one
portion of the rent money was given to the landowners
Both settlers and Ugwuaku people were also eligible
to hold office in the cooperative. The one-year
period of observation of the project unfortunately
did not permit a full assessment of the effectiveness

of these attempts to encourage social, economic, and geographic integration.

Despite the fact that the Eastern Nigeria government looked at the Ugwuaku project as an important and exciting experiment, the people of Ugwuaku, both landowners and settlers, were not impressed by the fact that they were serving as pathfinders. They were involved in the project because they had made shrewd calculations and come to the conclusion that their involvement was in their self-interest, and offered the only chance they had of realizing a somewhat better income so that they could buy a bicycle or a radio, and more importantly, so that they could pay school fees for their children and provide better educational facilities for their village.

After the settlers had been living in Ugwuaku for three months, Raymond Coatswith, who was closely associated with the Ugwuaku project as leader of the Ford Foundation rural development team, had the following to say about the motives and ambitions of the project participants:

> The Ugwuaku people are participating in this project only because they are intelligent enough to see that it is their only hope and because they believe it is best they can get. They would have much preferred, however, that Government take over their land and develop it for them. They are not so wedded to the practices of their forefathers that they would not be quite happy to see the land developed with new crops and mechanical equipment, provided perhaps by USAID and driven by Peace Corps Volunteers. For their own part, they would rather that Government hire them as established laborers at six shillings three pence a day, or failing, as Farm Settlers on a monthly subsistence and provide them with cement block houses. . . . This does not mean, however, that the Ugwuaku community is unreceptive to innovation or incapable of change.[18]

Elsewhere in the same report he states: "The man
who demonstrates that he has the skills that village
communities lack will invariably find a ready audienc
When he can show that what he demonstrates is profitable not only will the people copy what he does, they
will also adapt and continue to experiment."

RESETTLEMENT TO ACHIEVE MORE EFFECTIVE
SOCIAL ORGANIZATION AND ADMINISTRATION:
VILLAGE INTEGRATION IN ABAKALIKI

Probably more than any other group in Eastern
Nigeria, the people of Abakaliki Division (see Map
2, p. 228) have been a people in motion. For severa]
generations, they pushed in a north-easterly directic
displacing other groups of people by taking their
land. Recently, their tendencies toward mobility
and expansiveness have been constrained and confined
to annual migration as laborers and to redistributinc
themselves within the area already under their contrc

One side effect of their land-grabbing past is
that the Abakaliki people tend to live in scattered,
nonnucleated communities. Rather than grouping themselves into villages or hamlets, most people in
Abakaliki's rural areas prefer to spread themselves
out so that they can keep watch over and defend thei₁
land, in case the former owners try to regain posses-
sion. Most farmers' compounds in Abakaliki are
separated from each other by an eight to a quarter
of a mile or even more. Another reason for their
maintaining this dispersement is the scarcity of
water; water is only found in small, scattered ponds
or streams. One also gets the impression that
Abakaliki people believe there is something intrinsi-
cally improper and dangerous about living close to
one another. For instance, fortune tellers often
tell people that they should live at some distance
from their relatives and neighbors if they wish to
be prosperous and produce many children.

After a series of murders by the secret Odozi
Obodo Society between 1953 and 1958, the Eastern
Nigeria government decided in 1959 to try settling

the people of Abakaliki into nucleated communities,
somewhat analogous to what was attempted in Tanzania
with its "villagization" scheme. Officials though
that if people lived closer together they would not
be such easy prey for the rampaging escapades of the
Odozi Obodo. Although this motive provided the
initial impetus for integration, other benefits were
also envisaged. The rationale for the program in
later years has been more in terms of these other
benefits than for reasons of physical protection and
safety. The government, and particularly the provincial administration for Abakaliki, has believed
that for the rural areas of Abakaliki to develop
both economically and socially, the people will have
to be more effectively organized and greater social
cohesion will have to be achieved. In their scattered
state the communities of Abakaliki lack effective
systems of government and social control. In consequence community projects based on voluntary labor,
popular elsewhere in Eastern Nigeria, are generally
not encountered in Abakaliki. In addition to integration contributing to more effective local government and community action, it has also been hoped
that if people could be encouraged to live closer to
each other new agricultural innovations could be more
effectively introduced, and community economic projects, such as community rice plantations, could be
more easily established.

Following attempts in 1959 to coax the farmers
of Abakaliki to come together into nucleated communities, the village of Abina in Ikwo clan was the
first to indicate interest. While in 1959 the people
of Abina were scattered over a considerable area,
they now live on adjoining half-acre plots in a
relatively compact village. After its having achieved
integration, the government provided Abina with a water
reservoir and a filter pump, which the Abina people
believed were their greatest needs. The reservoir
and pump have now become the "prizes" offered other
villages that make substantial progress toward integration. Since water resources are so scarce, and
since untreated water is usually heavily infested
with guinea worm, the water reservoir and filter pump
offer powerful incentives. Until 1963 the government's

attempts to encourage integration were confined to
Ikwo Clan, but subsequently all four Abakaliki clans
have been involved in the program. By the time war
broke out in 1967, nine villages involving a population
of 12,000 were fully integrated. The total population
of Abakaliki's four clans exceeds 300,000.

To provide a basis for understanding the strength
and weaknesses of the integration program, it is
essential to comprehend the basic elements of the
traditional social and political organization of the
Abakaliki people.[19] The people of Abakaliki speak
a dialect of Ibo, but one that is mutually unintelligible with other Ibo dialects. Each of the four
clans of Abakaliki speaks a variation of the main
dialect, but these variants are mutually intelligible.
The people of this area are distinctive in other ways
than their language, in that they are among the least
acculturated people in Eastern Nigeria and the least
influenced by education and Christian missions.
Abakaliki is a savannah area, particularly suited to
growing yams and rice. The people are very able and
energetic farmers, but they have not been very interested in agricultural innovations.

Each of the four Abakaliki clans--Ikwo, Ezza,
Izi, and Ngbo--claims a common ancestor who symbolizes
the clan's unity. Although at the time of their
territorial expansion each of these clans was politically integrated and their political organizations
supported their expansion, no clan-wide political
structure of an effective nature existed in 1966,
except for the rather fragile system of representative
local government that the government of Eastern Nigeria
had introduced and was trying to strengthen. Nevertheless, clan differences are still clearly recognizable owing to dialect variations, differing cultural
traits, and self-identification by clan members.
Movements of individuals and families from village
to village within the clan area contribute to intra-
clan unity.

This unity is particularly characteristic of
the Izi, since every section of Izi clan contains
members of the same eight lineages. This means that

no matter where an Izi man travels or relocates within
the clan area, he can find members of his lineage to
which he can attach himself.

In many parts of Abakaliki, lineages constitute
more important social units than villages, despite
the fact that lineages are not residential units.
In Ezza the lineage is the principal landholding
body; individuals control pieces of land within the
lineage parcel, but no one can dispose of his piece
without consulting the other members of the lineage.
Moreover, lineage meetings are held more frequently
in Ezza villages than village meetings, age-group
meetings, or any other type of meeting.

In no part of Abakaliki are villages as closely
tied together by horizontal and associational ties
as they are in other parts of Eastern Nigeria. Seldom
do age-groups meet on a regular basis, and regular
village meetings are rarely held. Interest groups,
savings clubs, and other types of organizations that
tie villages together elsewhere are generally absent,
although in some Abakaliki communities the elders
meet regularly to discuss village affairs. As already
indicated, a principal aim of the village integration
program is to make the village a more effective and
active social and political unit.

The Eastern Nigeria government undertook the
village integration program on the assumption that
land in Abakaliki is all communally owned, but this
is a considerable oversimplification of the situation.
In Ezza one rarely finds land (other than sacred
forests) that is owned by the whole community. Land
is often divided up among lineages, but as indicated
above, individuals have firm control over pieces
within each lineage parcel. In some parts of Ezza
individuals so tightly control land that a community
must pay in order to obtain land from someone for a
community project, such as a school. In Ikwo and Izi
compound land is controlled individually; farm land
is controlled both individually and communally. Farm
land located adjacent to a farmer's compound is controlled by the individual farmer, while other farm
land is communally controlled and divided among the

farmers of the community on a annual basis. However,
to state that some land is communally controlled and
some is individually controlled does not mean that
there is a simple dichotomy and that individuals have
complete control over part of the land and the community has complete control over the rest--the situation is more complex and subtle than that. For
instance, in many communities it is believed that
individuals only control land because the community
has accorded them such control, and if the community
decides it has a better use for their land, it can
be taken back. This is what happened at the time
Abina was integrated, and it has happened in other
parts of Ikwo.

The people of Abakaliki have earned a reputation
for resistance to foreign ideas and for suspicion
of outsiders. For a long time they resisted the
introduction of new forms of local government, and
reluctance (even resistance) on the part of parents
to send their children to school has lingered on in
Abakaliki longer than elsewhere in Eastern Nigeria.
As new and more profitable rice-growing techniques
have been introduced, it is more often the outsiders
who lease rice land in Abakaliki who are the ones
to adopt the new techniques rather Abakaliki people.
Attempts to introduce other new farming techniques
have met with more suspicion and fear than one usually
encounters elsewhere in Eastern Nigeria.

In part this fear and resistance are because
contact with the outside world is more recent in
Abakaliki. It is difficult to determine, however,
the degree to which their conservatism is because of
relatively less exposure to outside influence and
how much it is because of differences in traditional
attitudes, beliefs, and social organization. In any
case, the premise lying behind the village integration
program is that following integration as a result
of improvement in internal and external communication
the people of Abakaliki will more readily accept and
utilize new ideas and developments.

Integration Achieved:
The Cases of Abina and
Igwenadoha in Ikwo Clan

Until the push toward integration commenced in
Abina and Igwenadoha, the people of both these villages
lived in scattered compounds. As a consequence of
integration, they now live in nucleated communities
served by networks of roads. Although before integration lineages did not constitute residential units,
the new settlements have particular sections set aside
for each lineage. Each resident has a half-acre
plot upon which to build his house, and each village
has a large water reservoir served by filter pumps.
Most of the construction of the roads and reservoirs
was done by the villagers on a volunteer basis, but
in Igwenadoha the government sent a bulldozer to
assist with the creation of the reservoir. The population of each village approximates 1,700 people.

Prior to integration some land in each village
was controlled individually and some controlled communally. For a man to achieve control over a piece
of land, he had to build a compound on the land, and
either he or a relative had to live there. If the
compound was abandoned, the land reverted to the
community. Because with integration everyone abandoned his compound and moved to the new village site,
everyone lost his claim to his individual land and
all farming land came under communal control. When
the residents of the two villages were asked about
the impact village integration made on their communities, communalization of land was one of the first
changes mentioned. In light of current interest in
Eastern Nigeria in moving toward individualized
tenure, the communalization of land is clearly a step
in the wrong direction. With land being divided up
annually and with no farmer being sure how much or
which piece of land he might have from one year to
the next, improvements in farming techniques and
farm management are difficult. It is pointless for
a farmer to contemplate permanent improvements to his

land or even attempt to increase soil fertility when
he is not sure if he will be farming that piece of
land the following year.

Despite these disadvantages of communalization,
most farmers in Abina and Igwenadoha are pleased
with the change. One reason is that some of the
larger landowners did not make full use of their
land, but were reluctant to allow others to farm it.
Since communal control permits more equitable distribution of land, the small landowners have more land
to farm than previously. Moreover, farmers in both
villages have the erroneous impression that the total
amount of farm land has been increased as a result
of integration. Since they are now farming areas
that were previously taken up by compounds, they
believe there must be more farm land, forgetting that
land previously farmed is now used for residential
plots. The villagers also maintain that communalization is justified by the fact that the place where
they decided to site the new village was owned by
only two individuals. Since they thought it would
be unfair to deprive two individuals of their land
and allow everyone else to benefit from their loss,
they felt justified in taking everyone's land and
putting it all under community control.

In addition to their satisfaction regarding the
communalization of land, the people of Abina and
Igwenadoha cited the following additional advantages
of integration:

1. They have a reliable, clean, and conveniently
located water supply.
2. With better roads they can get to and from
their farms more easily and they can transport their
produce to market more quickly and economically.
3. They now have a village market.
4. They see their friends and relatives more
often because they are living closer.
5. They know and trust their neighbors better,
and as a consequence they are able to reach decisions
more amicably at village meetings.
6. Committees that were organized to plan and
implement the integration scheme continue to help
manage village affairs.

7. Although village meetings are still not held
on a regular basis, they are called more frequently
and with considerably less difficulty and delay than
in preintegration times.

8. In both villages a farmers' cooperative has
been organized, which eventually will concern itself
with production, storage, processing, and marketing
of rice and other farm produce.

9. With the communalization of land, land disputes occur less frequently.

10. Such community projects as the organization
of a community rice project in Igwenadoha and the
building of a town hall in Abina have been facilitated
by integration.

11. Robberies and murders are less frequent now,
because people live close enough to each other to
come to each other's aid.

12. A campaign to eliminate yaws was conducted
without difficulty because those who were sick could
be easily located and treated.

There can be little question that integration
has made a significant impact on the character and
quality of community life in these two villages; the
impact is obvious to both villagers and outside
observers. A more difficult question is what effect
integration is having on the economies of the villages,
aside from the results of communalized tenure. One
cannot yet give a final answer to this question,
because at the last point in time that observation
was possible (1967) it was probably too early to
expect a substantial change in levels of productivity
and income. The expectation has always been that
village integration would have an indirect rather
than a direct effect upon the economies of the villages
being integrated. However, the agriculturalists
attached to the Norwegian Church Agricultural Project
(NORCAP), which is located in Ikwo, claim that farmers
in integrated villages tend to be more receptive to
agricultural innovations. They find that farmers in
integrated villages are less suspicious of outsiders
and more receptive to new ideas. This receptivity
results in part because people in close contact with
one another are better able to clear up confusion
and misunderstanding about what the agents of change
might tell them. Also, in an integrated village it

is easier to get people together to introduce new
ideas and practices to them. Although NORCAP is not
certain that the greater receptivity to new ideas on
the part of integrated villages is not the cause
rather than the effect of integration, their impressic
is that integration has made people more responsive
to the agricultural programs they are trying to
introduce. There can be no doubt that integration
facilitates communication, in that new ideas spread
more quickly in integrated villages.

NORCAP also finds it easier for those in an
integrated village to organize and manage such community agricultural projects as community rice farms
and community cattle pastures.[20] Farmers in unintegrated villages have had less experience planning
community projects, and the loose social structure
of these villages makes it more difficult for them
to undertake such cooperative projects. On the other
hand, where NORCAP has worked over a period of time
in nonintegrated villages, they have seen evidence
of increasing village cooperation and coordination.
Thus, integration is probably not an absolute prerequisite to the introduction of new practices in
Abakaliki or the organization of community projects.
In fact, villages that have thus far been resistant
to integration might be more receptive to the concept
following the introduction of agricultural programs.

In assessing the economic implications of village
integration, one of the most important questions is
the effect integration has on land-use patterns,
particularly whether concentrating the population
in nucleated villages will lead to exhaustion of the
soil close to the village. Some observers have feared
that if the Abakaliki farmers are pulled off their
farming plots, they will abandon their old farm lands
and only farm close to the new village. In the cases
of Abina and Igwenadoha this has not proved to be a
legitimate fear. Firstly, land is so scarce for these
two villages, as in most of Abakaliki Division, that
villagers have little choice but to use all the land
they have. In both Abina and Igwenadoha pressure on
the land is such that farmers are forced to use a
three-year rather than a longer fallow cycle.

Moreover, these communities are small, so that their
most distant farm land is only four miles from the
living area, which is not a prohibitive distance.
Even when they were living in scattered compounds,
most farmers cultivated several plots simultaneously
and had to walk considerable distances to reach them.
When asked about the impact of integration on land
use, the people of Igwenadoha said that in general
they walk about as far now to reach their farm land
as they did before integration. Where greater distances are entailed, the improved system of roads
makes travel easier and evacuation of produce considerably more efficient than previously. In Abina the
farmers said that since integration they have to walk
somewhat farther to reach their fields, but they apparently do not mind because they now have neighbors to
accompany them when they walk to their plots.

Just because integration has not had adverse
effects on land use in Abina and Igwenadoha does not
mean that this possibility should not be borne in
mind. The danger is particularly great when attempts
are made to integrate large communities that are
spread over wide areas. Plans devised in some parts
of Abakaliki to resettle people 7 to 12 miles from
their homes and farm lands could have serious consequences. If the farm land in such areas is controlled individually, then farmers will have to walk
excessive distances to reach their fields. This
could seriously jeopardize the village's economy.
If, on the other hand, land in these areas is communally controlled, then the fear is warranted that
farming activities will be concentrated close to the
village and that this in turn will lead to soil
exhaustion.

Integration in Process:
The Case of Ezza Clan

Despite the fact that those villages that have
been integrated recognize the benefits of integration,
most unintegrated villages, and particularly those
in Ezza Clan, remain strikingly unconvinced. Integration appeals to people in unintegrated areas almost

totally in terms of what the government might do for
them if they agree to integrate. Those villages that
have made a start toward integration have done so
primarily in response to the government's promise
that if they integrate their village, the government
will help provide them with a clean and conveniently
located water supply. They also hope that electricit'
and other amenities will follow on the heels of integration. Almost no appreciation whatever exists of
the benefits inherent in integration itself, such as
the impact integration can have on community life
and on the community's economic and social development.

This is one of the principal causes of the relatively slow progress of the integration program in
Ezza. Several communities have started relocating
their villages, building new roads and new houses in
order to get a water supply. However, they do not
see any relevant connection between what constitutes
the cause and what constitutes the effect, and as a
result their push toward integration is rarely sustained. Also, much of the work that is done is
motivated by fear of what might happen if they do
not cooperate. According to legislation passed by
the County Council, once a majority of people in a
given village indicate their approval of integration,
those who do not complete their apportioned share of
the road and house building can be, and often are,
fined or even imprisoned. While this sort of coercio
might bring a short-lived "cooperative" response, thi
is usually offset by the resentment and resistance
such a punitive approach breeds.

Lack of enthusiasm and apathy are not the only
difficulties integration faces in Ezza: Some people
actively oppose it. Some villagers fear that with an
improved road system and with people living closer
to one another it will be easier for tax collectors
to appear on village integration work days to apprehe
tax defaulters. Other villagers fear that improved
communications and transportation will encourage the
women of the community to run away to the cities.
In areas where outsiders have settled, the local
people sometimes fear that with integration they will

have to live too close to these strangers, whom they
do not trust.

In some villages opposition to integration results
from concern about having all the cattle in the village
brought to a central location. With everyone living
close together and with their cattle in proximity,
diseases can pass from one man's cows to another more
easily than if the cattle are scattered. They also
believe that if they move to a central location, either
the government or neighboring villages will attempt
to take their vacated land from them. Therefore in
several villages where integration is in progress only
young men are moving to the new site. The older men
are remaining in their original compounds to guard
their land. On the other hand, certain Ikwo villages
have opposed integration because they believe that
integration necessarily entails communalization of
land, as it has in Abina and Igwenadoha, and they wish
to maintain individual control over at least a portion
of their farming land.

Another obstacle to successful integration both
in Ezza and other parts of Abakaliki relates to the
acquisition of land to site the new village. Villagers
often support the idea of integration until they
realize that it may entail their losing a piece of
land. However as in the Igwenadoha case, where the
villagers decided to communalize all the land and
thereby not penalize any particular individual unduly,
land acquisition is usually not an insuperable problem.
Lineages in some villages that are being integrated
in Ezza have agreed to contribute sizable pieces of
land for new village sites.

Formation of the local committees to plan and
organize the work necessitated by integration also
presents problems. Some of these committees are
selected by the villagers themselves, while others
are appointed by the Village Planning Officer supervising the project. In many cases the Local Council
constitutes itself as the integration committee, and
in almost all cases integration committees are heavily
weighted with councillors, having the effect of putting
power in the hands of the young and the literate.

Elders tend to be excluded from these decision-making
processes and as a result they are often reluctant
to support what is decided. It is quite possible that
their natural conservatism would lead them to oppose
integration even if their views solicited, but to
exclude them from the beginning, as is often done
either by oversight or design, is almost sure to doom
the project to failure.

Assuring that all sections of a community are
adequately represented in decision-making relating to
integration is particularly important in Abakaliki,
since communities there tend to be sharply split by
factions and interest groups. Sometimes the split
is in terms of education. For example, in one Ezza
village a voluntary association whose membership is
confined to those who are literate has formed itself
into the village integration planning committee. In
another Ezza village the Christians plan and organize
the integration project; those who still adhere to the
traditional religion play no part in decision-making
relating to the project, but are forced to cooperate
in work projects by threats of court action brought
by the Christians.

A final difficulty facing integration in Ezza,
as in other parts of Abakaliki, arises from the fact
that only one water reservoir can be constructed at
a time. Because the government has only been able
to allocate a few pieces of earth-moving equipment
to the village integration program, the construction
of these large reservoirs is a slow and tedious process. This means that a community might work hard
to build roads and houses on a new site in hopes of
being rewarded for their efforts, and then they are
told that they will not get their reservoir for another
two years. When this happens, villages often lose
interest and slow the pace of work. Then when a
decision has to be reached over which village should
get water next, it is difficult to know whether to
construct a reservoir for a community that has not been
active for years, or to reward a community that has
been active recently and is probably prepared to
contribute substantial amounts of volunteer labor to
the construction effort.

The village integration program in Abakaliki has
the advantage over such comparable schemes as the
vil\.agization program in Tanzania of being inexpensive
for the government. The villagers are responsible
for building the roads and houses at the new village
site, as well as providing any other structures or
services they desire. The only capital contribution
from the government is in the provision of the filter
pump and the earth-moving equipment for the construc-
tior. of the water reservoir. Unlike most other resettlement schemes of this type, however, the Abakaliki
scheme has the disadvantage of not attempting to attack
directly the economic problems of the communities with
which it deals. Resettlement is merely seen as providing the basis for subsequent efforts to improve the
village economies. The main purpose of the scheme is
to improve government administration and enhance the
quality of community life.

The slowness with which integration has been
achieved can probably be explained in part by this
tendency to disregard the economic interests of the
people. Greater enthusiasm could undoubtedly be
generated for the program if a less punitive approach
were taken in encouraging participation and if integration were more effectively linked with an effort
to increase the incomes of Abakaliki's farm families.
Greater effort could also profitably be exerted by
government officals in attempting to understand the
fears that have caused villagers to hesitate to support
the integration of their villages. More careful
assessment is also required of both the economic and
social implications of integration for the villages
of Abakaliki, to assure both that the program as
currently organized actually does benefit those who
participate and to assure that the program in the
future is conducted in such manner that the maximum
possible benefits are derived.

NOTE ON RECENT DEVELOPMENTS

Of the 18 settlers residing at Ugwuaku at the
outbreak of the war, 8 remained in Ugwuaku throughout
the war and are currently participating as full members

of Ugwuaku's community agricultural projects. Both
settlers and Ugwuaka people are anxious for new
settlers to be selected and encorporated into the
community and its projects, so that the original
benefits envisaged as accruing from resettlement can
be fully realized. The community of Afam Nta, where
a second pilot resettlement scheme was launched
shortly before the outbreak of the war, is also eager
to start operations again. Although the division
of Eastern Nigeria into three states has made long-
distance resettlement more difficult, resettlement
from more-densely populated areas to less-densely
populated areas within each of the three eastern
states still holds considerable promise as a means
of increasing rural productivity and incomes.

     Efforts to stimulate village integration in
Abakaliki were revived soon after the end of the
war by the East Central State Government. Flooding
of the Cross River during the 1970 rainy season
forced many villagers in Abakaliki to abandon their
homes. The vulnerability of many Abakaliki villages
to renewed damaged by flooding has stimulated the
government to give high priority to the village integration program during the postwar period, and
it has also increased the willingness of many Abakaliki
people to agree to cooperate with the program.

                              NOTES

     1. Thayer Scudder, "The Kainji Lake Basin:
Research, Resettlement, and Development" (Lagos:
The Ford Foundation, 1965, mimeographed), p. 13.

     2. G. W. Amarteifio, D. A. P. Butcher, and David
Whitman, Tema Manhean: A Study of Resettlement
(Accra: Ghana Universities Press, 1966); Robert A.
Fernea and John G. Kennedy, "Initial Adaptations
to Resettlement: A New Life for Egyptian Nubians,"
Current Anthropology, 7 (1966), 349-354; Thayer
Scudder, "The Kariba Case: Man-Made Lakes and
Resource Development in Africa," Bulletin of the
Atomic Scientists, XXI (December 1965), 6-11; and
David R. Smock. "The Role of Anthopology in a

Western Nigerian Resettlement Project," in David Brokensha and Marion Pearsall, eds., The Anthropology of Development in Sub-Saharan Africa, Monograph No. 10, (Lexington, Kentucky: Society for Applied Anthropology, 1969), pp. 40-47.

3. "Volta Resettlement Symposium Papers" (Accra: Volta River Authority, 1965, mimeographed).

4. K. D. S. Baldwin, The Niger Agricultural Project (Cambridge, Mass.: Harvard University Press, 1957).

5. Robert Chambers, Settlement Schemes in Tropical Africa (London: Routledge and Kegan Paul, 1969).

6. Conrad C. Reining, The Zande Scheme (Evanston, Illinios: Northwestern University Press, 1966).

7. Richard S. Odingo, "Land Settlement in the Kenya Highlands," in James R. Sheffield, ed., Education, Employment and Rural Development (Nairobi: East Africa Publishing House, 1967), p. 146.

8. John C. de Wilde, et al., Agricultural Development in Tropical Areas, Vol II (Baltimore: The Johns Hopkins Press, 1967), p. 188. See also J. D. MacArthur, "Agricultural Settlement in Kenya" in G. K. Helleiner, ed., Agricultural Planning in East Africa (Nairobi: East African Publishing House, 1968), pp. 117-135; and K. H. Clough, "Some Economic Aspects of Land Settlement in Kenya" (Kenya: Egerton College, mimeographed, 1965).

9. de Wilde, op. cit., p. 217.

10. Aaron Segal, "The Politics of Land in East Africa," Economic Development and Cultural Change, XVl (January 1968), p. 279; See also Nikos Georgulas, "An Approach to the Economic Development of Rural Areas in Tanganyika with Special Reference to the Village Resettlement Program" (Syracuse, N. Y.: Program of African Studies, Syracuse University, 1963, mimeographed); and Nikolaus Newiger, "Village

Settlement Schemes," in Hans Ruthenberg, ed., <u>Small-holder Farming and Smallholder Development in Tanzania</u> (London: C. Hurst and Co., 1968), pp. 249-273.

11.   <u>Land Settlement Scheme-Farm Settlements</u> (Ibadan: Ministry of Agriculture and Natural Resource 1960); Dupe Olatunbosun, "Nigerian Farm Settlement and School Leavers' Farms" (East Lansing: Consortium for the Study of Nigerian Rural Development, Michigan State University, 1967, mimeographed); Carl K. Eicher, Reflections on Capital Intensive Moshav Farm Settle-ments in Southern Nigeria," paper presented at the Agricultural Development Council Seminar on Coopera-tives and Quasi-Cooperatives, University of Kentucky, Lexington, 1967, mimeographed); and M. Kreinen, "The Introduction of Israel's Land Settlement Plan to Nigeria," <u>Journal of Farm Economics</u>, 45 (August 1963), 535-546.

12.   Personal communication.

13.   For a description of these migratory pattern see R. K. Udo, "The Migrant Tenant of Eastern Nigeria, <u>Africa</u>, XXXIV (October 1964), 326-339.

14.   de Wilde, <u>op. cit.</u>, Vol. II, pp. 420-421.

15.   Daryll Forde and Richenda Scott, <u>The Native Economies of Nigeria</u> (London: Oxford University Press, 1946), pp. 109-111.

16.   John M. Brewster claims that the tendency to equate "predatory intentions with most of humanity outside the primary group" is virtually universal in the rural portions of developing countries.   See his "Traditional Social Structures as Barriers to Change," in Herman M. Southworth and Bruce F. Johnston eds., <u>Agricultural Development and Economic Growth</u> (Ithaca, N.Y.:   Cornell University Press, 1967), p. 80.

17.   H. A. Oluwasanmi, "Agriculture and Rural Development," paper presented at the Conference on National Reconstruction and Development in Nigeria, Ibadan, 1969, mimeographed, p. 10.

18.   Raymond Coatswith, "A Note on Village Atti-
tudes in Ugwuaku Project," Quarterly Report on the
Rural Development Project of Eastern Nigeria for the
Ford Foundation (Enugu: 1966, typescript).

19.   For a detailed description of the social
structure of the Abakaliki Ibo, see G. I. Jones,
"Ecology and Social Structure Among the North-Eastern
Ibo," Africa, XXXl (April 1961), 117-134.

20.   The cattle of Abakaliki are the dwarf short-
horn type (muturu) that are immune to tsetse-trans-
mitted trypanosomiasis.

10

MEASURING
ATTITUDES
TOWARD
DEVELOPMENT

One of the themes of this book is the effect
cultural and attitudinal factors have had on rural
development in Eastern Nigeria. In order to assess
fully the influence of cultural factors on rural
transformation, it is necessary to delineate in more
detail the contemporary attitudes of Eastern Nigerians
toward social, economic, and political development.
This chapter will describe a survey undertaken to
measure the attitudes toward development in 24 villages
and the resulting regional profile and individual
attitudinal clusters. Because Eastern Nigeria has
a variety of ethnic groups and has undergone an uneven
rate of change in the various portions of the region,
an analysis of the relationship between attitudes
toward development and the process of rural transformation also requires an evaluation of group
attitudinal patterns. Toward this end, Chapter 11
will appraise the divergences between groups based
on ethnic and demographic variables.

Since rural transformation is a multidimensional
process, attitudes relating to control over destiny,
change and innovation, optimism, education, work,
money, self-reliance, politics, and trust and cooperation all potentially mediate villagers' reactions
to specific projects and opportunities. Receptivity
to innovations and programs is not in all cases, of
course, dependent upon a systematically positive
orientation toward development. For example, a field

study of agricultural change in northern Katsina,
Nigeria, reported that despite the generally conservative predisposition of the Moslem population
there, the small farmers had responded to economic
incentives both in their changeover to the cultivation
of groundnuts since World War I and their more recent
adoption of chemical fertilizer. The acceptance of
other innovations in northern Katsina even in the
agricultural sector was, however, limited. For
instance, groundnuts emerged as an important cash
crop without any significant change occurring in the
traditional methods of cultivation.[1] Moreover, the
lack of enthusiasm for education (other than Koranic
education) and for other aspects of modern life in
northern Katsina augurs poorly for comprehensive
rural development.

Various analysts have dealt with the implications
of the peasant world view for development, albeit
to emphasize the obstacles it imposes.[2] These studies
it should be remembered, describe attitudes toward
development in specific non-African peasant societies
(Mexican, Asian, Italian) although some attempt to
generalize from a particular geographic locality to
a cognitive orientation common to all peasants. A
few of these analysts do either explicitly or
tacitly exclude African societies from these generali-
zations.[3] The features of the peasant world view,
according to these studies, which are detrimental
to development include the following traits: stress
on spiritual rather than material values, absence
of a perceived relationship between work and improved
economic conditions, lack of an achievement motivation
inability to cooperate, hostility to change, fatalism
fear of strangers, and a belief in a "limited good."
In a frequently quoted article George Foster asserts
that the cognitive model he terms the "idea of limited
good" best accounts for peasant behavior. According
to Foster,

> peasants view their social, economic, and
> natural universe--their total environment
> --as one in which all the desired things
> of life such as land, wealth, health,
> friendship and love, manliness and honor,

> respect and status, power and influence,
> security and safety, exist in finite
> quantities and are always in short supply
> as far as the peasant is concerned. . .
> there is no way directly within the
> peasant's power to increase the available
> quantity.[4]

In Foster's closed and limited universe of resources, individual or family improvement can come
only at the expense of others. Hence members of
such societies refrain from entering into cooperative
relations. Moreover, the peasant tends to perceive
himself as relatively powerless to increase his share
of the finite resources through his own efforts.

From a different perspective, David McClelland
stresses the psychological factors affecting economic
development. McClelland and other social scientists
endorsing his approach posit that economic development
depends on the incidence of "n" Achievement, i.e.,
the drive to excel, in a society. According to
McClelland, this psychological disposition particularly emerges in cultures that emphasize the need
for hard work. Entrepreneurial behavior then channels
this psychological drive into the energy that propels
economic development. The entrepreneur, as defined
by McClelland, perceives risk-taking as a function
of skill in decision-making rather than of chance,
anticipates future possibilities, accepts individual
responsibility, has energy, demonstrates organizational
skills, and measures results monetarily.[5] By cor-
relating economic development with the incidence of
"n" Achievement, McClelland implies that most underdeveloped countries have cultures that either do not
promote this trait in individuals or stifle the
entrepreneurial activities that should follow from
this proclivity.

It is not necessary to endorse Foster's model
of the "limited good" or McClelland's hypothesis
that rates of economic development reflect the incidence of the drive to excel to accept the more general hypothesis that attitudes act as subjective molds
to structure individual and group responses to

opportunities for development and change. Earlier
chapters in this study have indicated how certain
cultural perspectives have constituted assets or
posed problems for development and how attitudes
influenced and affected particular programs and
projects. To examine the possible relationships
between culture and development, social scientists
have adopted several approaches. Some of the case-
study material originated from traditional anthropolo
gical techniques of observation and selective interviewing. McClelland and his students generally
assess achievement motivation by analyzing the
narratives produced in response to the pictures in
the Thomatic Apperception Test (TAT). He has also
attempted to evaluate the propensity of cultures to
cultivate achievement motivation through rating the
imaginative stories used to teach children in the
third and fourth grades and the folk tales of primitive societies in terms of the amount of achievemer
imagery.[6] Robert LeVine compares the achievement
imagery in essays and dream reports of Ibo, Hausa,
and Yoruba schoolboys in his attempt to link patterns
of status mobility within these three ethnic groups
to expressed achievement motivation.[7]

For purposes of examining attitudes toward devel
ment, survey questionnaires have several advantages.
Interviewers can be trained more easily than for
psychological testing, and it is possible to question
a large sample of people in a relatively short durati
of time. In constructing a questionnaire, emphasis
can be placed on precisely those subjects about which
the analyst is interested in evoking data. If
properly handled, attitude surveys can usually provic
more precise and objective data than either the
impressionistic traditional anthropological technique
or the somewhat subjective interpretation of
narratives, stories, folk tales, essays, or dreams.
Furthermore the survey approach more readily permits
the quantification of data and the statistical
analysis of results.

Two other surveys with relatively large samples
have been conducted in Eastern Nigeria. In 1962
the Princeton Institute for International Social

Research undertook a nation-wide public opinion survey in Nigeria during which they interviewed 1,200 persons, 400 in each of the then three regions, to ascertain the "attitudes, hopes, and fears of Nigerians" pertaining both to. themselves and to the country.[8] Although the sample was supposed to be selected on a random basis, the fact that the rural population had to be accessible by road to interviewers somewhat biased the character of the sample. Since this survey did not have as its purpose an analysis of attitudes toward development, the questions asked do not easily lend themselves to this subject. Moreover, the published results do not distinguish between the responses of informants living in rural and urban areas or between the answers given by members of different ethnic groups.

Members of the Department of Communications at Michigan State University gathered data in the period 1965-67 from 71 villages in Eastern Nigeria, 52 of which were Ibo and 19 of which were Ibibio, in an attempt to ascertain the variables that distinguished villages in which agricultural change programs were relatively successful from those villages in which they were less successful. However, the research design for the survey permitted a village to be classified as innovative if only a very few people adopted any agricultural innovation. Thus in analyzing the results, villages with two or three innovative farmers were grouped with villages in which substantial portion of the cultivators took advantage of governmental agricultural programs. Moreover, few of the results turned out to be very illuminating. For instance, the most significant factor explaining variance in agricultural adoption turned out to be the index of contact with expert sources of information.[9] This index of contact reflected the organization and effectiveness of the extension service more than any characteristics of the village.

THE SURVEY METHODOLOGY

In order to explore, measure, and analyze attitudes toward social, economic, and political

development in Eastern Nigeria the authors conducted
a survey there in 1966 to obtain a sampling of attitude profiles of people in three parts of the region

    1.   the northern and eastern Ibo areas, which
are the more traditional Ibo areas;
    2.   the central and southern Ibo areas, which
are the more acculturated Ibo sections; and
    3.   minority (non-Ibo) ethnic localities.

The choice of the villages for the survey reflected the ethnic composition of the region. Accor
ing to the 1953 census (the last one for which detai
breakdowns were available), Ibos comprised approximately 61 percent of the population of the region,
Ibibios 15 percent, and Ijaws 3 percent. Of the 24
villages included in the sample, 16 (67 percent) wer
Ibo, 4 (17 percent) were Ibibio, 2 (8 percent) were
Ijaw, and 2 (8 percent) were Boki (one of the small
ethnic groups in the region).

Within the three large areas to be surveyed,
sub-areas were selected to give as broad a geographi
and ethnic spread as possible. To achieve this
distribution, four divisions within each of these
large areas were selected more or less randomly;
then a single county council area within each of the
divisions was selected. Within each of the county
council areas chosen, two villages were picked for
sampling. The eight villages in Group A, northern
and eastern Iboland, were located in Udi, Nsukka,
Afikpo, and Abakaliki Divisions. The eight villages
in central and southern Iboland, constituting Group
B, were located in Onitsha, Orlu, Owerri, and Awka
Divisions. The divisions in which the Ibibio, Ijaw,
and Boki villages of Group C were situated were
Uyo, Brass, Abak, and Ogoja.

A sample of 20 adult males in each of the villa
was interviewed with care being taken to assure that
they were representative of the total male populatio
The interviewers were given careful instructions
regarding the selection of the sample. One adult
male was to be picked from every fifth household.
If there was more than one adult male in a household
the interviewer was instructed to select a young man

in one household, a middle-aged man in the next, and
an old man in the next to assure an age spread within
the sample. With 24 villages and 20 persons interviewed in each, the total size of the sample was 480.

A 67-item questionnaire was prepared in English
and then, after selecting the villages to be surveyed,
the questionnaire was translated by bilingual native
speakers into the relevant languages. These included
Ibo (with a special translation for the Abakaliki
area), Ibibio, Boki, and Oloibiri-Ogbia, a dialect
of Ijaw. In order to check the accuracy of the
initial translation, a second native speaker was
asked to translate the questionnaire back into English
without showing him the original version. Some
translations went through this process several times
before their accuracy was satisfactory.

Students from the University of Nigeria who came
from the selected county council areas were recruited
to conduct the interviewing under the authors' supervision between March and June 1966. This method of
selecting interviewers obviously involved risks, as
do all techniques. It was thought, however, that
the advantages of interviewers being able to establish
quick rapport as a result of their working in their
home area outweighed the possible disadvantages of
this type of selection.

No attitude survey, however carefully designed
and administered, can be perfectly valid. The
authors are reasonably assured, though, that the
results of this attitude survey reflected the actual
views of the informants. Previous research projects
undertaken by the authors, as well as by other social
scientists, attest to the willingness of Eastern
Nigerians to cooperate and provide information. The
familiarity of the interviewers with the villages
they were surveying constituted another safeguard.
Since in Eastern Nigeria education evokes considerable
respect, the high status of university students
further induced the cooperation of the informants.
In addition, clusters of questions dealing with the
same subject in the questionnaire usually were not
asked in consecutive order to reduce the likelihood
of prompting artificially consistent answers. For

most of the questions informants were offered at
least three alternatives, and the interviewers were
instructed to read through the question and the opti
twice to acquaint the informant with them before
soliciting his answer.

The questionnaire incorporated items designed
to measure attitudes toward political, social, and
economic development, along with other items designe
to elicit demographic data on the age, wealth,
educational level, frequency of contact with mass
media, religion, occupation, and family migration.
In addition, the interviewer ranked each informant
in terms of his economic status relative to other
persons in his community, his willingness to coopera
and his understanding of the questions. Most of the
questions dealt with the following clusters of
attitudes: toward change and innovation, pertaining
to control over one's destiny, concerning optimism
for the future, toward work, toward money, with
reference to self-reliance, toward education, about
the political system, and relating to trust and
cooperation. A few of the questions were relevant
to more than one of these categories. A copy of the
questionnaire is reproduced as the Appendix to this
book.

Ten questions in the survey dealt with control
over one's destiny. In these questions informants
were asked such things as whether for the average
man it was useless to plan for the future, whether
success in life depends more on luck than on persona
ability, whether it is who you know more than what
you know or what you do that counts, whether a poor
man can become rich through his own efforts, whether
working harder will bring a higher standard of livir
whether a man's life should be guided more by the
demands of the present than by his visions of the
future, whether a contribution to a church or sacri-
ficing at traditional shrines will enable someone
to prosper, whether it is useless to try to change
one's own fate, and whether it is a wise man who
learns to forego immediate pleasures in order to
achieve more lasting satisfactions sometime in the
future. The large number of questions devoted to

control over one's destiny results from the importance
of these attitudes in reflecting one's overall attitudes toward development. Most delineators of a
peasant world view emphasize the pervading influence
of a fatalistic outlook. Obviously a group of people
who believe that they cannot determine their own
futures because their lives are completely manipulated
by capricious forces beyond their control will not
be responsive to opportunities to improve their
living conditions.

A second group of questions related to change
and innovation. These six questions included whether
one should return to the traditional life of one's
ancestors in order to have a better life, whether
life is changing too fast, whether it is difficult
to adopt new customs, whether the villager sided with
the the old-fashioned group or the modern group in
cases of conflict within his village, whether the
informant would be willing to be the first person
in his village to try a new and useful farming
technique, and whether the informant would be willing
to accept the recommendation of his son in learning
a new farming practice. Again many observers emphasize
the basic conservatism of peasants. This series of
questions sought to ascertain the receptivity, at
least on a verbal level, of Eastern Nigerians to
innovations and development efforts.

Other questions pertained to the degree of
optimism for the future. These asked the informants
whether five years from now they expected people in
the village to be better off or worse off (economically) or about the same as today, how they would
describe the progress of the village, what chance
they thought they would have to solve the problems
of their community, whether they believed that the
lot of the average man is getting worse, and if it
would be a long time before progress is achieved in
Nigeria. As Chapter 8 indicated, one of the factors
that distinguished communities responsive to the
introduction of community plantations from those that
expressed no interest was that inhabitants of the
responsive villages tended to be more optimistic
about their economic futures.

Four questions in the survey dealt with attitude
toward education. In these the informants were asked
whether through education a man or a woman could become anything he wanted to be, how he would spend
an extra £N100 in income--paying school fees for
children or relatives, entertaining people in the
villages, hiring labor to plant a bigger farm, making
improvements to his farm, buying a machine with which
he could go into business, saving the money, building
a better house, or buying a radio and a bicycle; and
whether a child should go as far as he could in schoo
The central role of education in providing skills and
in transmitting a knowledge of the world beyond the
village gave rise to this set of questions.

Two groups of questions in the survey inquired
into attitudes toward work on the one hand and toward
money on the other. Much of the literature on the
attitudes of backward and unresponsive peasants
stresses their lack of enthusiasm for work and the
pervasive character of their nonmaterial, otherworldl
concerns. Some descriptions of the world views of
African societies posit a negative attitude toward
work as characteristic of most Africans. For instanc
according to Robert LeVine,

> Africans aspire to wealth and status--in
> new as well as old forms--and many of them
> are also industrious farmers, craftsmen,
> and professionals, but they do not
> generally regard hard work as highly com-
> mendable in itself. On the contrary, their
> traditional status systems present ex-
> treme examples of what Thorstein Veblen
> called 'conspicuous leisure'--that is,
> the social pattern in which freedom from
> work is a prerogative of high status and
> is publicly displayed in order to rein-
> force one's position.[10]

Positive attitudes toward work contribute to
development, as demonstrated by McClelland's discover
of an association between the high incidence of
achievement-oriented individuals and societies whose
values emphasize the value of hard work. The questio

concerning work and money include the following:
in choosing a job, which of the following things is
most important--the pay, the prestige or status, the
easiness of the work, the interest of the work, or
the power it gives you over other people; would you
be willing to do any type of work for sufficient pay
or are there certain types of work that would be too
tedious, hard, or unpleasant; is it true that the
man who gets money finds happiness; if you worked
very hard, what would others in your community
think of you; if you were employed as a plantation
worker, do you think you should be hired as a laborer
or a supervisor; do men or women do more farm work
in this village; is it correct that a hard-working
man is a good man; would you be willing to learn to
climb a palm tree. While the significance of most
of these questions is rather obvious, a few require
some clarification. For instance, the willingness
to be hired as a plantation laborer or to learn to
climb a palm tree manifests a disposition to do hard
work considered to be of low status. When the women
in a community undertake most of the farm work, this
often reflects an unwillingness on the part of the
men to engage in most types of manual labor.

Many kinds of economic projects require villagers
to be self-starters and to be prepared to assume
initiative, thus making self-reliance an important
orientation for development. As Chapter 8 reported,
the question that produced the greatest difference
between the responsive and unresponsive communities
dealt with whether their respective members would
prefer to be employed by another person, be employed
by a company, or be self-employed. Of the informants
in responsive communities, 70 percent answered they
would prefer to start their own business while only
39 percent of those in the unresponsive communities
favored doing so. David McClelland and others also
claim that entrepreneurial behavior and attitudes
constitute requirements for economic development.[11]
In addition to the question concerning the preferred
type of employment, two others in the survey were
germane to this subject: should the building or
improvement of roads be mainly the duty of the government, the villagers themselves, or their joint

responsibility; and who should be responsible for
the building of a new school.

Several questions in the survey related to
attitudes toward politics and society or what some
social scientists term the political culture. Two
questions directly concerned with the political syste
asked whether the government was run for the benefit
of those in power or for the people, and what chances
the informant or persons like him would have of
getting justice in a court case. In many developing
countries the government is the major initiator of
projects to improve the economy and of efforts to
reform or modernize the society. A negative attitude
by the population toward the political system
obviously inhibits these governmental activities.
It is for this reason that political scientists consider a positive attitude toward the political syster
one of the necessary ingredients of a political
culture that promotes development.[12] Another such
attitude conducive to development is an acceptance
of the equality of individuals. According to Lucian
Pye, "Development demands effective leadership, but
it also encompasses sentiments about equality and
the absence of all arbitrary distinctions in status.
One question in the survey asked villagers whether
they agreed, partly agreed, or disagreed with the
statement that some have been born to command and
others to obey.

Five questions dealt with a related set of
attitudes pertaining to trust and cooperation. With
trust and without the ability for people to join
together in cooperative ventures most efforts to
improve a society are doomed. For that reason
political scientists often emphasize the importance
of trust in the development process.[14] Yet most
treatments of peasant society describe the existence
and debilitating effects of a pervasive distrust.[15]
To elicit data on the degree of trust and cooperatio
the survey included the following questions: whethe
in the past few years the people of the village
worked together on some kind of project, how well
the people cooperated on community projects, whether
a person knows someone he can count on in a difficul

situation, whether most, some, or few persons can
be trusted, and whether there were any people in
the village whom the informant would trust to be
treasurer of a cooperative.

REGIONAL PROFILE

Of those interviewed, 22 percent were between
the ages of 21 and 34, 31 percent between 35 and 44,
28 percent between 45 and 54, and 19 percent between
50 and 59. The largest single age bracket represented
in the sample were those between 40 and 44 who
constituted 17 percent of the total. Thirty-three
percent had houses with zinc or aluminum roofs, 23
percent with cement floors, and 18 percent with
cement walls, the remainder living in houses with
mud floors and walls and thatched roofs. Most of
the informants had several relatives living outside
the village, often in a city. Only 9 percent
answered that no members of their family were living
outside the village while 35 percent had eight or
more. Similarly 29 percent had no relatives then
living in a city, while 16 percent had up to eight
or more. An overwhelming portion of them, 69 percent,
hardly ever thought seriously about moving away
and living in another village or a township. As was
expected, full-time farmers constituted the most
numerous occupational grouping with 67 percent, of
which 79 percent did most of their own farm work.

Slightly more than half of the villagers (52
percent) had attended some school. Of those who
had attended school, 44 percent had completed no
more than four years, and only 10 percent had gone
beyond primary school. This was understandable
since there were few occupational opportunities in
the village for the more educated members of the
community, who usually migrated out to work in an
urban center. The survey results also reflected
the relatively low level of literacy in that only
one third answered that they could write a letter.
Approximately 59 percent of the informants listened
to the radio sometimes, and as many as 22 percent
did so every day. The religious composition of the

sample was as follows: 33 percent adhered to the
traditional religion, 36 percent were Catholic, and
29 percent were Protestant.

To make a rough numerical indication of the
gross nature of the responses given to a particular
set of questions, what is termed a development quotient was devised. The group being interviewed was
given a +1 score on a particular question if the
majority of the respondents answered the question in
a manner consistent with a positive attitude toward
development. What has been interpreted to constitute
a positive attitude toward development as revealed
in a particular question has already been explained
in the preceding section of this chapter. For
instance, if a majority of the respondents reveal
a positive attitude toward education in a question
dealing with education, they are given a +1 score
for that question. A negative attitude toward
education would be scored as -1. The development
quotient for a particular set of respondents on a
particular group of questions is calculated by adding
the scores for each of the questions in the set.
For instance, if a group of respondents answered
three questions dealing with education in such a
manner to indicate a positive attitude toward education and two other questions in such a manner to
indicate a negative attitude toward education, the
development quotient for this set of questions on
education is +1.

The cumulative attitudinal profile in the 24
villages, insofar as it was accurately reflected by
the survey, manifests a very striking commitment to
development. The development quotient for the total
sample on the whole questionnaire was +18. In other
words, out of the 48 questions in the questionnaire
that could be scored in terms of revealing a development orientation, a greater number of those interviewed revealed positive attitudes toward development
of 33 of these and negative attitudes toward development on only 15. The regional profile has positive
attitudinal clusters particularly in the following
groups of questions: those pertaining to education,
change and innovation, optimism, work, and self-

reliance. The informants also demonstrated an overall positive attitude in the sets of questions dealing
with control over one's destiny and trust and cooperation. Only on two groups of questions, those
relating to money and to the political system, did
the regional sample indicate an overall negative
score.

Of all the attitudes examined by this survey,
the villagers displayed a more striking commitment
to education than to any other aspect of development.
Each of the four questions about education evoked a
positive response from a large majority of the
informants (see Table 6). Most observers familiar
with Eastern Nigeria have perceived the almost total
faith the people there place in education. In the
survey conducted by the Institute of International
Social Research, next to the desire for an improved
standard of living, more (60 percent) of the Nigerians
interviewed chose education for their children as a
personal aspiration than any other goal.[16] The
Michigan State University survey results also demonstrated the high value placed on education. When
they asked the farmers about the level of education
they would have set out to obtain if they were young
again, 51 percent said university education, 33 percent
secondary education, and 13 percent primary education.
Yet only 27 percent of the same respondents mentioned
a job requiring a university degree when asked about
the occupation they would have preferred if they were
young again, thus indicating a somewhat tenuous
perception of the relationship between formal education
and occupational requirements.[17] It should be noted
that this wholesale commitment to education also had
some possible negative implications since an investment
in agriculture rather than school fees probably would
have brought about more immediate rural development.

On the six questions pertaining to change and
innovation, the regional profile showed a score of
+4 (see Table 7). A quotient of +4 on questions
relating to change and innovation was obtained because
answers to questions 1, 3, 4, 5, and 6 displayed a
generally positive attitude while the response to the
question 2 revealed a generally negative attitude.

TABLE 6

Attitudes Toward Education

	Percent
1. Through education a man in the future can be anything he wants to be.	
a. agree	88.33
b. partly agree	6.25
c. disagree	4.79
d. no answer	.63
2. Through education a woman in the future can become anything she wants to be.	
a. agree	79.38
b. partly agree	7.71
c. disagree	12.29
d. no answer	.63
3. Imagine that during this year your income is £N100 more than last year. Imagine that you could use the money for one of the following purposes. Which would it be?	
a. pay school fees for your children or relatives	80.21
b. entertain people in the village	.42
c. use it to hire labor so that you can plant a bigger farm next year	7.29
d. make some improvement to your farm	2.92
e. buy a palm-oil press or some other machine with which you could go into business	1.88
f. take a title or perform some traditional rites	.83
g. save the money	.63
h. build a better house	2.92
i. buy a radio and bicycle	.00
j. no answer	2.92
4. A child should go as far in school as he can.	
a. agree	88.13
b. partly agree	8.33
c. disagree	2.92
d. no answer	.63

TABLE 7

Attitudes Toward Change and
Innovation

Percent

1. We should return to the traditional life
    of our ancestors in order to have a better
    life.

    a. agree   32.29
    b. partly agree   13.13
    c. disagree   53.13
    d. no answer   1.46

2. Life is changing too fast.

    a. agree   64.58
    b. partly agree   12.50
    c. disagree   22.08
    d. no answer   .83

3. It is not difficult for a person to adopt
    new customs.

    a. agree   55.00
    b. partly agree   10.21
    c. disagree   33.54
    d. no answer   1.25

4. If a new and useful farming technique was
    made known to you, would you be willing
    to be the first person in this village to
    try it?

    a. yes   83.54
    b. no   3.33
    c. willing to try, but not first   11.46
    d. no answer   1.67

5. Suppose that such a new practice was
    learned by a son of yours. Do you think
    it would be good to accept his recommen-
    dation of this new practice, even though
    you are his father and are older?

    a. yes   96.25
    b. no   1.67
    c. no answer   2.09

6. With which group do you, yourself, usually
    side in conflict situations in the village?

    a. old-fashioned group   13.54
    b. modern group   48.96
    c. both about equally   3.33
    d. neither   .83
    e. no answer (most of these said
        there was no conflict of this
        nature in their villages)   33.33

275

On the questions revealing degrees of optimism
the regional profile had a similar score of +3 (see
Table 8). In this attitudinal cluster, a majority
of the responses were positive with the exception
of the responses to question 4.

The responses to the questions concerning attitudes toward work also produced a +3 rating (see Table
9). For this set of questions, all of the responses,
with the exception of question 4, were assessed as
displaying a positive attitude toward work. Questions
1 and 5 evoked particularly positive answers. On
question 2, only 17.50 percent of the respondents
believed that they were entitled to the high-status
position of a supervisor and the remainder were
willing to work as laborers. The responses to question
4 were considered to demonstrate negative attitudes.
The Michigan State University survey had similar
results with their items concerning work. As they
reported, "Questions on attitudes toward work confirmed the popular impressions about Ibo and Ibibio
people. More than eight tenths agreed that work
should come first (82 percent), and that one should
judge a man by his success in his occupation (81
percent) and that the most important qualities of a
real man are his determination and ambition (88 percent)."18

The respondents answered all three questions
pertaining to self-reliance in a manner consistent
with a positive orientation (see Table 10). Hence
the villagers in Eastern Nigeria did not exhibit the
dependence on the government for improvements so
typical of many other developing political systems.

The cluster of questions relating to attitudes
toward money was one of the two on which the regional
sample had an overall negative score. For the four
questions two produced negative responses and one a
positive response (see Table 11).

The questions relevant to the political culture
also gave rise to a -2 score (see Table 12). The
responses to the first two questions in this cluster
might reflect the general condemnation of the civilian

TABLE 8

Attitudes Toward
Optimism-Pessimism

Percent

1. Five years from now, do you expect people
   in this village to be better off or worse
   off (economically) or about the same as
   they are today?

a.	better off	75.42
b.	about the same	7.92
c.	worse off	7.92
d.	no answer	8.75

2. What would you say about the progress of
   the village? Would you say it is

a.	progressing rapidly	35.00
b.	progressing slowly	50.42
c.	not progressing	7.71
d.	going backward	5.83
e.	no answer	1.04

3. What chance do you and others like you have
   to solve the problems of this community?
   Would you say your chances are

a.	good	65.42
b.	fair	24.17
c.	poor	10.21
d.	no answer	.21

4. The lot of the average man is getting worse.

a.	agree	58.13
b.	partly agree	10.63
c.	disagree	29.79
d.	no answer	1.46

5. It will be a long time before much
   progress is made in Nigeria.

a.	agree	29.79
b.	partly agree	13.54
c.	disagree	49.38
d.	no answer	7.29

TABLE 9

Attitudes Toward Work

	Percent
1. If you worked very hard, what would others in your community think of you?	
a. that you are a fool because it is not worth it	5.63
b. they would respect you more for it	86.67
c. it would not make any difference at all	2.71
d. no answer	5.00
2. If you were employed as a plantation worker by ENDC or some other company, do you think you should be hired as laborer or as a supervisor?	
a. laborer	26.25
b. supervisor	17.50
c. it is not for me to decide	53.75
d. no answer	2.50
3. Who does more farm work in this village, men or women?	
a. men	61.38
b. women	34.03
c. no answer	4.59
4. (If you cannot climb a palm tree) Would you be willing to learn how to?	
a. yes	10.21
b. no	20.83
c. no answer (most of these already knew how to climb)	68.96
5. A hard-working man is a good man.	
a. agree	89.38
b. partly agree	5.63
c. disagree	4.58
d. no answer	.42

TABLE 10

Attitudes Relating to Self-
Reliance

Percent

1. If you could choose, would you rather work
for some person or a company or start your
own business?

a.	other person	6.04
b.	company	34.17
c.	start own business	58.54
d.	no answer	1.25

2. Suppose your village needed a new road built
or improvements on old roads. Should this
be mainly the duty of the government, mainly
the duty of the villagers themselves, or is
it the joint duty of both the government and
the villagers working together?

a.	government	18.33
b.	villagers	35.63
c.	both together	45.21
d.	no answer	.83

. What about building a new school. Who should
be mainly responsible for this sort of
project?

a.	government	17.50
b.	villagers	37.50
c.	both together	43.13
d.	no answer	1.88

TABLE 11

Attitudes Toward Money

	Percent
1. In choosing a job, which of the following things is the most important in your estimation:	
a. the pay	31.67
b. the prestige or status of the job	34.79
c. the easiness of the work	6.88
d. the interest of the work	14.58
e. the power it gives you over other people	8.54
f. no answer	3.54
2. If you were offered a job that paid well, would you be willing to do any type of work, or are there certain types of work that would be too tedious, hard, or unpleasant for you to be willing to undertake?	
a. I would undertake any type of work	42.29
b. there are some types of work I would not be willing to undertake	56.04
c. no answer	2.50
3. The man who gets money finds happiness.	
a. agree	73.33
b. partly agree	16.04
c. disagree	10.42
d. no answer	.21

TABLE 12

Attitudes Relevant to the Political
Culture

	Percent
Some say the government is run just for the benefit of those in power. Others say that the government is run to benefit the people. What do you say?	
a. for those in power only	45.21
b. for the people	43.75
c. undecided	7.92
d. no answer	3.13
Suppose you or another person like you became involved in a court case, what chance would you have of getting justice?	
a. good chance	29.79
b. fair chance	17.50
c. poor chance	50.83
d. no answer	1.88
Some have been born to command and others to obey.	
a. agree	44.58
b. partly agree	6.88
c. disagree	47.29
d. no answer	1.25

political system widely expressed in 1966. Interviewing for this survey began in March 1966, two
months after civilian politics became the casualty
of a military coup. In light of the egalitarian
nature of the traditional political systems in Eastern
Nigeria, the responses to the third question came
as something of a surprise. It is probable that the
respondents interpreted the question to mean that not
all men are born with the same ability, rather than
its meaning that high station in life and political
power should reside in particular royal or aristocrati
families.

     Even if there is such a thing as a peasant world
view based on an "idea of a limited good," the people
of Eastern Nigeria, according to the survey results,
do not adhere to the prototype. The regional profile
complied from the results of this survey reveal a
this-worldly, forward-looking rural population embracing positive attitudes toward development; a
people for whom the desired things of life can be had
through planning for the future and engaging in hard
work. According to the survey results, Eastern
Nigerians are willing to experiment with innovations
and do not fear change. Far from being constrained
in their efforts to improve their environment by a
pervasive distrust and antipathy toward other members
of their community, the Eastern Nigerians surveyed
displayed a willingness to cooperate in order to
achieve development. At the time of the survey in
1966 they combined a belief in their ability to
control their destinies with optimism for the future,
obviously unaware of the tragic events soon to follow

INDIVIDUAL ATTITUDINAL CLUSTERS

     The second phase of the analysis of the survey
data involved an effort to discover attitude clusters
by determining whether there was an inclination on
the part of the respondents to answer sets of questio
in similar or related fashion. It was also attempted
determine which questions proved particularly useful
in differentiating respondents who had a positive
orientation toward change and development from those

who tended to have a negative orientation. To do
this analysis cross-tabulations were run between the
responses given to a particular question and the
responses given to all the questions that revealed
attitudes toward development. A development index
score was then calculated to indicate the extent to
which those answering the question in a manner
revealing a positive attitude toward development were
likely to answer other questions in the questionnaire
in a manner revealing a positive attitude toward
development. As indicated in an earlier section of
this chapter, the total number of questions in the
questionnaire that revealed attitudes relating to
development is 48. All indications of significant
differences are at the .05 level using the "t" test.

To illustrate the type of analysis done, item
2 in Table 13 indicates that those who believe they
have a good chance of getting justice in court responded in significantly different fashion to 14 out of
the remaining 47 questions from those who believe
they had only a fair or poor chance of getting justice.
Out of these 14 questions, those who believed they
had a good chance of justice gave responses indicating
a more favorable inclination toward development on
8 and responses less favorable to development on 6,
than did those who believed they only had a fair or
poor chance of getting justice. Adding the negative
scores (-6) to the positive scores (+8), we arrive
at what we term the development index score for this
question (+2). This score of +2 indicates that those
who believe they can get justice in court are slightly
more likely to answer other questions in the questionnaire in a manner indicating a positive attitude
toward development. But this +2 score indicates that
this question is not a very good means of differentiating persons with positive attitudes toward development from those with less positive attitudes.
On the other hand item 1 in Table 13, which has
a +11 development index score, is a good differen-
tiator.

Three questions central to an assessment of the
political culture were cross-tabulated with responses
given to other attitudinal questions. The three were

TABLE 13

Cross-Tabulations of Responses to Questions Relating to
Political Culture with the Remaining 47 Attitudinal Questions

Response to Basic Question	Number of Significant Differences in Cross-Tabulations	Development Index Score
1. Government is run for the benefit of the people (question 22)	17	+11
2. There is a good chance of getting justice (question 23)	14	+2
3. Most people can be trusted (question 40)	10	+6
4. Very good cooperation (question 66)	11	+3

(1) whether the government is run just for those in power or for the people, (2) whether there is a good chance of getting justice in a court case, and (3) whether most people can be trusted. Along with these three questions, the results of one part of the interviewer's appraisal of the informants, the degree of cooperation, was included to give a concrete indication of the level of the informant's trust and willingness to cooperate. Table 13 indicates the extent to which those who responded positively in terms of those attitudes significant to the political culture also tended to respond to the other attitudinal questions in the questionnaire in a manner indicating a positive orientation toward development.

As is apparent from the table, of the four questions the one about the government being run for the benefit of the people proved to be the best in terms of dividing those who tend to be positively oriented toward social and economic change from those who are not. Questions 1 and 2 also proved to be closely related, in that those who responded that the government is run for the benefit of the people were also likely to respond that they have a good chance of getting justice in court, while those who thought that the government is run for the benefit of those doing the governing also believed that it is hard to obtain justice.

The characteristics of the respondents exhibiting positive social and political attitudes on these four questions offer some hope for the future. For instance, the villagers who believed that the government is run for the benefit of the people were more likely to be educated, literate, and Christian and to listen to the radio daily. Those answering that there is a good chance of getting justice tended to be those who had many relatives who had migrated from the village. The informants who cooperated very well in the interview had mostly attended school, were Christians, and had many relatives living outside of the village. Hence the greater the educational level and the exposure to the world beyond the village, the more likely it is that the respondent has absorbed a political culture conducive to development.

Most developing countries face the problem of
the proclivity of large numbers of rural residents
to emigrate into urban centers that lack the facilitie
to care for them and to provide them with jobs.   In
the survey of Eastern Nigeria, respondents answering
the question, "Do you ever think seriously about movir
away and living in another village or a township?"
with the response "often" or "sometimes" were particularly those between the ages of 30 and 44 with eight
or more of their relatives already resident in urban
areas.   Those answering in this fashion were also like
ly to have attended school and to listen to the radio
daily.   Those who indicated interest in emigrating
from the village were more likely to respond to other
attitudinal questions in a manner indicating a positiv
orientation toward economic and social development.
Of the 18 questions upon which those who said they
thought of leaving the village responded in significantly different fashion from those who said they do
not think about leaving their villages, on 12 they
gave responses more favorable to development while
on 6 they gave responses less favorable to developmen
giving those who contemplated leaving the village a
+6 development index score.   Those villagers considering emigration scored particularly high on question
dealing with the possibility of an individual's being
able to control his destiny.

When comparing the results of these cross-tabulations with the results reported in Chapter 8 regard
ing attitudinal differences between responsive and
unresponsive villages, it is important to bear in
mind that those communities were differentiated from
each other in terms of their responsiveness to community agricultural programs.   Thus, community cohesion
a folk-like society, and lack of out-migration contributed to the willingness of a community to engage
in a cooperative agricultural project engaging the
whole community.   In this chapter individual differences in attitudes toward development are being discussed, which means individual responsiveness to
individual activity, embracing both agricultural and
nonagricultural activities.

The responses given to two questions dealing wit

TABLE 14

Cross-Tabulations of Responses to Questions
Relating to Change with the Remaining 47
Attitudinal Questions

Response to Basic Question	Number of Significant Differences in Cross-Tabulations	Development Index Score
1. We should not return to the traditional life (question 34)	4	+3
2. It is not difficult to adopt new customs (question 36)	17	+9

287

commitment to change and innovation were also cross-
tabulated with responses given to the other attitudinal
questions. One of the questions asked whether the
informant thought his people should return to the
traditional life of their ancestors in order to have
a better life, and the other question asked whether
it is difficult for a person to adopt new customs.
As indicated in Table 14, the question concerning
the adoption of new customs had some value in dividing
those with generally favorable attitudes toward development from those with less favorable attitudes.

     Ever since the publication of Max Weber's theorie
about the Protestant ethnic,[19] many social scientists
have considered certain attitudes associated with
the entrepreneurial prototype as essential for economi
development. David McClelland, whose views were
mentioned at the beginning of this chapter, is one
of the foremost contemporary exponents of this hypothesis. Even without proof of a cause and effect
relationship between the incidence of entrepreneurial
behavior and national economic development, it is easy
to see how some traits like self-reliance, dedication
to work, willingness to defer consumption, and belief
in the utility of self-improvement efforts could contribute to development. As Chapter 8 indicated, the
question most clearly distinguishing those communities
desirous of establishing a community plantation from
those uninterested in doing so was one relating to
self-reliance, i.e., the preference of the former
group for starting their own businesses rather than
working for another person or a company. To make
some determination of the extent to which responses
to questions relating to the entrepreneurial spirit
were related to overall attitudes impinging on development, cross-tabulations of responses to entrepre-
neurial-related questions were analyzed with responses
to the whole set of attitudinal questions, the results
of which are given in Table 15. Only one of the questions listed in Table 15 appears to be of much value
in predicting responses to other items in the questior
naire. It is obvious, then, that what is referred to
as attitudes toward development are by no means unin-
dimensional. They cover a wide area on the attitudina
map. Moreover, even within several subsets of

Table 15

Cross-Tabulations of Responses to Questions Relating
to Entrepreneurial Behavior with the Remaining 47 Attitudinal Questions

Response to Basic Question	Number of Significant Differences in Cross-Tabulations	Development Index Score
1. Prefer to start own business (question 24)	8	0
2. Working harder can bring a higher standard of living (question 26)	23	+1
3. A poor man can become rich through his own efforts (question 28)	13	+1
4. Disagree that success depends on luck (question 30)	8	+6
5. A wise man learns to forego immediate pleasures for more lasting satis- factions in the future (question 50)	1	+1
6. A man who gets money finds happiness (question 62)	18	0
7. Willing to do any type of work that paid well (question 56)	14	+4
8. Willing to be a laborer on a plantation (question 55)	4	0

TABLE 16

Cross-Tabulations of Responses to 25 Questions
Relating to Entrepreneurialism

	Response to Basic Question	Number of Significant Differences in Cross-Tabulations	Development Index Score
1.	Prefer to start own business (question 24)	5	-1
2.	Working harder can bring a higher standard of living (question 26)	14	0
3.	A poor man can become rich through his own efforts (question 28)	9	+3
4.	Disagree that success depends upon luck (question 30)	6	+6
5.	A wise man learns to forego immediate pleasures for more lasting satisfactions in the future (question 50)	0	0
6.	A man who gets money finds happiness (question 62)	12	0
7.	Willing to do any type of work which paid well (question 56)	8	+2
8.	Willing to be a laborer on a plantation (question 55)	3	0

questions that appear to be assessing closely related
attitudes, what appears to be some inconsistency in
responses to similar questions has been discovered.
The questionnaire devised is not a highly sophisticated
instrument, and no effort has been made to try to
incorporate scaling features or to attempt factor
analysis. Whether the subject matter lends itself
to this kind of analysis will have to be tested by
other investigators.

Table 16 summarizes the results of cross-tabulations between responses given to particular questions
relating to the entrepreneurial spirit and all the
other questions in the questionnaire that relate to
the entrepreneurial spirit in an attempt to check
the consistency of responses to a variety of questions
relating to the same general subject. The 25 questions
in the questionnaire thought to relate to the entrepreneurial spirit are those regarding work, money,
control over one's destiny, self-reliance, and optimism.

The analysis of the Eastern Nigeria Rural Development Attitude Survey conducted in 24 villages during
the early months of 1966 showed generally positive
attitudes toward development in the region, particularly on questions relating to education, change and
innovation, optimism, work, and self-reliance. However,
cross-tabulations of the responses did not reveal
easily definable clusters of attitudes or core
attitudes whose adherents were the most favorably
inclined toward development. Only a few of the
questions proved to be of much value in predicting
the responses that would be given to other attitudinal
questions, and thus the authors did not discover a
few key attitudes that could serve as a shorthand
index to indicate whether an individual or group had
a positive orientation toward development.

NOTES

1. Kenneth Anthony and Bruce F. Johnston,
"Field Study of Agriculture Change: Northern Katsina,

Nigeria," (Stanford, Calif.:   Food Research Institute, Stanford University, 1968, mimeographed).

2.   See for example Philip M. Hauser, "Cultural
and Personal Obstacles to Economic Development in
Less Developed Areas," Human Organization, 18 (Summer
1959), 78-84; Arthur H. Niehoff and J. Charnel Anderso
"Peasant Fatalism and Socio-Economic Innovation,"
Human Organization, 25 (Winter 1966), 273-283; Edward
C. Banfield, The Moral Basis of a Backward Society
(Glencoe, Illinois: The Free Press, 1958); and
George M. Foster, "Peasant Society and the Image of
the Limited Good," American Anthropologist, 67 (April
1965), 293-315.

3.   Hauser, op. cit.; George M. Foster, "Interpersonal Relations in Peasant Society," Human
Organization, 19 (Winter 1960-61), 174-178.

4.   Foster, "Peasant Society and the Image of
the Limited Good," p. 296.

5.   David C. McClelland, The Achieving Society
(Princeton, N.J.:   Van Nostrand, 1961), particularly
p. 251.

6.   Ibid.

7.   Robert LeVine, Dreams and Deeds: Achievemen*
Motivation in Nigeria (Chicago: University of Chicag(
Press, 1966).

8.   Lloyd A. Free, The Attitudes, Hopes and Fear:
of Nigerians (Princeton, N.J.:   Institute for International Social Research, 1964).

9.   See Gerald D. Hursh, Niels G. Roling, and
Graham B. Kerr, "Innovation in Eastern Nigeria:
Success and Failure of Agricultural Programs in 71
Villages of Eastern Nigeria," and Joseph R. Ascroft,
Niels G. Roling, Graham B. Kerr and Gerald D. Hursh,
"Patterns of Diffusion in Rural Eastern Nigeria"
(East Lansing: Department of Communication, Michigan
State University, 1968 and 1969, mimeographed).

10. LeVine, op. cit., pp. 4-5.

11. McClelland, op. cit.

12. See, for example, Gabriel A. Almond and G. Bingham Powell, Jr., Comparative Politics: A Developmental Approach (Boston: Little, Brown and Company, 1966), pp. 50-57.

13. See Lucian W. Pye and Sidney Verba, eds., Political Culture and Political Development (Princeton, N.J.: Princeton University Press, 1965), particularly p. 22.

14. Pye and Verba, op. cit., p. 22; Almond and Powell, op. cit., p. 55; Gabriel A. Almond and Sidney Verba, The Civic Culture (Princeton, N. J.: Princeton University Press, 1963), pp. 208-243.

15. See for example Foster, "Interpersonal Relations in Peasant Society," and Banfield.

16. Free, op. cit., p. 27.

17. Ascroft, Roling, Kerr, and Hursh, op. cit., p. 41.

18. Ibid.

19. Max Weber, The Protestant Ethnic and the Spirit of Capitalism (New York: Charles Scribner's Sons, 1958). The work was originally published in 1904.

11

ETHNICITY
AND GROUP DIFFERENCES
IN ATTITUDES
TOWARD
DEVELOPMENT

Characterizations of the Ibo usually emphasize their exceptionally positive orientation toward development and modernization. In their attempts to account for the remarkable transformation of the Ibo, who in 40 years propelled themselves out of the isolation and improverishment of life in primitive, autonomous villages into a position among the leading ethnic groups in Nigeria's modern sector, analysts cite certain aspects of Ibo culture: equality of opportunity, stress on individual initiative and achievement, competition in every sphere of life, preoccupation with material concerns, acceptance of change, willingness to innovate, participation in politics, and pragmatism. Commentators also usually assume that the Ibo now share a common cultural orientation, even though the Ibo did not exist as a self-conscious and unified community prior to the colonial period. However, it seems unwarranted to suppose that a people who lived in approximately 600 autonomous village groups prior to the colonial period would have necessarily renounced all cultural differences when embracing an Ibo identity. Moreover, given the basic similarities in the traditional institutions and culture among Eastern Nigeria's various ethnic groups and the exposure to the same stimuli for change during the colonial period, it also seems unwarranted to assume that Ibo attitudes toward development are unique among groups from Eastern Nigeria.

Very few attempts have been made either to measure variations among various Ibo subgroups or to compare systematically Ibo attitudes with those of other ethnic groups. Robert LeVine's Dreams and Deeds, which compares Ibo, Yoruba, and Hausa school-boys, confirms in its conclusions the stereotype that the Ibo rank the highest in achievement motivation. One can, however, dispute whether LeVine's data justify this conclusion. For instance, half of his research data, i.e., the analysis of achievement and obedience values expressed in essays written by the schoolboys, resulted in a Yoruba-Hausa-Ibo ranking contrary to his conclusion of an Ibo-Yoruba-Hausa order on achievement.[1] In his depiction of the Ibo and the Efik in Calabar, W. T. Morrill attributes the immigrant Ibo economic ascendance to the willingness of the Ibo, in contrast to the Efik, to undertake any type of work.[2] Most descriptions contrasting the Ibo to other ethnic groups in Nigeria are based upon impressions rather than systematic research, and few analysts have compared the Ibo with other peoples specifically from Eastern Nigeria.

This chapter addresses itself to the following questions: whether the Ibo attitudes toward development are unique in Eastern Nigeria, whether it is meaningful to generalize about uniform Ibo orientation toward development, and whether factors other than ethnicity better account for differences in attitude toward development in the region. Using the data from the attitude survey described in the preceding chapter, group differences were determined on the basis of ethnicity, religion, wealth, literacy, frequency of radio listening, age, schooling, and number of relatives living in a city. As indicated in Chapter 10, the survey was conducted in three parts of Eastern Nigeria: Group A, the northern and eastern Ibo areas, which are the more traditional Ibo areas; Group B, the central and southern Ibo areas, which are the more acculturated Ibo sections; and Group C, minority (Ibibio, Boki, and Ijaw) ethnic localities. In each of these areas 160 people from 8 villages were interviewed. For the remainder of this chapter, the three sets of villages will be

designated Group A, Group B, and Group C. As in
the preceding chapter, for a difference between two
groups to be considered significant, it must be at
the .05 level using the "t" test. The focus of this
chapter is an attempt to contrast responses given by
various subgroups of the sample. The first comparison
is between the responses given to the questionnaire
by Ibo and non-Ibo respondents, which is followed by
a comparison of two Ibo subgroups. The final section
of the chapter compares the responses given by groups
distinguished in terms of differences in wealth,
literacy, and radio listening; and it attempts to
assess the relative importance of these factors as
opposed to ethnic identity as determinants of attitudinal differences. Analysis of responses given
by subgroups distinguished by differences in age,
schooling, and number of relatives living in a city
indicated that these differences did not give rise
to significantly different attitudinal profiles.

COMPARISON OF IBO AND NON-IBO ATTITUDES

    Contrary to established stereotypes, the results
showed the non-Ibo, i.e., the Ibibio, Rivers, and
Boki villages of Group C, to be significantly more
development oriented than the two groups of Ibo
villages when compared separately or when the two
Ibo groups are taken as a unit. On those questions
for which there were statistically significant differences between the responses of the Ibo and non-
Ibo villages, the latter (Group C) had the ranking
indicating a more favorable attitude toward development on the vast majority of them. When compared
with Groups A and B as a unit, Group C had a development index score of +15. Group C exhibited particularly strong commitments to development in the
following attitudinal clusters: money, change and
innovation, optimism, trust and cooperation, and
education. In addition, Group C manifested a more
favorable attitude toward the political system than
Groups A or B. Groups A and B had a more favorable
rating than Group C on only two groups of questions:
control over one's destiny and self-reliance. The
higher scores for the Ibibio, Boki, and Oliobiri-Ogbia

(Ijaw) villages do not, of course, mean that the
Ibo are not favorably inclined toward development.
As the regional profile demonstrated, all participating groups seemed to have very positive attitudes
toward development. However the results do undermine
the conception of the Ibo as being unique or as
being more receptive to development than the other
peoples of Eastern Nigeria.

When compared with the Ibo villages of Groups
A and B, Group C had a development index score of
+4 on questions concerning attitudes toward money.
Table 17 indicates the four questions relating to
money on which significant differences occur between
the Ibos and non-Ibos and on all four of these
questions Group C had the more favorable attitude.

As indicated in Table 18, the non-Ibos surveyed
proved to be more optimistic about the future.
Again, on the three items revealing the informants'
attitudes toward the future that gave rise to
significant differences between Group A-B and Group
C, Group C demonstrated a more favorable attitude
on all of them.

As Table 19 reveals, the people in Group C also
seemed to be more positively oriented toward education.

The three groups manifested consistent difference
with regard to their views on trust and cooperation,
as indicated in Table 20. Again Group C had the most
development oriented attitudes.

As shown in Table 21 Group C also displayed a
+3 development index score on questions relating to
change and innovation. Of the five questions in
this category that gave rise to significant differences between the two sets of informants, Group C
demonstrated a more positive orientation toward
development on four.

Discussions about politics in the former Eastern
Region frequently depict the minority ethnic groups
as being restive under the reputedly Ibo-dominated

TABLE 17

Comparison of Attitudes Toward Money
Among Ibo and Non-Ibo Groups

itude/Response	Response by Percentage			
	A^a	B^a	$A-B^b$	C^a
The man who gets money finds happiness (question 62)	58.1	79.4	68.8	82.4
Willingness to do any type of work that pays well (question 56)	40.0	36.9	38.4	49.7
In choosing a job pay is the most important consideration (question 47)	32.5	24.4	28.4	38.4
Would spend £N100 more in income in making improvements to farm (question 54)	0.6	0.6	0.6	7.5

a. In all tables in this section of the chapter, the following categories are
ained:

Group A was composed of traditional Ibo villages.
Group B was composed of more acculturated Ibo villages.
Group C was composed of non-Ibo villages.

b. In all tables in this section, A-B is the composite score of both Ibo groups.
ip differences are evaluated by comparing this composite score to the findings for
ip C.

TABLE 18

Comparison of Attitudes Toward the Future
Among Ibo and Non-Ibo Groups

itude/Response	Response by Percentage			
	A	B	A-B	C
Expect people in village to be better off in five years (question 18)	71.6	71.9	71.8	83.0
The village is progressing rapidly (question 19)	29.4	28.1	28.8	47.8
Good chance to solve problems of own community (question 21)	52.5	66.3	59.4	77.4

TABLE 19

Comparison of Attitudes Toward Education Among
Ibo and Non-Ibo Groups

Attitude/Response	Response by Percentage			
	A	B	A-B	C
1. A child should go as far in school as he can (question 63)	81.9	88.1	85.0	94.3
2. Through education a man in the future can become anything he wants (question 38)	89.4	83.0	86.3	92.5
3. Through education a woman in the future can become anything she wants (question 39)	71.9	77.5	74.7	88.7

TABLE 20

Comparison of Attitudes Toward Trust and Cooperation
Among Ibo and Non-Ibo Groups

Attitude/Response	Response by Percentage			
	A	B	A-B	C
1. Disagree that these days a person doesn't know whom to count on in a difficult situation (question 37)	16.3	16.9	16.6	26.4
2. Most people can be trusted (question 40)	3.8	8.1	5.9	20.8
3. People in village have worked together on a project recently (question 14)				

Comparison of Attitudes Toward Change and Innovation
Among Ibo and non-Ibo Groups

Attitude/Response	Response by Percentage		
	A	B	A-B	C
1. Disagree we should return to the traditional life of our ancestors (question 34)	52.5	45.6	49.1	61.6
2. It is not difficult for a person to adopt new customs (question 36)	39.4	50.0	44.7	76.1
3. Side with modern group in situations of conflict in village (question 52c)	48.8	33.8	41.3	64.2
4. Willing to be first in trying new farm technique (question 44)	75.0	80.0	77.5	95.6
5. Agree life is changing too fast (question 35)	53.1	62.5	57.8	76.1

TABLE 22

Comparison of Attitudes Toward the Eastern Nigerian
Government Among Ibo and Non-Ibo Groups

Attitude/Response	Response by Percentage		
	A	B	A-B	C
1. Government is run for the people (question 22)	31.9	36.3	34.1	63.5
2. There is a good chance of getting justice in a court case (question 23)	10.0	26.3	18.1	53.5

NCNC regional government and therefore seeking a
separate regional administration.[3] Far from being
restive under the NCNC regional government, the
results (see Table 22) suggest that the non-Ibo
villagers questioned in the survey had consistently
more positive attitudes toward the government than
the Ibo informants and seemed to manifest greater
confidence in the political system.

    Despite the more-favorable attitudes toward
development exhibited by Group C on many questions,
on some questions the Ibo informants in either
Group A or Group B responded equally to or more
positively than the non-Ibo informants. Groups A
and B combined scored better than Group C particular
on the questions dealing with self-reliance. Group
C had a O development index score for the category
of control over one's destiny (see Table 23) and
a -2 development index score for the cluster of
questions connected with self-reliance (see Table 24)
On the first five questions in Table 23 the responses
of Group C were considered to exhibit a less-positive
attitude toward development, and on the final
three questions their answers were evaluated as
being more positive, resulting in a -2 development
index score for the category of control over one's
destiny for Group C or a +2 for Groups A-B. For the
first question in Table 24 Group C had the highest
response to the non-self-reliant attitude that new
roads are the sole responsibility of the government
while for question 2 Group C had the lowest score
for the more self-reliant attitude that the government and the villagers should jointly build new
schools.

    Since the results of the survey contradict some
current notions about the uniqueness of the Ibo, it
is important to suggest possible sources of these
inaccuracies. Assumptions about the uniqueness of
the Ibo seem to result in part from the lack of
knowledge about other ethnic groups. Little research
has been done on the Ibibio, the second largest ethni
group in the Eastern Region, and virtually none on
some of the other groups. As Chapter 3 indicated,
the authors' information about the Ibibio and some

Comparison of Attitudes Relating to Control Over One's
Destiny Among Ibo and Non-Ibo Groups

Attitude/Response	Response by Percentage			
	A	B	A-B	C
1. Success in life depends on luck rather than ability (question 30)	58.1	68.1	63.1	73.0
2. It's who you know not what you know that counts (question 48)	64.4	54.4	59.4	89.9
3. Disagree that man should think more of present demands than visions of the future (question 51)	37.5	40.0	38.8	62.3
4. Disagree that for average man it is useless to plan for future (question 25)	86.9	90.0	88.4	75.5
5. Harder work helps get a higher standard of living (question 26)	72.5	90.0	81.3	41.5
6. Someone who sacrifices to the right shrines will prosper (question 43)	45.0	28.8	36.9	24.5
7. A poor man can become rich through his own efforts (question 28)	60.6	76.9	68.8	83.6
8. Disagree it is useless to try to change your fate (question 29)	30.0	27.5	28.8	40.3

303

of the other smaller ethnic groups depicts the
traditional social structure of the Ibibio and the
Ibo as being very similar. For most of the ethnic
groups in Eastern Nigeria, the lineage, age sets,
and autonomous village-group constitute the relevant
traditional social and political units. Both the
Ibo and the Ibibio had title societies constituted
by the wealthiest men in the community. Most groups
traditionally chose political leaders on the basis
of ability rather than according to the inheritance
of chiefly positions. Although many minor variations
are found, similarities exist in many important
categories of culture.

Furthermore, during the colonial period the
ethnic groups in Eastern Nigeria experienced roughly
similar stimuli for change. The colonial administration followed its basic policies in all parts of
the region. Since sections of the Ibibio territory
were almost as overcrowded as the extremely densely
populated Ibo communities, both groups responded to
new economic opportunities by flocking to cities in
the East and in other parts of Nigeria. Immigrants
from Ibibio and Ibo groups in the cities formed
ethnic unions to bring improvements to their home
villages and to endow scholarships for study abroad.

The stereotyped image of the modernistic,
achievement-motivated, and aggressive Ibo came into
vogue because it is to a great extent accurate.
Again it should be emphasized that the survey
profiles do not refute the favorable attitudes
toward change attributed to the Ibo. The survey
results do demonstrate, however, that some of the
other ethnic groups of Eastern Nigeria like the
Ibibios, Rivers people, and the Boki may have, at
least in their responses to the survey questions,
an even more favorable orientation toward development

IBO ATTITUDES TOWARD DEVELOPMENT:
A COMPARISON OF GROUP A AND GROUP B

Group A and Group B, the two Ibo groups, did
not have the same attitude profile. On the 48

TABLE 24

Comparison of Attitudes Toward Self-Reliance Among
Ibo and Non-Ibo Groups

Attitude/Response	Response by Percentage			
	A	B	A-B	C
New roads are the sole res- ponsibility of the govern- ment (question 16)	15.6	11.3	13.4	28.3
Building new schools should be the respon- sibility of both the government and the villagers (question 17)	50.6	42.5	46.6	36.5

TABLE 25

Comparison of Ibo Attitudes Toward Control Over One's
Destiny

Attitude/Response	Response by Percentage	
	A	B
A poor man can become rich through his own efforts (question 28)	60.6	76.9
Harder work results in a higher standard of living (question 26)	72.5	90.0
Disagree that success in life depends on luck rather than ability (question 30)	13.1	20.0
A contribution to church makes the donor prosper (question 42)	56.3	45.0
Disagree that someone who sacrifices to the right shrines will prosper (question 43)	39.4	60.0
Disagree that it's who you know not what you know that counts (question 48)	13.8	32.5

questions concerning attitudes toward development, the two Ibo groups gave significantly different responses to 26 of them. A major conclusion from the survey, therefore, is to warn against making general characterizations of the Ibo.

A comparison of the two Ibo groups shows Group B (the more acculturated Ibo communities) to be slightly more development oriented. For those questions on which a significant difference occurred between the responses of Groups A and B, Group B had a +4 development index score. Group B tended to have more favorable attitudes particularly when answering questions relating to control over one's destiny and optimism while Group A manifested a greater development orientation for the cluster of questions concerning work and change and innovation. As can be seen from Table 25, for the cluster of questions pertaining to control over one's destiny, Group B had a +6 development index score.

As indicated in Table 26, for the questions dealing with optimism, Group B had a +3 development index score and Group A inversely a -3.

Even more strikingly, Group A had a +5 rating for questions relating to work and inversely Group B a -5 (see Table 27). (In the analysis of the responses depicted in Table 27, the lower rate of refusal of Group A to learning to climb a palm tree was considered a more positive attitude.)

When the responses of Group B were compared with the combined answers to Groups A and C, Group B had the most development-oriented results on four questions dealing with control over one's destiny. When the answers of Group A were similarly contrasted with the combined totals for Groups B and C, these responses were evaluated as more development oriented on two questions pertaining to control over destiny, one concerning change and innovation, one relating to work, and one relevant to political attitudes.

The variations observed in the responses of the two Ibo subgroups can be explained as a persistence

Comparison of Ibo Attitudes Toward the Future

Attitude/Response	Response by Percentage	
	A	B
1. Disagree that lot of average man is getting worse (question 32)	23.8	35.6
2. There is a good chance to solve the problems of our community (question 21)	52.5	66.3
3. Expect village to be worse off in five years (question 18)	13.1	3.8

TABLE 27

Comparison of Ibo Attitudes Toward Work

Attitude/Response	Response by Percentage	
	A	B
1. Men do more work in village (question 61)	86.3	67.5
2. Not willing to learn to climb palm tree (question 60b)	20.0	30.0
3. In choosing a job the interest of the work is the most important consideration (question 47)	21.9	10.6
4. Willingness to be hired as planta- tion laborer (question 55)	23.8	11.9
5. If you worked harder others would respect you more (question 27)	91.3	83.8

of the precolonial fragmentation. Prior to the
colonial period the autonomous Ibo village-groups
did not share a common Ibo indentity or owe allegianc
to any common political superstructure. Missionaries
colonial officers, and anthropologists set the boundaries of the Ibo people primarily on the basis of
linguistic considerations. Even when the various
groups began embracing a common Ibo identity during
the last 30 years, each subgroup still maintained
its dialect and many of its distinctive customs.
Even today certain Ibo dialects remain mutually
unintelligible, and customs differ markedly from
area to area.

Furthermore, the development of a more inclusive
Ibo indentity did not displace the more parochial
clan subidentities, which contained to be more relevant in most situations. Within the micropolitical
community the same groups continued to compete
against each other. Only in border areas, in which
Ibo and non-Ibo groups lived contiguously, would
these local conflicts take on Ibo versus non-Ibo
dimensions. On the micropolitical level the character of competition between an Ibo subgroup and a
non-Ibo subgroup hardly differed from the rivalries
among Ibo subgroups. In the wider political arena
of the urban centers and on the regional level,
few political issues resulted in a simple Ibo/non-
Ibo division. The most significant political
divisions usually occurred between various Ibo subgroups, with each often organized on the basis of
colonial provincial boundaries and allied with
other Ibo subgroups and some minority groups. The
Ibo identity per se did not become critical until
shortly before the disintegration of Nigeria and
the attending persecution of Ibos on the basis of
ethnic indentity.

There has been an almost irresistible urge to
generalize about the entire Ibo linguistic group on
the basis of detailed research on one or a few villages or clans. Consequently, writing on the Ibo
more often stresses general (and unverified) Ibo
cultural characteristics rather than systematically
elucidating differences among subgroups. This
tendency for scholars and journalists to generalize

about the Ibo people has undoubtedly played some
part in fostering the stereotyped image of the Ibo.
Some classifications of the Ibo people do, however
correctly emphasize the existence of territorial
variations. Daryll Forde and G. I. Jones, for example, divide the Ibo into 5 main groups and 13 subgroups.[4] Some other scholars also emphasize the
distinctiveness of certain cultural traits and elements of the sociopolitical structure of the Ibo
subgroup that they are analyzing; but even when
scholars assume a micropolitical perspective and
resist generalizing to the entire Ibo-speaking people,
readers easily slip from the particular to the inclusive frame of reference. This predilection for the
more inclusive frame of reference probably reflects
several factors: the greater ease of dealing with
data in a macropolitical perspective, the absence
of a sufficient number of in-depth Ibo community
studies to make meaningful comparisons, and the
emergence of the Ibo on the world scene only after
the achievement of some pan-Ibo unity.

Overlaying the broad traits that Eastern Nigeria's
many ethnic groups shared, each community infused
distinctive customs, institutions, and attitudes to
meld a unique cultural unit. Thus there is a need
for systematic research to study subgroup variations
among large ethnic blocs like the Ibo. Before social
scientists can understand more precisely the relationships between cultural factors and development
orientations, additional research must be undertaken
on traditional and contemporary values in specific
communities so that these can be correlated with the
development process. When two Ibo groups can differ
more than they correspond in their scores on an
attitude survey, it does not make sense merely to
lump them together in a category designated "development oriented" and to mask the divergences and
uniqueness of each.

ETHNIC AND OTHER GROUP
DIFFERENCES COMPARED

The tendency among many observers of Africa has
been to stress ethnic variations in explaining group

differences. As one travels from place to place in
Africa, contrasts in settlement patterns, rituals,
inheritance, preferences, priorities, farming practices, and even appearance and dress often loom large
Surveys conducted in other parts of Africa have
verified the importance of ethnicity as a determinant
of attitudes. With an interview battery consisting
of an 85-item questionnaire, 10 Rorshach plates, 22
color slides, and 9 TAT-like value-pictures, a team
of anthropologists elicited internally consistent
and distinctive sets of responses from four ethnic
groups: the Kamba, Pokot, and Sebei in Kenya and the
Hehe in Tanzania. While the anthropologist assessing
the results found the relationship between ecology
and culture to be complicated and reciprocal, he
indicated that cultural factors arising from ethnic
differences were more decisive in determining values
attitudes, and personality.[5] Another East African
survey conducted in Kenya, Uganda, and Tanzania to
determine attitudes, ideas, and motives in connection
with issues relevant to social and economic development and particularly to family planning also resulte
in clear ethnic differences. Attitudes toward family
planning, for example, seemed to correlate with
ethnic origins, educational level, actual living conditions, and exposure to information and propaganda
on family planning. The rank order of favorable
dispositions to family planning among the ethnic
groups surveyed was as follows: Kikuyu (Kenya), Gand
(Uganda), Luo (Kenya), Jita (Tanzania), Kara (Uganda
Kerewe (Tanzania), and Sukuma (Tanzania).[6]

    The purpose of this section of the chapter is t
assess the relative importance of ethnic factors as
opposed to wealth, religious affiliation, and other
modernizing influences in shaping attitudes toward
change and development in Eastern Nigeria. As
already mentioned, such factors as age and education
are not discussed because they were found upon analy
not to give rise to significant differences in responses to items in the survey questionnaire.

    In terms of exposure and responsiveness to mode
izing influences, Group C was subjected to the great
exposure, followed by B and then A. Because of the

insufficient historical data, it is impossible to
rank these areas accurately as to when and to what
degree they had European contact, except to say that
the villages in Group A had less contact with
European and other acculturating agents than the
villages of Groups B and C. Evidence of the differing
degrees of modernizing influence is seen in variations
in the level of schooling, in literacy, in radio
listening, and in religious affiliation. While 65.6
percent of the villagers in Group A and 42.5 percent
of those in Group B had never attended school, only
37.1 percent in Group C had not received any formal
education. Some 16.4 percent of the villagers in
Group C had completed primary school (standard VI)
in comparison with 6.9 percent in Group B and 5.0
percent in Group A. A total of 40.3 percent of the
people in Group C answered that they could read and
write a letter, while in Groups B and A the respective
figures were 32.5 percent and 26.9 percent. Similarly,
32.1 percent of the respondents in Group C listened
to the radio daily in contrast to 21.3 percent in
Group B and 11.3 percent in Group A. Only 12.6 percent
of the people in Group C had not become Christians
while 26.9 percent in Group B and 58.7 percent in
Group A still practiced their traditional religion.
In Group A 20.0 percent were Catholic and 21.3 Protestant; in Group B 43.1 were Catholic and 25.0
Protestant; and figures for Group C were 44.0 and
41.5 respectively.

     Many of these differences between Groups A, B,
and C, however, are not statistically significant.
For instance, in terms of school attendance and
literacy, the somewhat higher percentages for Group
C do not differ with Group B at the .05 level. In
terms of radio listening, there was not a significant
difference between the number of villagers in Group
C and Group B who never listened but there was in
the number who listened daily. While Group C and Group
B did have a significant variation in the percentage
of informants who adhered to Christianity, they did
not in the percentage that were Catholic.

     In order to contrast the responses of individuals
from relatively poor and relatively wealthy villages

(see Table 28), what proved to be the clearest and
most easily determinable indicator of wealth, i.e.,
house types, were used. An analysis of the materials
used for the walls, roofs, and floors of the houses
of the informants indicated that Group B was the
wealthiest, followed by C and then A. While 29.4
percent of the villagers in Group B had walls of
concrete in their homes, 17.0 percent in Group C and
only 8.8 percent of Group A had them. The remainder
had mud walls. Similarly, 53.1 percent of the
respondents in Group B had zinc or aluminum roofs
in comparison with 24.5 percent in Group C and 20.6
percent in Group A. The remainder had thatched roofs.
In contrast to the 36.3 percent in Group B who had
concrete floors, 22.0 percent in Group A had them,
and the remainder had mud floors. Using house types
as the basis for differentiation, the 24 villages
surveyed were divided into two groups: one relatively
poor and the other relatively wealthy. The category
of rich villages was constituted as follows: two
villages from Group A, seven villages from Group B,
and three villages from Group C. The two villages
from Group A came one each from Udi and Nsukka
Divisions; of the seven from Group B, two were located
in Onitsha Division, one in Orlu Division, two in
Owerri Division, and two in Awka Division. Two
villages from Ogoja Division and one from Abak Division
comprised the three rich villages in Group C. The
category of poor villages was composed of six villages
from Group A, one from Group B, and five from Group
C. Group A's contributions came one from Udi Division
one from Nsukka Division, two from Afikpo Division,
and two from Abakaliki Division. The sole poor
village from Group B was in Orlu Division, and the
five poor villages from Group C were located two
each in Uyo and Brass Divisions and one in Abak
Division.

Another factor analyzed in the survey results
is differences in responses given by Christians and
non-Christians, i.e., those still practicing the
traditional religion (see Table 28). Except where
religious differences coincide with traditional cultural patterns and conversion occurred during an
early period, as in the Islamic reinforcement of

Hausa-Fulani social and political structure in
northern Nigeria, most analysts believe that contemporary religious affiliation to imported faiths does
not substantially affect attitudes. For example,
Angela Molnos, the author of the survey on family
planning in East Africa, states, in response to the
lack of a correlation in her survey between Christianity and positive attitudes toward development, that
traditional value systems operate at a deeper and
more effective level.[7] Many people suppose that
conversion to Christianity frequently entails only
a nominal profession of dogma and doctrine and that
traditional religious beliefs infuse the practice
of the new religion. Since education in most parts
of Africa could be obtained until recently only or
primarily in church schools, conversion seemed to
be motivated by the desire to acquire schooling.

    Table 28 also gives the results of the analysis
of the possible impact of literacy and radio listening
on attitudes toward development. Initially, colonial
administrators and social scientists assumed that
literacy and exposure to modernizing influence would
not be compatible with the maintenance of traditional
cultural bonds and thought patterns. This was the
era during which residents of urban centers and
school graduates were termed "detribalized" individuals. More recent research has demonstrated that
urbanization and modernization does not erode ethnic
loyalties.[8] This study mentions, for example, the
significant contribution the "sons abroad" made to
the development of their home communities in Eastern
Nigeria. Some recent studies also show that many
individuals retain traditional attitudes and values
while they acquire more modern ones, even when the
two would seem to be logically inconsistent.[9] Few
social scientists would deny though that the bridges
to the modern world provided by literacy and radio
listening do effectuate at least subtle and perhaps
some fundamental cognitive and evaluative modifications.

    Contrary to the many assumptions concerning the
superficiality of Christian conversion, the cross-
tabulations according to group differences (Table 28)
indicate that religion gives rise to the highest

TABLE 28

Group Differences in Attitudes
Toward Development

Group	Number of Signif-icant differences	Development Index Score
Christians (vs. non-Christians)	28	+20
Group C (vs. Group A-B)	37	+15
Literates (vs. Illiterates)	17	+14
Radio Listeners (vs. Nonlis-teners)	18	+12
Rich Villages (vs. Poor Villages)	19	+ 7

development index score followed by ethnic identity,
literacy, radio listening, and wealth. Christians
scored particularly high on questions revealing a
positive attitude toward change and innovation,
toward education, and toward optimism for the future
(see Table 29). Literates manifested especially
positive attitudes in the cluster of questions relating to control over one's destiny and change and
innovation. Radio listeners exhibited strong positive attitudes in the categories of control over
one's destiny and optimism. Informants in rich
villages also had a very high score for the responses
to questions pertaining to control over one's destiny

As a result of the high development index score
of the Christians, responses given by Catholics and
Protestants were also compared. In the regional
sample 35.63 percent of the informants were Catholic

TABLE 29

Selective Group Differences in Attitudes
Toward Development

Group	Development Index Scores			
	Change	Optimism	Control over Destiny	Education
Christians (vs. non-Christians)	+4	+4	+2	+4
Group C (vs. Group A-B)	+3	+3	-3	+3
Literates (vs. Illiterates)	+2	0	+7	0
Radio Listeners (vs. Nonlisteners)	+2	+3	+4	+1
Rich Villages (vs. Poor Villages)	+1	+1	+5	0

315

and 29.38 percent Protestant.   Since the publication
of Max Weber's The Protestant Ethic and the Spirit
of Capitalism, Protestants have been assumed to be
more disposed to entrepreneurship and hence to develo
ment than Catholics.   Contrary to this stereotype,
the findings point to the Catholic informants as the
more development oriented.   The 19 significant differences between the Catholics and the Protestants
yielded a +7 development index score for the Catholic
This means that in the survey Catholics statistically
constituted the single most development-oriented
group in Eastern Nigeria.

The interpretation of this data regarding group
differences is not as clear-cut as the statistical
findings seem to indicate.   In the vast majority of
localities in Eastern Nigeria religious affiliation
parallels ethnic variations because the missionary
societies initially working there partitioned the
region among themselves.   More recently missionaries
have begun to compete for converts, but in most communities one Christian denomination still predominate
and some are virtually homogeneous in terms of Christian affiliation.   The rate of conversion sometimes
has depended on two historical accidents: the date of
contact with missionaries and the intensity of missio
ary activity in the area.   Of course it also reflects
the receptivity of the group since at least in some
cases missionary societies concentrated on promising
localities.   Many of the minority ethnic groups in
Eastern Nigeria have become highly Christianized, exceeding the conversion rate of the Ibos.   This is
attested to in the survey by the fact that 87.4 perce
of the informants in Group C are Chrsitian as compare
with 73.1 percent of Group B and 41.3 percent of Grou
A.   It is possible, in fact likely, that the development index score of the Christians reflects in large
part underlying ethnic differences.   Moreover, since
access to education and conversion to Christianity
usually went hand in hand, literacy, Christianity,
and ethnicity are all related.

Reciprocally, Group C's higher level of adheren
to Christianity, literacy, and radio listening raise
the question whether their exposure to certain

aspects of modern life accounts for their development orientation. Christianity, literacy, and radio listening probably have accentuated the cultural factors favorable to change. However, without an initially favorable orientation to development, the villagers in Group C would have resisted conversion and school attendance. Moreover, given the relatively small differences between Group C and Group B in levels of education, literacy, radio listening, and Catholicism, it is unlikely that the slight variations in exposure to modernizing influences can explain the rather substantial disparity existing between the two groups in their attitudes toward development.

Although differences in frequency of conversion and in exposure to other modernizing influences apparently do play some part in explaining distinctions in attitudes toward development held by the three groups, it is believed these factors are not sufficient explanations. It seems likely that were it possible to hold these factors constant, differences between Groups A, B, and C would remain, although they would most likely not be as great. The cognitive universe endowed by the cultural bonds uniting members of an ethnic group does mold their attitudes and values. The issue is one of identifying accurately the boundaries of this culture. In 1966 the Ibo lingustic unit did not constitute the most meaningful cultural unit for its members. Only a less inclusive unit could provide the more homogeneous perspective characteristic of strong cultural bonds.

In terms of ascribing the respective importance to ethnic and religious distinctions, ethnicity was hypothesized as the primary determinant even though the group profiles from the survey show the Christian/non-Christian contrast to give rise to the highest development index score. In view of the tendency for rates of conversion to reflect the intensity of missionary activity in any given area and for specific denominational affiliation to depend largely on the identity of the first missionaries to arrive, the five-point differential between religion and ethnicity does not seem to be conclusive. Receptivity to Christianity itself followed from the nature of the

traditional culture. Moreover, Christianity most
likely attracted many of the most development-oriented
individuals in any community. The greater access
of these converts to schooling, and with it contact
with the outside world, further accentuated their
development orientation. Therefore, as the end
result in a causal chain, Christians were more development oriented but not solely or even primarily because
of their faith.

Despite the variations found between the ethnic
groups of the region, a systematic comparison of
the attitudes of ethnic groups in Eastern Nigeria,
which are generally favorable to development, with
those of other peoples in Nigeria would probably
underline the similarities among the ethnic groups
analyzed in this survey.

NOTES

1. Robert LeVine, Dreams and Deeds: Achievement
Motivation in Nigeria (Chicago: University of
Chicago Press, 1966), p. 67. According to LeVine
the differences between the groups were not statisti-
cally significant. His dream analysis did show the
Ibo to be the most development oriented.

2. W. T. Morrill, "Immigrants and Association:
The Ibo in Twentieth Century Calabar," Comparative
Studies in Society and History, V (July 1963),
424-448.

3. For example, see James S. Coleman, Nigeria:
Background to Nationalism (Berkeley and Los Angeles:
University of California Press, 1958), pp. 386-396;
Frederick A. O. Schwartz, Jr., Nigeria: The Tribes,
the Nation, or the Race (Cambridge: M.I.T. Press,
1965), pp. 82-100; Richard L. Sklar, Nigerian Polit-
ical Parties (Princeton, N.J.: Princeton University
Press, 1963), pp. 138-140.

4. Daryll Forde and G.I. Jones, The Ibo and
Ibibio-Speaking Peoples of South-Eastern Nigeria
(London: Oxford University Press, 1950), p. 10.

5. Robert B. Edgerton, "'Cultural' versus
'Ecological' Factors in the Expression of Values,
Attitudes, and Personality Characteristics," American
Anthropologist, 67 (April 1965), 442-447.

6. Angela Molnos, Attitudes toward Family Planning in East Africa (London: C. Hurst and Co., 1968).

7. Ibid., p. 176.

8. On Nigeria, for example, see P. C. Lloyd,
A. L. Mabogunje, and B. Awe, The City of Ibadan (Cam-
bridge: Cambridge University Press, 1968); Leonard
Plotnicov, Strangers to the City: Urban Man in Jos,
Nigeria (Pittsburgh: University of Pittsburgh Press,
1967); Howard E. Wolpe, "Port Harcourt: Ibo Politics
in Microcosm," The Journal of Modern African Studies,
VII (October 1969), 469-494.

9. See, for example, David W. Brokensha, Social
Change in Larteh, Ghana (Oxford: Clarendon Press,
1966); Plotnicov; David R. Smock, "From Village to
Trade Union in Africa: A Study of Power and Decision-
Making in the Nigerian Coal Miners' Union and in the
Villages from which the Coal Miners Migrated," unpub-
lished dissertation, Cornell University, 1964; Audrey
C. Smock, Ibo Politics: The Role of Ethnic Unions in
Eastern Nigeria (Cambridge, Mass.: Harvard University
Press, 1971); Hugh H. and Mabel M. Smythe, The New
Nigerian Elite (Stanford, Calif.: Stanford University
Press, 1960); and C. S. Whitaker, Jr., "A Dysrythmic
Process of Political Change," World Politics, XIX
(January 1967), 190-217.

12

**TOWARD
A DEVELOPMENTAL
STRATEGY
FOR THE FUTURE**

Although the bulk of this study deals with the
situation prevailing in Eastern Nigeria prior to the
outbreak of the war in 1967, any discussion of a
developmental strategy must naturally refer to the
period of postwar reconstruction. The most immediate
problem facing the Nigerian government is one of
assisting farmers to reestablish themselves and
their farms, so that at the minimum a subsistence
level can be regained. Roads and bridges have to
be reconstructed and other services made operational
once again. Only after minimal needs have been
satisfied can attention be turned to the kinds of
developmental issues that will provide a basis for
greater prosperity in the long term. Obviously,
these are not completely separable phases, and if
imaginative approaches that are immediately applicable
can be devised to the developmental problems of the
three states of the former Eastern Nigeria, the
rehabilitation stage can be passed more readily and
the economy of the area will begin to revive at an
earlier date. This chapter is not concerned with
the immediate problems, but with somewhat longer-term
approaches to economic and social growth. Moreover,
the social, cultural, and political aspects of rural
development will continue to be emphasized as has
been done throughout this study. In addition, the
chapter does not detail a strategy in programatic
terms, it rather suggests an approach to development

problems. For the sake of brevity, this chapter does not repeat the suggestions already made in earlier chapters regarding the implications of the findings for development policy.

No one can question the enormity of the tasks facing the people and government of Nigeria. Writing nine months before the end of the war, Ukpabi Asika, Administrator for the predominantly Ibo East Central State, stated:

> From my experience I can state without equivocation that these problems of peace will be much greater and more complex than the problems of the present war. The processes of rehabilitation and resettlement contain a crucial even if less tangible socio-psychological dimension. They involve not merely the restoration of the capacity for economic well-being to persons, the restoration of destroyed or disrupted materials and services, but also in the circumstances of a civil war also include the need to re-assure the people that they do in fact have a future.[1]

The investment required is not only financial; the gravity of the situation demands innovative ideas and imaginative solutions to the novel problems being faced. Although the poverty and misery created by the war will probably linger on for several years, the war does not seem to have traumatized the people of Eastern Nigeria to the point that they are not prepared to respond in innovative fashion to the demands made upon them for the revival of their area. Moreover, the drive for survival among Eastern Nigeria's peasant families, along with their preparedness to work hard and be responsive to new ideas should make the period of reconstruction somewhat shorter than might otherwise be necessary.

Although throughout this book the unit of analysis has been Eastern Nigeria (for reasons discussed in Chapter 2), Eastern Nigeria is now divided into three separate Nigerian states (see Map 1 on page 2).

The ethnic composition, the population distribution, and the physical setting of the three new states differ. The East Central State with its Ibo population comprises the parts of the old Eastern Region with the highest population densities; it is devoid of a coastline or port and contains only a minor portion of the region's petroleum resources. Much of this area, with prewar densities of up to 1,632 persons per square mile in some divisions and generally poor soil, could not sustain its population through farming before the war. The South-East State, consisting of Ibibios, Efiks and the numerous small ethnic groups in the Ogoja area, includes the lower Cross River basin and the adjacent lowlands. It combines low population density with much fertile farming land, some of which has not yet been exploited. The Rivers State is the home of the Ijaws, but before the war also had a very substantial Ibo population. Most of the known oil-producing areas in Eastern Nigeria now form part of this state. Despite the location of the major oil installation here, at its creation it was the least economically developed of the three carved out of Eastern Nigeria, because the Niger Delta with its swamps and many small inlets presented special problems to development.

The analysis and recommendations in this book have relevance primarily for the East Central and South-East States; the ecology of the Rivers State has made the people there primarily fisherman and traders rather than farmers. As Chapter 3 indicated, the traditional sociopolitical structures and attitudes of the Ibo and Ibibio peoples are very similar. Moreover, the attitude survey discussed in Chapters 10 and 11 suggests that Ibibio villages, which constituted half of those in Group C, might be even more development oriented than the Ibos, who have been renowned for their ability to take advantage of change and innovation. The programs and projects described and assessed in the preceding chapters were formulated and implemented with regard to the areas now incorporated in both the East Central and South-East States. Community plantations, for instance, met with roughly equal success in Ibo and Ibibio communities.

Obviously with the creation of three states, development strategies prescribing region-wide co-operation in Eastern Nigeria cannot easily be implemented. In particular, hostility engendered during the war period between those on the opposing sides has probably lessened the likelihood of success in the immediate future for projects involving cooperation between the East Central State and states adjacent to it. Migration and resettlement from one state to another will be more problematic than in the prewar period, and the notion of the commonweal will most likely be defined on the basis of states, especially in relation to those states whose populations opposed each other during the war. There is no reason, however, that the three states should not profit from their joint experience and pursue agricultural policies pioneered by the Eastern Nigerian government. Informal cooperation between the governments of the states may be possible in the not too distant future.

The major recommendation the authors would like to make here, that future development strategy be based on the economic benefits of particular projects, does not merely arise from the area's serious economic predicament in the postwar period. Throughout this study the need for government expenditure on projects that will secure increased incomes for those living in the rural areas has been stressed. Expanded social services can only be sustained if rural incomes are increased and if in turn the tax base is strengthened. As Hans Singer has written, "In the poorer countries we have a movement of 'original welfare,' not . . . derived from previous development. . . . Where an attempt is made to start with welfare, the effort may inhibit economic growth and be a formidable obstacle to development."[2] Moreover, with increased incomes village dwellers can satisfy many of their own needs for expanded services and can program and finance the development of their villages.

Many of those concerned with the development of rural Africa do not focus their attention on projects with economic potential or even on the provision of services, but rather on activities that will

presumably lead villagers to "believe" in themselves
and their ability to shape their destinies. The
literature of community development is filled with
the notions that development agencies should satisfy
"felt needs" and assist villagers with those projects
for which they request assistance, regardless of the
particular economic or social benefits that may accrue
from the project. Charles Erasmus, after surveying
a sample of the community development literature,
expresses dismay at the number of authors who "tend
to view material measures of accomplishment as spurious
and destructive."[3] As an illustration of this attitude he quotes from an article written about the Vicos
Project in Peru:

> Its people still live in adobe huts. They
> have no bathrooms. Their drinking water is
> impure. Their food is primitive. They
> weave their own clothes and wear them Indian
> style. 'But we didn't set out to change
> these people outside,' Professor Holmberg
> says. 'We weren't putting on a show. We
> wanted to change the inside, where it
> matters.'[4]

Although this quote probably gives a one-sided
view of the Vicos Project and of Holmberg's intentions,
it nevertheless illustrates much of the thinking in
the community development field.

A few administrative officers in Eastern Nigeria
have been imbued with this type of community development thinking and they have had an unfortunate
influence on more hard-headed development efforts
and in turn on the economic development of rural
Eastern Nigeria. In the late 1950's a village in
Orlu Division was anxious to establish a community
agricultural project. Despite the fact that the land
available had little potential, the divisional officer
for Orlu and his agricultural officer did not want
to disappoint the villagers or dampen their desire
for progress, so they decided to help them establish
a cashew farm on the sandy soil they had available.
When the trees came into full bearing mid-sixties the
villagers realized a gross income of £N116 per annum

for the 37 acres they had devoted to the project,
which meant earnings of a mere £N3 per acre for all
the land and labor invested. Not only have these
farmers not received a good return from their investment, but it is doubtful that they will have much
faith in future projects advocated by government
officials. A village in Udi Division had seen the
success of a truck-farm project in a neighboring
village and asked for government assistance to establish a similar project. Even though an agricultural
technician who assessed the project advised against
it, another government official wanted to help the
village satisfy its felt needs, and so the project
was established with government assistance. The
project finally had to be abandoned when the dam
constructed for irrigation purposes washed out for
the third time (something the agricultural technician
had predicted would happen) and when it became obvious
that the soil was not suitable for vegetables. It
is clear from cases like these that it is better to
refuse to respond to felt needs on occasion in order
not to waste resources and to preserve what self-con-
fidence the villagers have in themselves and what
confidence thay have in the government.

     To reiterate a point already made several times
in this study, the state governments of the former
Eastern Nigeria need to give more attention to the
economic needs of the peasant farmers of the area.
Expenditures during the sixties in the agricultural
sector emphasized high-capital farm settlements and
ENDC plantations. The success of the Oil Palm
Rehabilitation Scheme in increasing productivity and
incomes at relatively little expense to the government
suggests the potential pay-off of programs aimed at
the smallholder. The success of the smallholder
fertilizer program in Northern Nigeria provides
additional evidence of an agricultural development
strategy that focusses on benefits to the peasant
farmer. In addition to government schemes directed
at the smallholder being more economical and proving
to be sounder investments, they also benefit much
larger numbers of individual farm families and in turn
provide a basis for the steady transformation of the
rural areas of Eastern Nigeria, and for Africa as a
whole.

The special needs of the reconstruction period
dictate a development strategy through which the
government can reach a large number of smallholders
at a relatively low cost. The war disrupted agricultural cycles and seriously reduced productivity
in many areas. Until recently many farmers lacked
even seeds to replant their crops. Under such
circumstances the successor governments cannot afford
the luxury of the highly capitalized agricultural
programs financed by the Eastern Nigerian government.
Compounding the economic burdens of the postwar era
is the reduction in anticipated revenues, which imposes
an additional reason for frugality. Even if the
Nigerian government changes the basis of revenue
allocation from derivation to need, the East Central
and South-East States will not receive anywhere near
the portion of income contributed by oil earnings to
the Eastern Nigerian government. Prevailing economic
dislocations will further diminish government income
until restoration of productivity of the smallholders,
and with it the tax base, is achieved. Hence economic
necessity and proper development strategy both point
to the need for agricultural programs designed to
increase the productivity and income of the small
farmer.

Early efforts to encourage Eastern Nigerian
farmers to accept new farming practices that met with
initial but unsustained success led many officials
to conclude that the farmers were not responsive to
innovations or to economic incentives. Under such
circumstances the development strategy proposed here
does not make much sense. However, in a manner
similar to the reactions of Asian farmers to the
introduction of dwarf rice and wheat, Eastern Nigeria's
farmers have proven that they are responsive to
economic incentives when those incentives are sufficiently large to be easily recognizable and to
justify the increased investment of time and resources
that the introduction of innovations usually requires.
A 5- or -10 percent increase in yields or earning is
hardly noticeable to a farmer whose family consumes
most of what he produces and who does not keep records
of yields or earnings. On the other hand, farmers
may not be aware that the improved variety of oil
palms being introduced through the Oil Palm

Rehabilitation Scheme produces five times as much oi
as wild palms, but the vigorous growth pattern of th
trees in their first years easily convinces the farm
who see them that the trees offer considerable potential and are worth the investment.

The response to the prospect of increased incom
was clear in the pilot community plantations observe
over a two-year period. To get the clearing of land
and planting done in the first year of the project
required almost continual encouragement and supervis
by Rural Development Officers (RDO's), Divisional
Officers, and Peace Corps Volunteers. The participa
responded much more, however, in the second year, af
they had seen how the trees thrived and they had
realized the potential profitability of the project.
In the second year, very little encouragement was
required to assure that tasks were performed. Anoth
example of responsiveness to economic incentives
came in a community plantation project in Bende
Division, where the RDO encouraged the women of the
project village to interplant maize with the oil pal
their husbands were planting. At first the women
could not imagine making much money on maize, and di
not realize the potential productivity of the new NS
seed that the government was distributing. Moreover
the women contended that maize would not grow on the
type of soil available. Nevertheless, after conside
able encouragement they agreed to try. Some of the
women were so casual about the project that they jus
threw their seed on the ground. But after watching
the maize grow and realizing how much profit could b
made from selling the harvested maize to the Ministr
of Agriculture, the women became wildly enthusiastic
The following year, they demanded more seed than the
Ministry had available, and they managed what they
had planted with considerable care.

The realization that a primary stimulus to productive activity among the farmers of Eastern Nigeri
is economic self-interest led the Ministry of Rural
Development to place as much emphasis as it did on
the individual approach to the organization of work
in community plantation projects. Despite the fact
that a sense of community spirit is generally not

sufficient to sustain communally operated economic
projects, pride in one's village and a desire to make
it praiseworthy constitute important motivators of
change as well. One of the forces motivating the
people of Ugwuaku to want to establish their resettlement project and encourage strangers to come and settle
in their village was that they wanted Ugwuaku to
increase in size and wealth to the point that it would
be put on the map, both literally and figuratively.
An important stimulus to those participating in two
community plantations in Onitsha Division was competition between the two villages in terms of which
project would be successful. In the early days of
the community development movement in Eastern Nigeria,
Divisional Officers made effective use of intervillage
competition to encourage the building of such amenities
as roads and maternities. E. R. Chadwick, Divisional
Officer of Udi Division in the 1940's, often promised
several bags of cement to the village that could
complete its part of a road first. Villages were
motivated by a desire to win the cement, but they
also wanted to best the other villages.

On the other hand, community pride and competition
can on occasion be exacerbated to the point of being
petty and destructive. The Divisional Officer for
Okigwi in 1965 told the residents of an Okigwi village
that their community projects were so successful and
their village was making such rapid progress that in
time the people of surrounding villages would be their
servants. This statement and the success of the project so incensed those living in adjacent villages
that they started a land dispute over the ownership
of the project land and they refused to allow the project participants to do any more work on the project.

Pride in one's community and concern over its
status is largely what motivated sons abroad to assist
their home villages with development projects. The
continuing interest sons abroad take in their home
communities has been one of the most important contributing forces to the development of rural Eastern
Nigeria. Sons abroad in Eastern Nigeria have probably
contributed more money, ideas, and leadership to
village development projects than in any other part
of Africa.

Many development planners point with alarm to
the so-called school leaver problem, by which they
mean the lack of employment opportunities for those
who have received some formal education and migrate
to urban areas rather than taking up the family
occupation of farming. Despite the undoubted fact
that the economy of Eastern Nigeria, and the economies of most other African countries, can only
absorb a small proportion of those being turned out
by the educational system, to concentrate on absorbing
these individuals into the economy as an end in itself
is to emphasize the wrong problem. Although school
leavers who are unemployed and discontented can
potentially create political problems for an African
state, the cure proposed is often more harmful than
the illness, in that the inclination of governments
is generally to absorb these individuals into relatively unproductive activities. The cost of supporting these make-work programs is usually so great that
valuable resources are drained from the economy, which
might be used to stimulate productive employment.

The authors' recommendation would be that those
planning the development of the three eastern states
concentrate not upon the school-leaver problem, but
on making farming adequately remunerative and village
life sufficiently attractive that school leavers will
be encouraged to remain in the fields of agriculture,
rather than joining the ranks of the unemployed.
Significantly, several community plantation projects
managed to entice school leavers back to their rural
homes. Urban migration is not as much a function
of the comforts and excitement offered by city life
as of the urban-rural differentials in wages and
income potential. Although in itself the community
plantation program can not achieve these ends, it
makes one step in the right direction. As one of
its principal recommendations, the Consortium for
the Study of Nigerian Rural Development proposes
that for tax purposes greater reliance be placed on
Nigeria's oil production and less upon export taxes
imposed on agricultural commodities.[5] If a higher
proportion of the export prices for such commodities
as palm oil and kernels went to the producer and
less went to the government, rural incomes could

increase significantly and farming would become a more
attractive occupation to young people. This is not
the place to attempt to prescribe (or to reiterate
those approaches already suggested) all that needs
to be done to stimulate the economy of the rural
sector in Eastern Nigeria. The point being made is
that stagnation of the rural economy is the problem
that needs to be attacked, rather than the problem
of providing work for unemployed school leavers. If
the former problem is successfully approached, the
latter problem will no longer loom so large.

While for both political and humanitarian reasons
it is important to achieve some regional balance in
development by assuring that all parts of the state
benefit to some degree from government-sponsored
development programs, it is also important that scarce
resources be invested in areas where the greatest
return is likely to be realized. Especially in the
early and experimental stages of a rural development
program, those villages that offer the best chance
for success should be given priority in the selection
process. In addition to assessing the physical and
economic feasibility of a project in a particular
locality, the potential responsiveness of the population can also be tested by the kinds of instruments
described in Chapter 8. Eastern Nigeria's new rural
development program was in jeopardy at the outset in
1964 because some government officials believed that
the villages selected as sites for community plantations
did not offer sufficient geographic and ethnic spread.
But if geographic and ethnic spread had been the
criteria used in project selection rather than potential for success, the program would have fizzled.

Particular approaches to rural development might
have special appeal and might be especially appropriate
for certain ethnic groups or ecological settings.
In recognition of this, it is important to develop
a variety of programs or to adapt a particular program
to local requirements. The social and cultural
variations found in different parts of Eastern Nigeria
must be taken into account when projects are planned.
One sphere in which significant differences exist is
that of self-images--how the people of a village view

themselves. A somewhat extreme example of such differences can be drawn from a portion of Ogoja Provin
now part of the South-East State, where an ENDC
plantation is located, the land for which is owned
half by one village and half by another. The people
in these two villages speak two different languages
and their cultures differ significantly. Persons
from both villages have been hired to work on the
plantation, but their responses to their jobs contra
sharply. The workers from one village work hard and
are willing to undertake any type of task requested
of them, regardless of how menial. The workers from
the other village think of themselves only as supervisory material. They believe that being farm labor
is beneath their dignity, even though most of them
lack the requisite qualifications for supervisory
posts. Those who have accepted positions as laborer
complain continually about how hard and tedious the
work is.

If a development agency were considering siting
rural development projects in these two villages, it
would be judicious to think in terms of different
types of projects. As is typical with many Ogoja
villages, the people in one of the villages dislike
physical labor, but they might make good entrepreneu
and managers. They might usefully be assisted with
the organization of a limited liability company that
could operate a plantation on a commercial basis
utilizing hired laborers. The standard community
plantation in which the participants do most of the
work would probably not be appealing or appropriate.
Those from the other village would probably be responsive to the community plantation concept. Not
to recognize such differences between villages and
ethnic groups and not to modify a program to adjust
to such differences can easily lead to the introducti
of inappropriate projects and a high failure rate.
The realm in which the most crucial cultural variations exist is that of land tenure. For this reason
no standard lease agreement can be drawn up for
community plantations; each lease must be adapted
to local traditions and practices to make sure that
it will receive broad and sustained support and not
be declared invalid by local governing bodies.

It is quite possible that one will find significant differences in motivation in patrilineal and
matrilineal areas. The desire to pass on wealth and
property to one's sons constitutes an important stimulus to economic advancement in patrilineal areas.
For instance, old men participated in community
plantation projects that will not yield any profit
until these men are dead in order to have a farm to
pass on to their children. However, in matrilineal
societies such as one finds in parts of Rivers State
and South-East State, a man is often less interested
in investing in an enterprise from which he will not
benefit directly. Farmers in these areas are often
reluctant to plant a farm that will benefit only their
sister's children. Consequently, it probably would
be advisable to establish projects with a short-term
pay-off in communities that have a matrilineal system
of inheritance, so that the man who does the work
will realize the profit. Alternatively, in some
localities moves are afoot to circumvent the traditional matrilineal rules of inheritance, and these
developments might be encouraged.

The authors' expected to encounter a lack of
sensitivity to the significance of cultural variations
among foreign technical assistance personnel working
in Eastern Nigeria. What came as a shock was the
realization of how provincial otherwise sophisticated
Nigerian government officials often were and how
unaware they were of the range of cultural variation
found in Eastern Nigeria. Despite a vague realization
that villages and ethnic groups did differ from one
another, their lack of detailed knowledge of villages
and ethnic groups other than their own often prompted
them to assume that in most respects other villages
resembled the one with which they were familiar.
Such an assumption is not only unwarranted but action
based upon this assumption could undermine development
efforts in the rural areas.

Despite the need to adapt a program to the local
cultural context, certain basic elements in the project
design should be applied universally. In 1964 some
government officials in Eastern Nigeria contended that
rural development projects should be offered to

villages on terms laid down by the villagers. In
other words, the government should assist projcets,
but the character of the project and how it is
organized should be left to the villagers themselves
to determine. The organizers should help the community do what it wants to do and avoid imposing
their own ideas. However, to accept this approach
implies that villagers know more about organizing
rural development projects than representatives of
a government agency or ministry. This view never
seemed to be expressed in discussions of farm settlements: No one claimed that the settlers themselves
should completely shape the settlement's plan. But
in proposals regarding community projects, some
officials believed that the community's will should
prevail. The experience of the Ministry of Rural
Development with community plantations demonstrates
quite clearly that certain basic elements have to be
incorporated in every project if a minimal level of
success is to be assured. This is not to say that
project organizers should be rigid or that adaptations
should not be made to local conditions, but it does
mean that certain organizational and technical
requirements must be met. For instance, in the
organization of successful community plantations a
legal survey of the land has to be conducted and a
valid lease agreement drawn up if land disputes are
to be avoided and the tenants and landowners are both
to be assured that their rights will be respected.
To have a survey requires the use of cement pillars
as boundary makers, and to finalize a lease the
parties to the agreement must sign the document.
But one Divisional Officer proposed that cement pillar
not to be used in one project in his division because
the people in that village believed that the pillars
would poison the soil. Another Divisional Officer
recommended that no lease be prepared for one project
village because the people of that village, most of
whom were illiterate, feared putting ink on their
thumbs to make thumb imprints on the lease document.[6]
Objections by villagers to such innovations as cement
pillars and legal agreements derive from their new-
ness, and through patient persuasion and education,
project organizers can overcome fears of what hitherto
has been unknown. A development program has no impact

if it does not change attitudes, practices, and techniques. If the Eastern Nigerian government had accepted the traditional fear of strangers expressed
by the people of Ugwuaku, no attempt would have been
made to establish a pilot resettlement project there.
Educational efforts and government participation in
the project assured the people of Ugwuaku that they
could afford to radically alter village traditions
regarding the absorption of outsiders and the leasing
of unused land to strangers on a long-term basis.

In various portions of this book the general
receptivity of Eastern Nigerians to innovations and
their preparedness to participate in development
projects has been referred to. Although these
predispositions are on the whole advantageous to
development efforts, they entail certain dangers as
well. Because peasant farmers have little basis for
critically evaluating new ideas presented to them,
they often accept what is recommended out of a naive
and almost blind faith in those with ideas to offer,
whether these are agricultural extension personnel,
RDO's, or divisional administrators. When one farmer
participating in a community plantation project was
asked whether he would accept all the advice given
him by the RDO and Peace Corps Volunteer attached
to the project, he stated, "When someone doesn't
know something and someone teaches him, he has to
do it. It is like going to shcool." When another
farmer was asked whether all the advice he had been
given by the RDO and PCV was sound, he asked
rhetorically, "How can you find fault with the advice
of your teacher?" Trying to pose an extreme example,
a group of participants in a truck farming project
were asked whether they would pull all the leaves
off their tomato plants if the supervising RDO and
PCV advised doing so. All the farmers questioned
said that they would follow the advice and defoliate
their tomato plants.

Because of this prevailing naive receptivity in
Eastern Nigeria, it is tempting for change agents to
push farmers to accept unproven or untested techniques
and materials. For instance, the Ministry of Agriculture recommended the application of fertilizer to

yam plots in 1965--before adequate experimental data
had been amassed to assure that use of fertilizer on
yams was justified both agronomically and economically
To say that farmers in Eastern Nigeria tend to be
naively receptive to new ideas should not be taken
to imply that they are uncritical of results, for
Eastern Nigeria's farmers usually are very concerned
about the benefits that accrue from new investments
or risk-taking. If farmers are persuaded to try what
turns out to be a bad investment or a bad risk, they
may not be receptive again to the advice of change
agents for many more years. The current receptivity
is based on a faith in those proffering new ideas,
and if that faith is undermined it may be difficult
to instill it again.

     Another danger resulting from the receptivity
of Eastern Nigerians to innovations is the inclination
for government officials and departments to view the
success of a few pilot projects as sufficient grounds
for rapid expansion of a program. After most of the
pilot community plantations developed successfully
over their first two years of operation and many
additional villages expressed interest in obtaining
government assistance in establishing similar projects
the Ministry of Rural Development attempted to satisfy
most of these requests for assistance. This eagerness
to contribute to village development and to replicate
what has turned out to be a successful and popular
project design is quite understandable. But the too-
rapid expansion of operations by the Ministry of Rural
Development in 1966 meant that projects could not
be screened with the care that was required, that
the supervision needed from the RDO and the agricultural extension worker could not be offered in
adequate measure, and that the materials needed for
the project, such as oil palm seedlings and fertilizer, could not be supplied in requisite quantity
or delivered with sufficient speed. The long-term
success of the rural development program could have
been more adequately assured if expansion had pro-
ceeded more slowly.

     Some of the openness and naivete regarding
technological innovations applies to organizational

innovations as well. Evidence of this came in 1965
when the pilot community plantations were visited at
the end of one year of operation to ask the participants whether they thought any part of the project
should be organized differently in 1966. Some helpful
suggestions were anticipated about how communal work
days could be organized, how disciplinary control
could be exerted over those who did not do their work
regularly, how the individual parcels of land in the
project area might be more efficiently and equitably
distributed, how the money earned by the project
participants during the first year in subsidies under
the Oil Palm Rehabilitation Scheme might be divided
most sensibly, etc. Some of the farmers questioned
did make suggestions, particularly concerning whether
project work should be done on an individual or a
communal basis, but for the most part they had no
ideas to contribute. Many farmers said that they did
not know enough about the modern world in general or
about community plantations in particular to be able
to suggest alternative modes of operation; they were
waiting for those who were supervising the project
("their teachers") to decide whether they should
organize the project differently and then to instruct
them in the new patterns to be followed. Statements
such as these were not evidence of indifference or an
unwillingness on the part of the farmers to think
for themselves. Their experience in such matters
was so limited and their horizions so narrow that they
could not even imagine alternative means of organizing
the project.[7]

The organizational forms with which most Eastern
Nigerian villagers are familiar and which can be
productively incorporated into community projects are
village work groups, reciprocal work arrangements,
age-grade organizations, village meetings, and ethnic-
improvement unions. Villagers generally feel at ease
functioning within these contexts and these organizational forms can constitute important elements in
development projects, either operating by themselves
or as adjuncts to such innovative forms as cooperatives. In the more acculturated communities, ethnic-
improvement unions hold particular promise as sources
of innovative concepts, leadership, and money in

support of village development projects.   In several
villages for example, ethnic-improvement unions took
the inititative in organizing community plantations.

    At various points in this study the advantages
for rural development that accrue from the relative
solidarity, homogeneity, and self-sufficiency of
most village-groups in Eastern Nigeria and the continuing vitality of many traditional features of
village social and political organization have been
emphasized.   This group solidarity and isolation,
however, entail difficulties for organizing development projects that encompass or require the cooperation
of units larger than the village-group.   Evidence of
this could be seen in the discussion in Chapter 9
to the difficulties involved in resettling persons
from high-population density areas in places with
lower population density, since strangers, even if
they speak the same language and are of the same
ethnic group, are frequently distrusted.   Further
evidence of the difficulties created for intervillage
cooperation by the traditional isolation and autonomy
of Eastern Nigeria's villages can be seen in the
responses to two questions given by 60 persons
interviewed in a village in Udi Division, East Central
State.   These informants were first asked whether
they would respect someone from their village who
became wealthy by cheating people from the village.
They were virtually unanimous in stating that they
would not respect such an individual.   However, when
they were asked whether they would respect someone
from their village who went to Enugu or another city
in Nigeria and made a great deal of money by illegal
means and cheating people, 70 percent said that they
would respect the man, and only 30 percent answered
they would not respect him.[8]   Clearly a double standard
is applied, depending upon whether someone is cheating
his own people or strangers.   Admittedly, generali-
zations about the whole of Eastern Nigeria are unwarranted on the basis of a questionnaire administered
in a single village, but the tendency to restrict
one's moral frame of reference to a limited group
of people, usually those to whom one can trace
geneological relationships, does appear to be fairly
widespread, at least in the prewar period.

Despite the terrible loss of life during the war period, the state governments of the area also need to give priority attention following the reconstruction period to the organization of a family planning program. Eastern Nigeria has long been overpopulated; with the possibilities of migration to other parts of Nigeria curtailed (although not eliminated) the population problem during the next decade will be particularly severe. Moreover, population growth must be reduced from its prewar rate of 2.5-3.0 percent annually to a rate more in line with the pace of economic development and the ability of the economy to absorb or otherwise provide for those newly entering the work force each year. A family planning program can have an enormously beneficial impact on both the economy and the families of the area if only unwanted births are prevented. Given the high value placed on children, the fear that the high mortality rate will end the family line unless there are many children to reduce the risk, the dependence of parents upon their children for support in their old age, the large number of Catholics in the area, and the understandable desire of families whose children died during the war to replace them, the forces working against the government's being able to mount a successful family planning program are considerable. But any long-term solution to the area's economic problems will be virtually impossible without a reduction in the rate of population growth. Ghana recently issued a population policy and established a government family planning program despite the same high value placed on children and a large family in that country as in Eastern Nigeria. The Ghana experiment will be well worth watching by Nigerians, and it may suggest an approach to the problem that will be both palatable to its citizens and beneficial to its economy.

Chapter 5 reported some of the deficiencies of the Eastern Nigerian political system for promoting rural development: the consumptionist political orientation, the inability of the county councils to assume economic functions, the problems of coordinating planning and implementation, and the weak linkages between levels resulting in a low degree of

effectiveness of the regional government with regard
to effecting change. Since many of these deficiencies
were bound up with the general condition of political
underdevelopment, no simple prescription for reori-
enting and reorganizing the political system can enable
the successor governments to overcome all of these
defects. For a start, though, the new governments
should categorically demonstrate a change of priorities
from merely providing social services to promoting
economic development. The pauperization resulting
from the war necessitates a change in orientation.
At the same time the need for austerity provides an
opportunity for the state governments to mold a new
image of the political system with correlative expectations that will have repercussions far beyond the
period devoted to rehabilitation. By taking the
initiative and demonstrating a productionist set of
priorities, the new governments can promote an image
of the political system as a mobilizer for development
and as an economic benefactor, instead of as a
dispenser of amenities.

     Decentralization of political authority would
seem to constitute the best strategy for strengthening
the linkages between state level institutions and
local communities. Such a decentralization should
differ considerably from the relative autonomy many
local communities had during the life of the Eastern
Nigerian political system. As envisioned here,
decentralization would involve a fundamental restructuring of the political system incorporating a
redistribution of responsibility and a reapportionment
of resources and personnel commensurate with this
realignment. Decentralization of authority, as distinct from the confirmation of autonomy, should be
through institutions designed to operate primarily
as agents of the state political system rather than
as representatives of localities. Since most African
political systems have not developed sufficient
capabilities to be able to centralize power and still
ensure implementation and control, power for assuming
functions should be constitutionally or legally vested
in intermediary and local bodies. By reducing lines
of control through transforming intermediary and local
bodies into agents of the state administration and

vesting them with a broad panoply of functions, this
reform should increase the overall effectiveness
of the political system. This approach would also
bring the political system closer to the people in
a manner relevant to their lives. In so doing, it
should stimulate greater political awareness and
hopefully a positive image of the political system.

After revision of the concept of community
development in 1963 from the addition of amenities
to the improvement in the economic base of rural
communities, the Eastern Nigerian government moved
toward a decentralization of political authority
similar to what is proposed here. Provincial and
divisional officers were assigned responsibility
for community development. In conjunction with the
RDO's from the Ministry of Rural Development, Divisional Officers selected potential project sites
and prepared communities for participation. Moreover,
the intention was for the Provincial and Divisional
Officers to establish development committees and then
together with these committees formulate a development
program for their area. A few months before the war
began in 1967 the Eastern Nigerian Military Government announced it would create more provinces and
then endow the provinces with a wider range of
responsibilities to be exercised through newly established provincial executives. By so doing, the
Eastern Nigerian Military Government hoped to satisfy
the demands of minority groups for greater control
over their affairs short of dismembering the region.

A decentralization scheme was proposed for Ghana
in 1967, which has potential relevance to the drafters
of the revised systems of administration for the new
states in Nigeria.[9] The scheme proposed for Ghana
attempted to balance representative and administrative
prescripts. On the two most important levels, the
region and the district, there would be an elected
council, a professional staff, and a chief executive
selected by the council from a short list submitted
by the central government. The chief executive, who
would most likely be a career civil servant, would
provide an element of professional management, and
the elected council with its centrally appointed

chairman, who would be the agent of the governing
political party, would allow for participation. The
commission that proposed the scheme compared the
role of the chief executive to that of a managing
director of a business organization.[10] The functions
suggested for the council included the approval of
the budget and of rates and fees, the passing of by-
laws, and the appraisal of the manager's performance.
As the third tier, councils or committees corresponding
to traditional authorities would be initiated to
undertake discretionary local projects. Ultimately
the scheme called for decentralization primarily
to the districts. The district authority would be
the basic administrative and executive institution
for the provision of government services, and the
region would be the planning and coordinating body.
In order to be able to staff the decentralized units
with qualified functionaries, the commission also
proposed to unify the civil service so that personnel
attached to all levels of the political system would
be part of a single public service with standards for
recruitment, promotion, discipline, and salaries
determined by a central public service commission.
Therefore the staffs of the regional and district
authorities would in effect be employees of the
central government rather than of the local councils,
as they were previously both in Ghana and in Eastern
Nigeria.[11]

Decentralization in the three states formed
from Eastern Nigeria would necessitate establishing
new institutions in place of the ineffective county
and local councils as the agents of decentralization.
County and local councils neither afforded an opportunity for meaningful participation nor maintained
the sophisticated social services they were empowered
to furnish. Hence it would be unwise to redistribute
resources and to assign still more functions to these
bodies without altering their purpose and composition.
The authors propose that intermediary and local
political institutions be constituted with the
expressed intention of promoting productive economic
development, undertaking the functions and services
supplied by all governmental agencies at that level
of the political system, and linking rural communities

with the state government. Councils or committees
in which administrators and professional agents of the
central ministries rather than political representatives predominate would be more suitable executors
of this new concept of local government.[12] Hence
the authors advocate that the post-1964 format in
Eastern Nigeria vesting civil servants with responsibility for development be continued and strengthened
by assigning to them significant administrative
functions as well. The ratio of civil servants to
population should be considerably reduced, thus
enlarging the public service, and its composition
should be altered so that a higher proportion of pro-
fessionals and specialists are recruited along with
generalists.

Of the organizational patterns in force in the
Eastern states at the time of this writing, the
model adopted by the South-East State most closely
approximates the blueprint for decentralization.
Nevertheless the system in the South-East State
differs in several respects, mainly in that the
civil servants are not attached to the planning committees but instead operate autonomously. Thus the
planning committees lack professional guidance,
and the administrators implementing policy do not
have the legitimizing sanction of popular participation through direct committee support.

Another inadequacy in the Eastern Nigerian
political system, which any effort at reform should
attempt to surmount, is the excessive fragmentation
of local political units that results in their being
too small to sustain development functions and to
serve as a link with the regional government.
Decentralization down to an intermediary unit of
approximately 300,000 would seem to be the best compromise between the conflicting aims of bringing
the political system closer to the population and of
providing a realistic resource base. In the eastern
states this would mean a unit smaller than the old
districts and larger than the county council areas.
Units slightly less inclusive than the former provinces
should translate state priorities and programs into
concrete guidelines for the area. Until a sufficient

number of development administrators and technicians
become available, some administrative and development
functions might also have to be assigned to the provinces. In addition the provincial authorities could
permanently manage secondary schools, hospitals,
water systems, electricity, and road construction.

Below the intermediary authorities or districts
(if they are so designated), the governments might
establish committees in groups of villages to act as
a communications and information link between the
people and the administrators. Administrators could
institute a regular schedule for consultations with
members of the village committees to explain programs
and objectives, to ascertain their views, and to
secure their cooperation when necessary. This interchange between the village and district levels would
be extremely important, especially if the district
authority, as envisioned here, were organized in
such a manner as to ensure administrative ascendance
Consultation with village or clan committees would
provide an element of popular participation and would
capitalize on the traditions of communal self-relian
Because the popularly elected county councils and th
politicians were so thoroughly discredited during
the life of the Eastern Nigerian political system,
the people there would probably welcome a radical
departure in local administration, even if that new
order reduced the representative element, but they
would most likely strenuously object to being denied
any voice. Village or clan committees could also
organize communal projects that the district authori
ties could then assist.

The size of the provincial, district, and local
authorities advocated here can only be temporary
approximations pending experimentation. All adminis
trative units within the eastern states will have to
be compromises between the popular demand for fragmentation and the exigencies of large units for effe
tive governance. Hopefully the lessons of past fail
and the current inclination for people to be more
flexible will be capitalized on to bias the compromi
in the latter direction. South-East State's divisio
development councils and area development committees

represent a very positive departure in that direction. East Central State's community councils, on the contrary, seem like something of an attempt to resurrect relics from the past.

This outline differs from the Ghanaian blueprint in the following respect: the districts being larger units in terms of population, the greater number of responsibilities permanently assigned to the provincial level authority, the role of the village committees, and the greater emphasis on administrative dominance. To reiterate points made earlier, no organizational changes can by themselves overcome historical problems or the condition of political underdevelopment. Furthermore, any extensive political and administrative reforms will of necessity require some experimentation.

Another consideration in restructuring the political system should be the rationalization of responsibility for rural development at the state level in order to minimize conflicts and to facilitate coordination. The problems of coordination in Eastern Nigeria derived in part from the number of agencies concerned with rural development: The Ministry of Rural Development initiated and directed some rural development projects but also was dependent on other ministries, particularly the Ministry of Agriculture, for supplies and specialist services; moreover, the Ministry of Agriculture had its own programs for developing the rural areas. As Chapter 5 indicated, no restructuring of the political system could possibly overcome all of the organizational problems, since a meaningful rural development program hinges on the cooperation of many different government agencies. A cabinet-level superministry for rural development would have to incorporate up to three fourths of all government agencies, and thus would be unwieldy.

The establishment of a special office directly under the chief executive of the state that would plan for rural development and would coordinate programs of the various ministries with the authority to issue instructions to the ministries seems the best alternative. The field administration

including divisional and provincial officials could
also report to this office. No administrative arrange
ment can assure cooperation, but this proposal would
at least institutionalize binding mediation between
the conflicting claims of the ministries. This refor
would preserve the benefits demonstrated by the
Ministry of Rural Development as a nonspecialist
coordinator and would overcome many of its liabilitie
through the ability to operate as a kind of czar of
rural development.

It is far more difficult to reform components
of a political culture than to restructure a politica
system. As a dimension of the overall cultural herit
age and historical experience of a people, the political culture tends to resist drastic efforts at socia
engineering. But the political attitudes, values,
and orientations of a community are not hardened
fossils forever fixed in a set form. There is reason
to hope that some of the attitudes inhibiting rural
development in Eastern Nigeria may be modified as a
result of the experiences of the last few years and
through efforts of the governments to educate the
people. Ironically, the traditional, social, and
political values and attitudes of the former Eastern
Nigerians tend to be conducive to development while
many of the more recently acquired ones give a consumptionist orientation to the political system.
This consumptionist orientation, which views the
political system as a dispenser of amenities rather
than as a mobilizer for economic development, is to
a great extent a legacy of terminal British colonialism. The roles that the British reforms assigned
to regional government and local councils, and the
priorities that colonial administrators set, fostered
expectations that the primary role of the political
system was to provide social services. A reorientati
in the goals and operational style of the political
system should have the educational effect of reversin
some of these expectations.

*   *   *

The economic, social, and political landscape of
Eastern Nigeria has undergone a radical transformatio

since the departure of the civilian administration in 1966. In the interim the region has been devastated by war, plagued by fighting and hunger, and pauperized at least temporarily by economic dislocations. Yet there is still some basis for optimism for the future. This optimism derives from its human resources: commitment to development, resiliency, receptivity to innovation, and ingenuity. Unless the war and its aftermath have permanently scarred the cultures and peoples of Eastern Nigeria, the future should bring recovery and further development.

NOTES

1. Ukpabi Asika, "Rehabilitation and Resettlement," paper presented at the Conference on National Reconstruction and Development in Nigeria, (Ibadan: 1969), p. 18.

2. Hans Singer, International Development: Growth and Change (New York: McGraw-Hill, 1963), pp. 63-64.

3. Charles J. Erasmus, "Community Development and the Encogido Syndrome," Human Organization, 27 (Spring 1968), 72.

4. Ibid.

5. Glenn L. Johnson, Orlin J. Scoville, George K. Dike, and Carl K. Eicher, Strategies and Recommendations for Nigerian Rural Development, 1969/1985 (East Lansing: Consortium for the Study of Nigerian Rural Development, Michigan State University, 1969), pp. 55-57.

6. Ruthenberg has an interesting discussion of when pressure for conformity to certain standards should be exerted as part of attempts to introduce innovations into smallholder farming. See Hans Ruthenberg, ed., Smallholder Farming and Smallholder Development in Tanzania (London: C. Hurst and Co., 1968), p. 347.

348   RURAL TRANSFORMATION

7. A similar phenomenon was discussed in a
study of the Nigerian Coal Miners' Union. See David
R. Smock, Conflict and Control in an African Trade
Union (Stanford, Calif.: Hoover Institution Press,
1969) p. 114.

8. David R. Smock, "From Village to Trade
Union in Africa: A Study of Power and Decision-
Making in the Nigerian Coal Miners' Union and in
the Villages from which the Coal Miners Migrated,"
unpublished dissertation, Cornell University, 1964,
p. 350.

9. The Ghanaian government is implementing
decentralization in a form somewhat different from
the model proposed by the commission.

10. Report of the Commission on the Structure
and Remuneration of the Public Service in Ghana
(Accra-Tema: Ministry of Information, 1967), p. 5.

11. See also on Ghanaian decentralization,
T. J. Barrington and M. A. B. Sarpong, "The Development of Local Government in Ghana," unpublished
report submitted to the Commission on the Structure
and Remuneration of the Public Services in Ghana,
1967 (mimeographed); Report of the Commission of
Enquiry into Electoral and Local Government Reform,
3 vols. (Accra: Ghana Publications Corporation, 1968
"White Paper on the Report of the Commission on the
Structure and Remuneration of the Public Services
in Ghana," Working Paper No. 6 (Accra-Tema: Ministry
of Information, 1968); "White Paper on Part III of
Report of the Commission of Enquiry into Electoral
and Local Government Reform," Working Paper No. 2
(Accra: Ghana Publishing Company, 1969).

12. The authors disagree with Guy Hunter's
assertion that the system of decentralization in
India, panchayati raj, which is based on political
control, constitutes the best type of rural administration for peasant societies. For his views see
Guy Hunter, Modernizing Peasant Societies: A Comparative Study in Asia and Africa (London: Oxford

University Press, 1969), pp. 208-215. Panchayati
raj has inhibited rural development by aggravating
factionalism in Indian villages, by precipitating
unending conflicts between politicians and the
development personnel supposed to operate under
their direction, by enabling politicians to dispose
of development resources for patronage purposes, and
by failing to stimulate programs to raise economic
productivity. For a comparison of the defects of
panchayati raj with the greater success of basic
democracies in Pakistan, which contrary to the
implications of its name affords a much larger role
to administrators, see A. T. R. Rahman, "Rural
Institutions in India and Pakistan," Asian Survey,
VIII (September 1968), 792-805.

APPENDIX

RURAL DEVELOPMENT ATTITUDE
SURVEY QUESTIONNAIRE

1. Age

    1. 21-25
    2. 26-29
    3. 30-34
    4. 35-39
    5. 40-44
    6. 45-49
    7. 50-54
    8. 55-59
    9. 60 or over
    No Answer

2. Of what material is your house?

    Walls

    1. mud
    2. concrete
    3. other
    No answer

3. Roof

    1. grass
    2. mat
    3. zinc or aluminum
    4. other
    No answer

4. Floor

    1. earth
    2. concrete
    3. wood
    4. other
    No answer

5. How many members of your family (mother, father,
    children, uncles, aunts, and first cousins)
    are now living outside of this village?

0. none
1. one
2. two
3. three
4. four
5. five
6. six
7. seven
8. eight or more
No answer

6.   (If some live outside) How many of those live
      in a city?

0. none
1. one
2. two
3. three
4. four
5. five
6. six
7. seven
8. eight or more
No answer

7.   Have you ever attended school?   (If so) For
      how many years?

1. no
2. yes, one year or less
3. yes, two to four years
4. yes, four to seven years
5. finished standard VI
6. some secondary
7. completed secondary
8. went beyond secondary
No answer

8.   Can you read and write--for example, can you
      write a letter?

1. yes
2. not really, just a little
3. no
No answer

9.   What is your occupation?

        1.   farmer
        2.   fisherman
        3.   artisan
        4.   trader
        5.   other
        No answer

10.   Besides your principal occupation, do you
        often work in another activity that brings
        you some money?

        1.   no
        2.   yes (in what type of activity?)
        3.   artisan
        4.   selling
        5.   fishing
        6.   other
        No answer

11.   Where were you born?

        1.   in this village
        2.   in another village
        3.   in a township
        No answer

12.   How often do you listen to the radio?

        1.   never
        2.   once a month or less
        3.   every two weeks or less
        4.   once a week or less
        5.   two to four times a week
        6.   every day
        No answer

13.   Do you ever think seriously about moving away
        and living in another village or a township?

        1.   often
        2.   sometimes
        3.   never or hardly ever
        No answer

14.   In the past few years, have the people of
        this village all worked together on some
        project, such as road building, building a
        maternity, etc.?

        1. yes
        2. no
        No answer

15.   When it comes to cooperating on some community
        project, how well do the people cooperate?
        Would you say there is...?

        1. much cooperation
        2. fair cooperation
        3. poor cooperation
        No answer

16.   Suppose your village needed a new road built
        or improvements on old roads. Should this be
        mainly the duty of the government, mainly the
        duty of the villagers themselves, or is it
        the joint duty of both the government and the
        villagers working together?

        1. government
        2. villagers
        3. both together
        No answer

17.   What about building a new school. Who should
        be mainly responsible for this sort of project?

        1. government
        2. villagers
        3. both together
        No answer

18.   Five years from now, do you expect people in
        this village to be better off or worse off
        (economically) or about the same as they are
        today?

        1. better off
        2. about the same

3.   worse off
No answer

19.   What would you say about the progress of the
      village? Would you say it is...?

      1.   progressing rapidly
      2.   progressing slowly
      3.   not progressing
      4.   going backward
      No answer

20.   If a member of your family had a dispute with
      somebody else in the village, would you always
      support the member of your family?

      1.   yes
      2.   no
      No answer

21.   What chance do you and others like you have
      to solve the problems of this community?
      Would you say your chances are...?

      1.   good
      2.   fair
      3.   poor
      No answer

22.   Some say the government is run just for the
      benefit of those in power. Others say that
      the government is run to benefit the people.
      What do you say?

      1.   for those in power only
      2.   for the people
      3.   undecided
      No answer

23.   Suppose you or another person like you became
      involved in a court case, what chance would
      you have of getting justice?

      1.   good chance
      2.   fair chance

3.   poor chance
No answer

24.   If you could choose, would you rather work for
       some person or a company or start your own
       business?

       1.   other person
       2.   company
       3.   start own business
       No answer

25.   Some say that for the average man it is useles
       to plan for the future. Do you...?

       1.   agree
       2.   partly agree
       3.   disagree
       No answer

26.   Some say that through working harder, you will
       have a higher standard of living. What would
       you say....?

       1.   I don't believe it
       2.   it would help a little but not enough to
            be worth the effort
       3.   yes, it would definitely help
       No answer

27.   If you worked very hard, what would others in
       your community think of you?

       1.   that you are a fool because it is not
            worth it
       2.   they would respect you more for it
       3.   it would not make any difference at all
       No answer

28.   A poor man can become a rich man through his
       own efforts.

       1.   agree
       2.   partly agree
       3.   disagree
       No answer

29.   It is useless to try to change your own fate.

       1. agree
       2. partly agree
       3. disagree
       No answer

30.   Success in life depends more on luck than on
       personal ability.

       1. agree
       2. partly agree
       3. disagree
       No answer

31.   Some have been born to command and others to
       obey.

       1. agree
       2. partly agree
       3. disagree
       No answer

32.   The lot of the average man is getting worse.

       1. agree
       2. partly agree
       3. disagree
       No answer

33.   It will be a long time before much progress
       is made in Nigeria.

       1. agree
       2. partly agree
       3. disagree
       No answer

34.   We should return to the traditional life of
       our ancestors in order to have a better life.

       1. agree
       2. partly agree
       3. disagree
       No answer

35.   Life is changing too fast.

         1. agree
         2. partly agree
         3. disagree
         No answer

36.   It is not difficult for a person to adopt new
         customs.

         1. agree
         2. partly agree
         3. disagree
         No answer

37.   These days a person doesn't really know whom
         he can count on in difficult situations.

         1. agree
         2. partly agree
         3. disagree
         No answer

38.   Through education a man in the future can
         become anything he wants to be.

         1. agree
         2. partly agree
         3. disagree
         No answer

39.   Through education a woman in the future can
         become anything she wants to be.

         1. agree
         2. partly agree
         3. disagree
         No answer

40.   Some people say that most people can be truste
         Others say you can't trust people. How do
         you feel about it?

         1. most people can be trusted
         2. some people can be trusted

3. rarely do you find a person you can trust
No answer

41.   What is your religion?

1. Catholic
2. Protestant
3. traditional religion (pagan)
4. atheist or agnostic
5. other
No answer

42.   If someone gives a contribution to the church,
he will prosper.

1. agree
2. partly agree
3. disagree
No answer

43.   It is said that someone who sacrifices to the
right (traditional) shrines will prosper.

1. agree
2. partly agree
3. disagree
No answer

44.   If a new and useful farming technique was made
known to you, would you be willing to be the
first person in this village to try it?

1. yes
2. no
3. willing to try, but not first
No answer

45.   Suppose that such a new practice was learned
by a son of yours. Do you think it would be
good to accept his recommendation of this new
practice, even though you are his father and
are older?

1. yes
2. no
No answer

46.   Suppose that a villager has committed a crime
        and is caught. Which do you think would be
        worse for him:

        1. the shame of exposure before his friends
            and neighbors
        2. his own personal knowledge of his guilt
        No answer

47.   In choosing a job, which of the following
        things is most important in your estimation:
        1. the pay
        2. the prestige or status of the job
        3. the easiness of the work
        4. the interest of the work
        5. the power it gives you over other people
        No answer

48.   It's who you know more than what you know or
        what you do that counts these days.

        1. agree
        2. partly agree
        3. disagree
        No answer

49.   Do you get upset if someone criticizes you?

        1. I get very upset
        2. I get a bit upset
        3. I don't get upset
        No answer

50.   It is a wise man who learns to forego immedi-
        ate pleasures in order to achieve more lasting
        satisfactions sometime in the future.

        1. agree
        2. partly agree
        3. disagree
        No answer

51.   Man's life should be guided more by the demand
        of the present than by his visions of the futu

1. agree
2. partly agree
3. disagree
No answer

52. a. In this village is there much conflict between
       people who want to do things in the old ways
       and those who want to do things in the new
       ways?

       1. much conflict
       2. some conflict
       3. hardly any or no conflict
       No answer

    b. If much or some, which group usually gets
       what it wants?

       1. old fashioned group
       2. modern group
       3. sometimes one group, sometimes the other--
           success about equal
       No answer

    c. With which group do you, yourself, usually side?

       1. old fashioned group
       2. modern group
       3. both about equally
       4. neither
       No answer

53.   If your 10-year old son has done something bad
       and you try to punish him, but he runs too fast
       and you can't catch him, would you eventually

       1. give him the original punishment
       2. punish him more severely
       3. let him get away
       No answer

54.   Imagine that during this year your income is
       £N100 more than last year. Imagine that you
       could use the money for one of the following
       purposes. Which would it be?

1. pay school fees for your children or relatives
2. entertain people in the village
3. use it to hire labor so that you can plant a bigger farm next year
4. make some improvement to your farm
5. buy a palm oil press or some other machine with which you could go into business
6. take a title or perform some traditional rites
7. save the money
8. build a better house
9. buy a radio and bicycle
No answer

55. If you were employed as a plantation worker by ENDC or some other company, do you think you should be hired as a laborer or as a supervisor?

1. laborer
2. supervisor
3. it is not for me to decide
No answer

56. If you were offered a job that paid well, would you be willing to do any type of work, or are there certain types of work which would be too tedious, hard, or unpleasant for you to be willing to undertake?

1. I would undertake any type of work
2. there are some types of work I would not be willing to undertake
No answer

57. Do you do most of your own farm work, or do hired laborers do most of it?

1. myself
2. hired laborers
No answer

58. Are there any people in this village whom you would trust to be treasurer of a cooperative

and to handle hundreds of pounds without taking
any for himself?

1. yes, there are some people I would trust
2. no, there are no such people
No answer

59.   Do you and your wife together plant more yams
       or cassava?

       1. yams
       2. cassava
       No answer

60.   a. Can you climb a palm tree?

       1. yes
       2. no
       No answer

       b. (if not) Would you be willing to learn how to?

       1. yes
       2. no
       No answer

61.   Who does more farm work in this village, men or
       women?

       1. men
       2. women
       No answer

62.   The man who gets money finds happiness.

       1. agree
       2. partly agree
       3. disagree
       No answer

63.   A child should go as far in school as he can.

       1. agree
       2. partly agree
       3. disagree
       No answer

64.   A hard-working man is a good man.

        1. agree
        2. partly agree
        3. disagree
        No answer

Answered by Interviewer

65.   Based on your observations of the informant,
        his house, and his family, what would be your
        evaluation of his economic status, comparing
        him only with other persons in the same
        community.

        1. high
        2. medium
        3. low
        No answer

66.   What was your impression of the cooperation
        of the informant?

        1. very good
        2. good
        3. fair
        4. poor
        5. very poor
        No answer

67.   Did the informant understand the questions?
        Estimate his level of understanding.

        1. very good
        2. good
        3. fair
        4. poor
        5. very poor
        No answer

BIBLIOGRAPHY

Official Sources

Agricultural Development in Nigeria, 1965-1980, Rome: Food and Agricultural Organization, 1966.

"Agricultural Sample Survey of 1963-64," Lagos: Federal Office of Statistics, 1965.

"Agriculture Division Programme of Work, 1966-67," Technical Bulletin No. 12, Enugu: Ministry of Agriculture, 1966, mimeographed.

"Background Brief for District Officers on the Rural Development Program," Enugu: Ministry of Internal Affairs, 1965 (mimeographed).

Barrington, T. J. and M. A. B. Sarpong, "The Development of Local Government in Ghana," unpublished report submitted to the Commission on the Structure and Remuneration of the Public Services in Ghana, 1967, mimeographed.

Eastern Nigeria Development Plan, 1962-68, Official Document No.8 of 1962, Enugu: Government Printer, 1962.

"Eastern Nigeria Farm Settlement Scheme," Technical Bulletin No.6, Enugu: Ministry of Agriculture, n.d..

Eastern Region of Nigeria, Revised Development Programme, 1958-1962, Official Document No.13 of 1960, Enugu: Government Printer, 1960.

Estimates of the Government of the Federation of Nigeria, 1964-1965, Lagos: Government Printer, 1965.

Jones, G. I., Report on the Position, Status and Influence of Chiefs and Natural Rulers in the Eastern Region of Nigeria, Enugu: Government Printer, 1956.

Kenya Development Plan, 1966-1970, Nairobi: Government Printer, 1966.

Land Settlement Scheme-Farm Settlements, Ibadan:
     Ministry of Agriculture and Natural Resources,
     1960.

Meek, C. K., Land Tenure and Land Administration in
     Nigeria and the Cameroons, Colonial Research
     Studies, No.22, London: HMSO, 1957.

"Policy for Community Development," Official Document
     No.27, Enugu: Ministry of Internal Affairs, 1963.

Population Census in the Eastern Region of Nigeria,
     1953, Lagos: Census Superintendent, 1954.

Population Census in the Western Region of Nigeria,
     1952, Lagos: Government Statistician, 1953.

Report of the Commission of Enquiry into Electoral
     and Local Government Reform, 3 volumes, Accra:
     Ghana Publications Corporation, 1968.

Report of the Commission on the Structure and Remuner-
     ation of the Public Services in Ghana, Accra-
     Tema: Ministry of Information, 1967.

"Report of the Seminar on Rural Development for Ad-
     ministrative Officers in Eastern Nigeria," Enugu:
     Community Development Division of the Ministry
     of Internal Affairs, 1965, mimeographed.

Second National Development Plan (1970-1974), Lagos:
     Federal Ministry of Information, 1970.

Udoji, Chief J. O., "Objectives and Concepts of the
     Rural Development Programme," address given to
     Provincial Secretaries Conference on Rural Devel-
     opment, 1965, mimeographed.

"Volta Resettlement Symposium Papers," Accra: Volta
     River Authority, 1965, mimeographed.

"White Paper on Part III of Report of the Commission
     of Enquiry into Electoral and Local Government
     Reform," Working Paper No. 2, Accra: Ghana Publi-
     ing Company, 1969.

"White Paper on the Report of the Commission on the
    Structure and Remuneration of the Public Services
    in Ghana," Working Paper No.6, Accra-Tema: Min-
    istry of Information, 1968.

                            Books

Abernethy, David B., The Political Dilemmas of Popular
    Education: An African Case, Stanford, Calif.:
    Stanford University Press, 1969.

Achebe, Chinua, A Man of the People, London: William
    Heinemann, 1966.

Allan, William, The African Husbandman, Edinburgh:
    Oliver and Boyd, 1965.

Almond, Gabriel A. and G. Bingham Powell, Jr., Com-
    parative Politics: A Developmental Approach,
    Boston: Little, Brown and Company, 1966.

_____ and Sidney Verba, The Civic Culture, Prince-
    ton, N. J.: Princeton University Press, 1963.

Amarteifio, G. W., D. A. P. Butcher and David Whitman,
    Tema Manheam: A Study of Resettlement, Accra:
    Ghana Universities Press, 1966.

Apter, David E., The Politics of Modernization,
    Chicago: University of Chicago Press, 1965.

Baldwin, K. D. S., The Niger Agricultural Project,
    Cambridge, Mass.: Harvard University Press, 1957.

Banfield, Edward C., The Moral Basis of a Backward
    Society, Glencoe, Illinois: The Free Press, 1958.

Bascom, William R. and Melville J. Herskovits, eds.,
    Continuity and Change in African Cultures,
    Chicago: University of Chicago Press, 1962.

Brokensha, David W., Social Change in Larteh, Ghana,
    Oxford: Clarendon Press, 1966.

_____ and Marion Pearsall, eds., The Anthropology of Development in Sub-Saharan Africa, Monograph No.10, Lexington, Kentucky: Society for Applied Anthropology, 1969.

Chambers, Robert, Settlement Schemes in Tropical Africa, London: Routledge and Kegan Paul, 1969.

Chubb, L. T., Ibo Land Tenure, Ibadan: Ibadan University Press, 1961.

Coleman, James S., Nigeria: Background to Nationalism, Berkeley and Los Angeles: University of California Press, 1958.

_____ and Carl G. Rosberg, Jr., eds., Political Parties and National Integration in Tropical Africa, Berkeley and Los Angeles: University of California Press, 1964.

Dean, Edwin, The Supply Responses of African Farmers, Amsterdam: North-Holland Publishing Co., 1966.

Dike, K. Onwuka, Trade and Politics in the Niger Delta 1830-1885, London: Oxford University Press, 1956.

Dumont, Rene, False Start in Africa, New York: Frederick A. Praeger, 1966.

The Economic Development of Nigeria, Baltimore: The Johns Hopkins Press, 1955.

Eicher, Carl K., Research on Agricultural Development in Five English-Speaking Countries in West Africa New York: The Agricultural Development Council, 1970.

_____ and Carl Liedholm, eds., Growth and Development in the Nigerian Economy, East Lansing: Michigan State University Press, 1970.

Elias, T. O., Nigerian Land Law and Custom, London: Routledge and Kegan Paul, 1962.

Fallers, Lloyd A., Bantu Bureaucracy: A Century of Political Evolution among the Basoga of Uganda, Cambridge: W. Heffer and Sons, Ltd., 1956.

Floyd, Barry, Eastern Nigeria: A Geographic Review, New York: Frederick A. Praeger, 1969.

Forde, Daryll, ed., Efik Traders of Old Calabar, London: Oxford University Press, 1965.

_____ and G. I. Jones, The Ibo and Ibibio-Speaking Peoples of South-Eastern Nigeria, London: Oxford University Press, 1950.

_____ and Richenda Scott, The Native Economies of Nigeria, London: Oxford University Press, 1946.

Free, Lloyd A., The Attitudes, Hopes and Fears of Nigerians, Princeton, N.J.: Institute for International Social Research, 1964.

Geertz, Clifford, ed., Old Societies and New States: The Quest for Modernity in Asia and Africa, New York: The Free Press of Glencoe, 1963.

Green, M. M., Ibo Village Affairs, 2nd ed., New York: Frederick A. Praeger, 1964.

Hagen, Everett, On the Theory of Social Change, Homewood, Illinois: The Dorsey Press, 1962.

Helleiner, G. K., ed., Agricultural Planning in East Africa, Nairobi: East African Publishing House, 1968.

_____, Peasant Agriculture, Government and Economic Growth in Nigeria, Homewood, Illinois: Richard D. Irwin, Inc., 1966.

Hellen, John A., Rural Economic Development in Zambia 1890-1964, New York: Humanities Press, 1968.

Hien, S. C. and T. H. Lee, An Analysis and Review of Agricultural Development in Taiwan: An Output

and Productivity Approach, Taipei: Chinese-
American Joint Committee on Rural Reconstruction,
1958.

Hill, Polly, The Migrant Cocoa Farmers of Southern
Ghana, Cambridge: Cambridge University Press,
1963.

Horton, Robin, Kalabari Sculpture, Apapa, Nigeria:
Department of Antiquities of the Federation of
Nigeria, 1965.

Hoselitz, B. F. and W. E. Moore, eds., Industrialization and Society, The Hague: UNESCO-Mouton,
1963.

Hunter, Guy, Modernizing Peasant Societies: A Comparative Study in Asia and Africa, London:
Oxford University Press, 1969.

Huntington, Samuel P., Political Order in Changing
Societies, New Haven, Conn.: Yale University
Press, 1968.

Jackson, C., Advance in Africa: A Study of Community
Development in Eastern Nigeria, London: Oxford
University Press, 1956.

James, R. W. and A. B. Kasunmu, Alienation of Family
Property in Southern Nigeria, Ibadan: Ibadan
University Press, 1966.

Johnson, Glenn L., Orlin J. Scoville, George K. Dike,
and Carl K. Eicher, Strategies and Recommenda-
tions for Nigerian Rural Development 1969/1985,
East Lansing: Consortium for the Study of
Nigerian Rural Development, Michigan State
University, 1969.

Jones, G. I., The Trading States of the Oil Rivers:
A Study of Political Development in Eastern
Nigeria, London: Oxford University Press, 1963.

LaPalombara, Joseph, ed., Bureaucracy and Political
Development, Princeton, N. J.: Princeton
University Press, 1963.

Leighton, Alexander, et al., Psychiatric Disorder
Among the Yoruba, Ithaca, N.Y.: Cornell University Press, 1963.

LeVine, Robert, Dreams and Deeds: Achievement
Motivation in Nigeria, Chicago: University of
Chicago Press, 1966.

Leys, Colin, ed., Politics and Change in Developing
Countries, London: Cambridge University Press,
1969.

Lloyd, P. C., Yoruba Land Law, London: Oxford
University Press, 1962.

_____, A. L. Mabogunje, and B. Awe, The City of
Ibadan, Cambridge: Cambridge University Press,
1968.

Mackintosh, John P., ed., Nigerian Government
and Politics, London: George Allen and Unwin,
Ltd., 1966.

Mann, H. S., Land Tenure in Chore, Addis Ababa: Haile
Sellassie I. University Press, 1965.

McClelland, David C., The Achieving Society, Princeton,
N. J.: Van Nostrand, 1961.

Meek, C. K., Law and Authority in a Nigerian Tribe,
London: Oxford University Press, 1937.

Miracle, Marvin P., Agriculture in the Congo Basin:
Tradition and Change in African Rural Economies,
Madison: University of Wisconsin Press, 1967.

Molnos, Angela, Attitudes toward Family Planning in
East Africa, London: C. Hurst and Co., 1968.

Moseman, Albert H., ed., Agricultural Sciences for
the Developing Nations, Washington, D. C.:
Association for the Advancement of Science,
1964.

Obi, S. N. C., Ibo Law of Property, London: Butterworths, 1963.

Ogura, T., ed., Agricultural Development in Modern
    Japan, Tokyo: Fugi Publication Co., 1963.

Oluwasanmi, H. A., Agriculture and Nigerian Economic
    Development, London: Oxford University Press,
    1966.

_____, I. S. Dema, et al., Uboma: A Socio-Economic
    and Nutritional Survey of a Rural Community in
    Eastern Nigeria, Bude, Cornwall: Geographical
    Publications, Ltd., 1966.

Parsons, K. H., F. J. Penn, and Philip Raup, eds.,
    Land Tenure, Madison: University of Wisconsin
    Press, 1956.

Plotnicov, Leonard, Strangers to the City: Urban
    Man in Jos, Nigeria, Pittsburgh: University
    of Pittsburgh Press, 1967.

Pye, Lucian W., and Sidney Verba, eds., Political
    Culture and Political Development, Princeton,
    N. J.: Princeton University Press, 1965.

Reining, Conrad C., The Zande Scheme, Evanston,
    Illinois: Northwestern University Press, 1966.

Richards, A. I., Land, Labour, and Diet in Northern
    Rhodesia, London: Oxford University Press, 1937.

Rogers, Everett, Diffusion of Innovations, New York:
    The Free Press of Glencoe, 1962.

Rosen, George, Democracy and Economic Change in India,
    Berkeley and Los Angeles: University of Cali-
    fornia Press, 1966.

Ruthenberg, Hans, ed., Smallholder Farming and Small-
    holder Development in Tanzania, London: C. Hurst
    and Co., 1968.

de Schlippe, Pierre, Shifting Cultivation in Africa,
    London: Routledge and Kegan Paul, 1956.

Schwartz, Frederick A. O., Jr., Nigeria: The Tribes, the Nation, or the Race, Cambridge: M. I. T. Press, 1965.

Scudder, Thayer, The Ecology of the Gwembe Tonga, Manchester: Manchester University Press, 1962.

Sheffield, James R., ed., Education, Employment and Rural Development, Nairobi: East African Publishing House, 1967.

Singer, Hans, International Development: Growth and Change, New York: McGraw-Hill, 1963.

Sklar, Richard L., Nigerian Political Parties, Princeton, N. J.: Princeton University Press, 1963.

Smock, Audrey C., Ibo Politics: The Role of Ethnic Unions in Eastern Nigeria, Cambridge, Mass. Harvard University Press, 1971.

Smock, David R., Conflict and Control in an African Trade Union, Stanford, Calif.: Hoover Institution Press, 1969.

Smythe, Hugh H. and Mabel M., The New Nigerian Elite, Stanford, Calif.: Stanford University Press, 1960.

Sorrenson, M. P. K., Land Reform in the Kikuyu Country, Nairobi: Oxford University Press, 1967.

Southworth, Herman M., and Bruce F. Johnston, eds., Agricultural Development and Economic Growth, Ithaca, N.Y.: Cornell University Press, 1967.

Spence, C. F., The Portuguese Colony of Mocambique: An Economic Survey, Cape Town: A. A. Balkema, 1951.

Stephenson, Robert F., Population and Political Systems, New York: Columbia University Press, 1968.

Stolper, Wolfgang F., <u>Planning without Facts: Lessons</u>
    <u>in Resource Allocation from Nigeria's Develop-</u>
    <u>ment</u>, Cambridge, Mass.: Harvard University
    Press, 1966.

Tang, Hui-Sun, <u>Highlights of Land Reform in Taiwan</u>,
    Taipei: Joint Commission on Rural Reconstruc-
    tion, 1957.

_____, <u>Land Reform in Free China</u>, Taipei: Joint
    Commission on Rural Reconstruction, 1967.

Uchendu, Victor C., <u>The Igbo of Southeast Nigeria</u>,
    New York: Holt, Rinehart and Winston, 1965.

Weber, Max, <u>The Protestant Ethic and the Spirit of</u>
    <u>Capitalism</u>, New York: Charles Scribner's Sons,
    1958.

Weiner, Myron, <u>The Politics of Scarcity</u>, Chicago:
    University of Chicago Press, 1962.

Whyte, William F., and Lawrence K. Williams, <u>Toward</u>
    <u>an Integrated Theory of Development</u>, Ithaca:
    New York State School of Industrial and Labor
    Relations, Cornell University, 1968.

de Wilde, John C., <u>et al.</u>, <u>Agricultural Development</u>
    <u>in Tropical Africa</u>, 2 vols., Baltimore: The
    Johns Hopkins Press, 1967.

Yudelman, Montague, <u>Africans on the Land</u>, Cambridge,
    Mass.: Harvard University Press, 1964.

                            Articles

Ashford, Douglas E., "The Politics of Rural Mobilisa-
    tion in North Africa," <u>The Journal of Modern</u>
    <u>African Studies</u>, VII (July 1969), 187-202.

Asika, Ukpabi, "The Structure of the Ibo Community,"
    <u>The Renaissance</u>, March 14, 1971, pp. 3, 12, 16,
    and 17.

Coatswith, R. W., "Establishing a Rural Development
    Programme in Eastern Nigeria," Administration,
    III (October 1968), 9-12.

Dyson-Hudson, Rada and Neville, "Subsistence Herding
    in Uganda," Scientific American, 220 (February
    1969), 76-89.

Edgerton, Robert B., "'Cultural' versus 'Ecological'
    Factors in the Expression of Values, Attitudes,
    and Personality Characteristics," American
    Anthropologist, 67 (April 1965), 442-447.

Eicher, Carl K., "The Dynamics of Long-Term Agri-
    cultural Development in Nigeria," Journal of
    Farm Economics, 49 (December 1967), 1158-1170.

Erasmus, Charles J., "Community Development and the
    Encogido Syndrome," Human Organization, 27
    (Spring 1968), 65-73.

Fernea, Robert A., and John G. Kennedy, "Initial
    Adaptations to Resettlement: A New Life for
    Egyptian Nubians," Current Anthropology, 7
    (1966), 349-354.

Fogg, C. Davis, "Economic and Social Factors Affecting
    the Development of Smallholder Agriculture in
    Eastern Nigeria," Economic Development and
    Cultural Change, XIII (April 1965), 278-292.

Foster, George M., "Interpersonal Relations in
    Peasant Society," Human Organization, 19 (Winter
    1960-61), 174-178.

_____, "Peasant Society and the Image of the
    Limited Good," American Anthropologist, 67
    (April 1965), 293-315.

Geertz, Clifford, "Religious Belief and Economic
    Behavior in a Central Javanese Town," Economic
    Development and Cultural Change, IV (January
    1956), 134-158.

Hauser, Philip M., "Cultural and Personal Obstacles to Economic Development in Less Developed Areas," Human Organization, 18 (Summer 1959), 78-84.

Henderson, Richard N., "Generalized Cultures and Evolutionary Adaptability: A Comparison of Urban Efik and Ibo in Nigeria," Ethnology, V (October 1966), 365-391.

Homan, F. D., "Consolidation, Enclosure and Registration of Title in Kenya," Journal of Local Administration Overseas, I (January 1962), 1-11.

Horton, Robin, "The Kalabari World View: An Outline and Interpretation," Africa, XXXII (July 1962), 197-220.

Jones, G. I., "Ecology and Social Structure Among the North-Eastern Ibo," Africa, XXXI (April 1961), 117-134.

_____, "Ibo Age Organizations with Special Reference to the Cross River and the North-Eastern Ibo," Journal of the Royal Anthropological Institute, XCII (July-December 1962), 191-211.

Jones, William O., "Economic Man in Africa," Food Research Institute Studies, I (May 1960), 107-134.

_____, "Manioc: An Example of Innovation in African Economies," Economic Development and Cultural Change, V (April 1957), 97-117.

Kreinen, M., "The Introduction of Israel's Land Settlement Plan to Nigeria," Journal of Farm Economics, 45 (August 1963), 535-546.

Leis, Philip E., "Palm Oil, Illicit Gin, and the Moral Order of the Ijaw," American Anthropologist, 66 (August 1964), 828-838.

"Local Government in West Africa," Four parts, West Africa, January 30-February 5 issue to March 6-12 issue, 1971.

Malinowski, Bronislaw, "The Primitive Economics of
    the Trobriand Islanders," The Economic Journal,
    XXXI (March 1921), 1-16.

Mellor, John W. and T. V. Moorti, "Farm Business
    Analysis of 30 Farms; Midhakur, Agra District,
    U.P. 1959-1960," Research Bulletin I, Agra:
    The Balwant Vidyapath, 1961.

Messenger, John C. Jr., "Religious Acculturation
    Among the Anang Ibibio," Comparative Studies in
    Society and History, V (July 1963), 424-448.

Morrill, W. T., "Immigrants and Associations: The Ibo
    in Twentieth Century Calabar," Comparative
    Studies in Society and History, V (July 1963),
    424-448.

Netting, Robert, "Household Organization and Intensive
    Agriculture," Africa, XXXV (October 1965), 422-
    429.

Niehoff, Arthur H., and J. Charnel Anderson, "Peasant
    Fatalism and Socio-Economic Innovation," Human
    Organization, 25 (Winter 1966), 273-283.

Okediji, Oladejo O., "The Role of Rational Planning
    in Economic Development: A Nigerian Example,"
    Human Organization, 28 (Spring 1969), 42-49.

Onitiri, H. M. A., "Presidential Address--A Proposal
    for Nigerian Rural Development," The Nigerian
    Journal of Economic and Social Studies,
    VIII (March 1966), 1-8.

Ottenberg, Simon, "Ibo Oracles and Intergroup Rela-
    tions," Southwestern Journal of Anthropology,
    XIV (Fall 1958), 294-317.

_____, "Local Government and Law in Southern
    Nigeria," Journal of Asian and African Studies,
    II (January and April 1967), 26-43.

Porter, Philip W., "Environmental Potentials and
    Economic Opportunities--A Background for Cultural

Adaptation," American Anthropologist, 67 (April 1965), 409-420.

Rahman, A. T. R., "Rural Institutions in India and Pakistan," Asian Survey, VIII (September 1968), 792-805.

Redfield, Robert, "The Folk Society," The American Journal of Sociology, LII (January 1947), 293-308.

Rweyamau, Anthony, "Managing Planned Development: The Tanzanian Experience," The Journal of Modern African Studies, IV (May 1966), 1-16.

Schuman, Howard, "Economic Development and Individual Change: A Social-Psychological Study of the Comilla Experiment in Pakistan," Occasional Papers in International Affairs, No. 15, Cambridge, Mass.: Harvard University Center for International Affairs, 1967.

Scudder, Thayer, "The Kariba Case: Man-Made Lakes and Resource Development in Africa," Bulletin of the Atomic Scientists, XXI (December 1965), 6-11.

Segal, Aaron, "The Politics of Land in East Africa," Economic Development and Cultural Change, XVI (January 1968), 275-295.

Simons, Donald C., "Sexual Life, Childhood and Marriage among the Efik," Africa, XXX (April 1960), 153-165.

Smith, M. G., "Historical and Cultural Conditions of Political Corruption among the Hausa," Comparative Studies in Society and History, VI (January 1964), 164-196.

Smock, David R., "Changing Political Processes among the Abaja Ibo," Africa, XXXVIII (July 1968), 281-292.

Uchendu, Victor C., "Socioeconomic and Cultural
    Determinants of Rural Change in East and West
    Africa," Food Research Institute Studies, VIII
    (No. 3, 1968), 225-242.

Udo, R. K., "The Migrant Tenant of Eastern Nigeria,"
    Africa, XXXIV (October 1964), 326-339.

Versluys, J. D. N., "The Gezira Scheme in the Sudan
    and the Russian Kolkhoz: A Comparison of Two
    Experiments," Economic Development and Cultural
    Change, II (April 1953) 32-59.

Welsch, Delane E., "Response to Economic Incentive
    by Abakaliki Rice Farmers in Eastern Nigeria,"
    Journal of Farm Economics, 47 (November 1965),
    900-914.

Whitaker, C. S., "A Dysrhythmic Process of Political
    Change," World Politics, XIX (January 1967),
    190-217.

Williamson, Kay, "Changes in the Marriage System of
    the Okrika Ijo," Africa, XXXII (January 1962),
    53-60.

Wolpe, Howard E., "Port Harcourt: Ibo Politics in
    Microcosm," The Journal of Modern African Studies,
    VII (October 1969), 469-494.

                    Unpublished Manuscripts

Ascroft, Joseph R., Niels G. Roling, Graham B. Kerr,
    and Gerald D. Hursh, "Patterns of Diffusion in
    Rural Eastern Nigeria," East Lansing: Depart-
    ment of Communications, Michigan State University,
    1969, mimeographed.

Asika, Ukpabi, "Rehabilitation and Resettlement,"
    paper presented at the Conference on National
    Reconstruction and Development in Nigeria,
    Ibadan, 1969.

Adedeji, Adebaya, "Federalism and Development Planning
    in Nigeria," paper presented at the Conference
    on National Reconstruction and Development in
    Nigeria, Ibadan, 1969.

Anthony, Kenneth, and Bruce F. Johnston, "Field Study
    of Agricultural Change: Northern Katsina,
    Nigeria," Stanford, Calif.: Food Research Insti-
    tute, Stanford University, 1968, mimeographed.

Boston, J. S., "The Igala Oil-Palm Industry," Nigerian
    Institute of Social and Economic Research, Con-
    ference Proceedings, March 1962, Ibadan: 1963,
    mimeographed.

Clark, Robert C., and I. A. Akinbode, "Factors Asso-
    ciated with the Adoption of Three Farm Practices
    in Western Nigeria," n.p., 1967, mimeographed.

Clough, K. H., "Some Aspects of Land Settlement in
    Kenya," Kenya, Egerton College, mimeographed,
    1965.

Coatswith, Raymond, "A Note on Village Attitudes in
    Uguwaku Project," Quarterly Report on the Rural
    Development Project of Eastern Nigeria for the
    Ford Foundation, Enugu: 1966, typescript.

Eicher, Carl K., "Reflections on Capital Intensive
    Moshav Farm Settlements in Southern Nigeria,"
    paper presented at the Agricultural Development
    Council Seminar on Cooperatives and Quasi-Coop-
    eratives, University of Kentucky, 1967, mimeo-
    graphed.

_____, "Reflections on West Africa's Rural Develop-
    ment Problems of the 1970's," paper presented at
    the Symposium on Africa in the 1980's, Adlai
    Stevenson Institute of International Affairs,
    Chicago, 1969, mimeographed.

_____, "Transforming Traditional Agriculture in
    Southern Nigeria: The Contemporary Experience,"
    paper presented at the Annual Meeting of the
    African Studies Association, Bloomington, Indiana
    1966, mimeographed.

Gaitskell, Arthur, "Observations on Agricultural
    Development Plans in Eastern Nigeria," 1962,
    mimeographed.

Georgulas, Nikos, "An Approach to the Economic Develop-
    ment of Rural Areas in Tanganyika with Special
    Reference to the Village Resettlement Program,"
    Syracuse, N.Y.: Program of African Studies,
    Syracuse University, 1963, mimeographed.

Harbison, Frederick H., "Priorities in External Aid
    for African Higher Education," 1969, mimeo-
    graphed.

Henderson, Richard N., "Onitsha Kingship Succession:
    Traditional and Contemporary Patterns in Ibo
    Politics," paper presented at the Annual Meeting
    of the African Studies Association, Philadelphia,
    1965.

Herrmann, Omer W., "Nigerian Agricultural Research,"
    East Lansing: Consortium for the Study of
    Nigerian Rural Development, Michigan State Uni-
    versity, 1968, mimeographed.

Hrabovszky, J. P., and T. D. Moulik, "Economic and
    Social Factors Associated with the Adoption of an
    Improved Implement: A Study of the Olpad Thresher
    in India," Agricultural Development Council
    Paper, 1967.

Hursh, Gerald D., Allan Hershfield, Graham B. Kerr,
    and Niels G. Roling, "Communication in Eastern
    Nigeria: An Experiment in Introducing Change,"
    East Lansing: Department of Communication,
    Michigan State University, 1968, mimeographed.

_____, Niels G. Roling, and Graham B. Kerr, "Inno-
    vation in Eastern Nigeria: Success and Failure
    of Agricultural Programs in 71 Villages of East-
    ern Nigeria," East Lansing: Department of Com-
    munication, Michigan State University, 1968,
    mimeographed.

Huth, William P., "Traditional Institutions and Land

Tenure as Related to Agricultural Development Among the Ibo of Eastern Nigeria," Research Paper No. 36, Madison: Land Tenure Center, University of Wisconsin, 1969, mimeographed.

Jones, G. I., "From Direct to Indirect Rule in Eastern Nigeria," seminar paper presented at the Institute of African Studies, University of Ife, Nigeria, 1964.

MacFarlane, David L., and Martin A. Oworen, "Investment in Oil Palm Plantations in Eastern Nigeria," Enugu: Economic Development Institute, University of Nigeria, 1965, mimeographed.

Okoko, Olatunde, "A Study of Socio-Economic Factors Affecting Agricultural Productivity in Annang Province, Eastern Nigeria," Ibadan: Nigerian Institute of Social and Economic Research, n.d., mimeographed.

Okurume, Godwin, "The Food Crop Economy in Nigerian Agricultural Policy," East Lansing: Consortium for the Study of Nigerian Rural Development, Michigan State University, 1967, mimeographed.

Olatunbosun, Dupe, "Nigerian Farm Settlement and School Leavers' Farms," East Lansing: Consortium for the Study of Nigerian Rural Development, Michigan State University, 1967, mimeographed.

Oluwasanmi, H. A., "Agricultural and Rural Development," paper presented at the Conference on National Reconstruction and Development in Nigeria, Ibadan, 1969 mimeographed.

Purvis, Malcom J., "Report on a Survey of the Oil Palm Rehabilitation Scheme in Eastern Nigeria-- 1967," East Lansing: Consortium for the Study of of Nigerian Rural Development, Michigan State University, 1968, mimeographed.

Scudder, Thayer, "The Kainji Lake Basin: Research, Resettlement, and Development," Lagos: The Ford Foundation, 1965, mimeographed.

Smock, David R., "From Village to Trade Union in
    Africa: A Study of Power and Decision-Making
    in the Nigerian Coal Miners' Union and in the
    Villages from which the Coal Miners Migrated,"
    unpublished dissertation, Cornell University,
    1964.

Takes, C. A. P., "Socio-Economic Factors Affecting the
    Productivity of Agriculture in Okigwi Division,"
    Ibadan: Nigerian Institute of Social and Eco-
    nomic Research, 1963, mimeographed.

Wells, Jerome C., "Government Agricultural Invest-
    ment in Nigeria: 1962-1967," Ann Arbor: Center
    for Research on Economic Development, University
    of Michigan, 1968, mimeographed.

ABOUT THE AUTHORS

DAVID R. SMOCK has had considerable experience with rural development in Africa. He spent two years as a Ford Foundation adviser to the Eastern Nigeria Ministry of Rural Development, following which he spent a year as a Ford Foundation adviser on resettlement to the International Institute of Tropical Agriculture in Ibadan, Nigeria. Prior to his period as adviser to the Ministry of Rural Development, he spent a year conducting research for rural and urban institutions in Eastern Nigeria. A portion of the data collected during that period is contained in a book entitled Conflict and Control in an African Trade Union (Stanford, Calif.: Hoover Institution Press, 1969).

Dr. Smock received his academic training at Oberlin College, the School of Oriental and African Studies of the University of London, and received his Ph.D. in cultural anthropology from Cornell University. His articles have appeared in such journals as Foreign Affairs, Africa Report, The Journal of Developing Areas, Economic Development and Cultural Change, and Midstream.

Following his departure from Nigeria in 1967 Dr. Smock became Program Officer for North and East Africa for the Ford Foundation in New York, and he is currently Assistant Representative for the Ford Foundation in West Africa, in charge of the Foundation's activities in Ghana.

AUDREY C. SMOCK is a political scientist specializing in the relationship of traditional culture to political development. She has spent three years in Africa teaching and doing research. The results of her research in Nigeria are contained in the book Ibo Politics: The Role of Ethnic Unions in Eastern Nigeria (Cambridge, Mass.: Harvard University Press, 1971) and in several journal articles.

Dr. Smock received her academic training at Wellesley College and Columbia University, from which she received her Ph.D. Formerly an assistant professor of government at Barnard College, Columbia University, she is now a lecturer in the Department of Political Science, University of Ghana.